OTHER TITLES OF INTEREST FROM ST. LUCIE PRESS

Quality Government

Designing, Developing, and Implementing TQM

JERRY W. KOEHLER
JOSEPH M. PANKOWSKI

S_L^t

St. Lucie Press
Delray Beach, Florida

TABLE OF CONTENTS

PREFACE

Soon after being elected Governor of the State of Florida in 1990, Governor Lawton Chiles appointed the Commission for Government by the People, chaired by Bill Frederick, former Mayor of Orlando. The purpose of the Commission was to design a "road map" that the Governor could use to transform a state government operated by "bloated, ineffective, distant bureaucracy into a state government operated by and for the people."

One member of the Commission, James Apthorp, President of the Apthorp Management Group, asked the first author if he would speak to the Commission and explain to them how the total quality management principles and practices that he applied at Honeywell Space Systems, as an internal consultant, could work in government. During his presentation, he suggested that Total Quality Management would, in all probability, remain only a buzz word in government, since the bureaucracy was too far removed from the customer, and he doubted that a government leader would be willing to invest the time and energy required to work with front-line workers to thoroughly understand customer needs and expectations.

Following the meeting, the first author informed Commissioner Frederick and his friend Apthorp that he would only be willing to work with government if they would find a top echelon bureaucrat who was willing to focus on meeting or exceeding customer expectations. He was quite confident that he would never hear from the Frederick Commission again.

To his surprise, Commissioner Frederick called him to tell him that Frank Scruggs, recently appointed as Secretary of Labor and Employment Security, would be coming to Tampa and would be willing to listen. Scruggs was Ivy-League educated with a Law Degree from Harvard. He came to Tampa, along with Apthorp and Frederick, to meet with a focus group composed of front-line workers who administered unemployment benefits. Scruggs listened attentively to every comment. His legal pad was completely full by the end of the day. Ideas flowed, and opportunities for improvement emerged one after the other.

One suggestion, which later led to a merger of two divisions, related to the need for an applicant for employment benefits to have to travel to another office, often miles away, to complete a similar application to prove that he or she was actively seeking employment. By integrating two processes into one, the applicant did not have to take another day to complete the process. In fact, a two-day process, that frequently took more than four hours each day in two different locations, became one process that took less than an hour. In selected offices that emphasized continual improvement, the whole new process took less than 15 minutes. The customers saved time and energy, and the taxpayers saved money.

Scruggs recruited the first author as a consultant to help him improve the Department of Labor and Employment Security. While serving as a consultant, the first author became friends with the second author, who was a Bureau Chief in the Division of Vocational Rehabilitation in the Department of Labor and Employment Security. Both shared the philosophy and interest in implementing Total Quality Management in government.

After serving a brief time as an external consultant to Secretary Scruggs, the first author took a leave of absence from the University of South Florida to serve as a full-time consultant to Tom Herndon, Executive Director of the Department of Revenue, who was truly committed to improvement, and empowered a team to determine how the department might implement TQM.

A year later, Secretary Frank Scruggs resigned as Secretary and Governor Lawton Chiles appointed Shirley Gooding as Secretary of Labor and Employment Security. Secretary Gooding appointed the first author as Deputy Secretary and charged him with the responsibility of implementing Total Quality Management in the department. She appointed the second author as TQM Administrator.

Quality Government: Designing, Developing and Implementing Total Quality Management was an outgrowth of the experiences the authors encountered while implementing TQM in the state agencies. The authors were truly impressed with, and amazed at, the many people in government who were willing to change to a TQM culture to manage government more efficiently and effectively.

However, it is not an effortless task to change any organization. It is certainly not an easy task to make the change from putting the needs of the top echelon first to putting the needs of the customer first. This requires tremendous energy, time and perseverance. Two departments did exactly this, and the authors are proud of both the Department of Revenue and the Department of Labor and Employment Security. Just this past year, the Division of Unemployment Compensation in the Department of Labor and Employment Security became the first state government agency to be selected for a site visit by the Sterling Award (Florida's state award similar to the Baldridge National Quality Award) examiner.

This book would not have been possible without the assistance of many people. First, we would like to thank James Apthorp, Bill Frederick, Jack

Critchfield, Thom Dupper, Representative Buddy Johnson, Mike Kiviek, Senator John Grant, Representative Marjorie Turnbull, Chery Burbano, John Pieno, Bill Laney, Duane Meeter, Carolyn Aidman, Mark Gibbons, Belden Daniels, Don Whyte, Steve Powell, Al Kreischer, Jeff Huenink, John "Bunk" Berry, Bill Talley, Lois Jordan and John Brown for their encouragement. We would like to thank Frank Scruggs, Shirley Gooding, Doug Jamerson, Tom Herndon, Governor Lawton Chiles, Lieutenant Governor Buddy McKay, Chancellor Charles Reed and University of South Florida President Betty Castor, for without their commitment to Total Quality Management, this book would not have been possible.

We owe a special debt of gratitude to the internal consultants in the Department of Labor and Employment Security: Joy Barber, Duane Underwood, John Wold, Don Bassett, Lee Weaver, Rick Maiello, Rebecca Rust, Brian Poloniecki, Franklin Sands, Stan Ford, Peter Hoffman, Tom McCauley, Ken Reecy, Vincent Edwards, Sam Brooks, Al Herndon, Louise Sadler, and Theresa Mullin who kept us all on track. Also we would like to thank the Department of Labor and Employment Security training team: Sharon La Couture, Morris Rose, Charles Chester, Linda Scowden, Ann Loadholtz, John Cummings, Anita Richardson, Gene Wilson and Dale Ward.

Many quality leaders emerged from the time we started our TQM initiatives in the Department of Revenue and the Department of Labor. For all of those leaders we owe a debt of gratitude. However, a special thanks goes to those who contributed directly to our book: Jim Zingale, Jeff Warner, Perry Barrett and Jim Everett, Jessie Durand and Gerald Johnson in the Department of Revenue. In the Department of Labor and Employment Security we thank: Ken Holmes, Ann Clayton, James Blount, Bob Bradner, Robert Whaley, Everette Beckman, Maria Risco, Lois Scott, Barbara Griffin, Renee Benton, Cassandra Wiggins, Bill Gorbett, Willie Robinson, Nancy McCurdy, Cindy James, Ted Behn, Jeff Green, Bethany Kemp, Moe Johnson, Dan Newman, Mickey Stopko, Ann Sullivan, Kim Polasky, John Alrich, Linda Chandler, Mike Murphy, Emma Mobley, Bill Wood, Reuben Patrick, Bill McQueen, Bill Reynolds, Letizia Morales, Sandy Patch, Barbara Wisher, Mary Ann Plake, Alan Stucks, Sam Copeland, Robert Lynn, Beverly Boatwright, Paul Lewis, Ed Bennett, Jimmie Hall, Julie Sanon, Carole Massey, Henrietta Francis, Tom Maher, Tom Carson, Fran Fisher, David Sellars, Jean Casali, Patti Strickland, Ron Clark, Pam Wilson, Randy Touchton, Steve Hill, Linda Davis, David Perkins, Jerry Reeves, Efrain Saurez, Laura Eslinger, Edson Kline, Jerome Dilworth and Jerry Henderson.

We owe a special debt of thanks to Belinda Padgett for typing the manuscript, Dennis Buda, Editor in Chief, St. Lucie Press, and our editors Sandy Pearlman and Sandra Koskoff.

Jerry W. Koehler
Joseph M. Pankowski

ABOUT THE AUTHORS

Dr. Jerry W. Koehler recently returned to the faculty in the Department of Management at the University of South Florida in Tampa after serving the past three years as Deputy Secretary in the Florida Department of Labor and Employment Security.

Dr. Koehler has authored numerous books and has served as consultant to government agencies and leading business organizations. He is co-author with Joseph Pankowski of another book, *Continual Improvement Methods and Tools for Government*, (St. Lucie Press, 1996), and two additional St. Lucie titles, *Teams in Government* and *Leadership in Government*.

Joseph M. Pankowski is no stranger to quality improvement efforts, having directed the Bureau of Quality Assurance in the Florida Department of Labor and Security for five years prior to working with Dr. Koehler. He continues serving as a consultant to the Department on quality management, and conducts seminars on customer expectations, teams, tools, and presentation skills.

During his 31 years of work with government, he has experience as a first-line rehabilitation counselor, state supervisor and assistant director, in addition to other assignments. He has directed teams studying innovative approaches in service delivery, and under his guidance the Bureau of Quality Assurance was recognized by the federal government for its excellence.

*This book is dedicated to
all of our associates in
the Department of Labor and Employment Security
and the Department of Revenue, State of Florida,
who share our commitment to quality.*

1

INTRODUCTION

"History is not kind to those who hurry it."
—source unknown

Following World War II, the United States of America experienced productivity gains that no country had previously ever experienced. These phenomenal gains launched the U. S. as, without a doubt, the world's industrial leader. With few exceptions, most Americans prospered from corporations' successes. In fact, in the 1950s, 75 percent of all world goods and services were produced in the United States. The United States, whose citizens valued education and hard work, was a very fortunate country with essentially only one language. Most people prospered from U.S. productivity gains. They were able to afford quality homes and automobiles and to participate in many valued activities such as vacations, sports, religious life, etc.

At the same time, government grew significantly since people were on the move and required extensive investments by our government. Many laws were made just to prevent uncontrollable growth, protection of worker rights, etc. It seemed as though the growth of industry and the growth of government would never stop. Many American dreams were being fulfilled. A quality educational system evolved from Head Start through a comprehensive program of higher education.

The biggest concern was whether or not another country, such as Russia, would start a war and interfere with America's freedom and prosperity. Most Americans were eager to protect what they had achieved and wanted to keep the same opportunities available for their children. Most people believed that the number one threat was the military force of another country. Therefore, few argued against military build-up and military intervention in other parts of the world to protect what the United States had as a country. The feeling was that prosperity would continue as long as no other nation took liberties from us.

What few people understood was that the threat to U.S. dominance of worldwide productivity and prosperity was not from a military takeover, but rather was from international competition. The real threat to freedom and prosperity was not military but rather from foreign manufacturing. While we were prospering, other countries began to sell goods and services to the United States. Since we were experiencing such phenomenal growth in the 1960s and 1970s, only a few were concerned about international competition, and most of those who were concerned did not suggest that manufacturing processes be changed, they argued instead to limit goods and services from other countries. For example, when the Japanese began selling cars in the United States, the U. S. automakers and their labor unions were lobbying Congress to prohibit the sales of Japanese autos. They argued that if we did not prohibit Japanese automobiles, the least we could do would be to levy tariffs against these imports so that their price would not be competitive with U.S. automakers.

Most of the attempts made by organized labor and U. S. automakers to limit Japanese automobiles failed largely because Japanese automobiles seemed to meet the American consumer needs. During the early 1970s after inflation became a serious problem in the United States and gas prices soared astronomically often propelled by the scarcity of gas in some cases, American consumers didn't seem to care where the automobile was made as long as the automobile they purchased gave them good gas mileage. Also, the American consumer did not want to pay astronomical costs for automobile repair, and wanted a car that was reliable and would last much longer than the one that they had previously purchased.

In other words, Americans were redefining the word "quality." They wanted an automobile that worked right the first time, and when it worked, was economical to drive. It seemed as though foreign manufacturers understood what the American consumer wanted. Consumers no longer wanted what the executives in the automobile industry wanted to sell the American people. Instead, consumer demands were going to drive consumer behavior.

PUTTING THE CUSTOMER FIRST

While American manufacturing was dominated by management by objectives as its approach, foreign competitors were manufacturing items by a process designed around the principles of Total Quality Management. Management by objectiveswas no doubt a very successful management approach when the primary objective was productivity. Top management would identify the productivity objectives for the organization and the rest of the managers in the organization were to align their objectives with top management. It became a very effective method for producing goods and services. For example, top management would design the automobiles that they wanted the American consumers to purchase. They would then determine how many automobiles they could make and set up production systems that proved to be very successful. They were able to produce more cars faster than their international competition. The problem was that U. S. automobile makers were unable to compete with the international manufacturers because American consumer buying habits were changing rapidly. American consumers wanted small economical cars that were very reliable. Furthermore, since U. S. automobile makers were producing automobiles with many defects, they had to charge considerably more for their cars because they knew they would have to spend more money in order to live up to the guarantees that they had to provide. For example, while an American automobile manufacturer was charging $1,000 more per car just to cover the guarantee, the Japanese automobile maker was only charging $150.

Since Congress was unable to agree on how to stop the import of foreign automobiles, the American automobile manufacturer had to learn to compete at an international level. The effect of foreign competition on the American automobile manufacturer was practically devastating. For example, on January 1, 1989, Ford Motor Company employed a little more than 200,000 workers. Eighteen months later on June 30, 1981, Ford Motor Company only employed 87,000 workers. Thousands of people lost their jobs. Why? Because foreign competitors had adopted the principles of Total Quality Management.

What makes the matter even worse is that countries that not long ago experienced complete devastation due to World War II were becoming prosperous because they were willing to adopt management principles that were developed in the United States and used to defeat them during World War II. These principles were largely attributed to two Americans who worked in the Defense Department during World War II, W. Edwards Deming and Joseph Juran. It was during World War II that Americans adopted the principles of Total Quality Management.

The American Defense Department knew that quality products and services were needed to win the war. Airplanes that flew right the first time, and tank and guns that didn't fail in combat were required. Furthermore, American workers were willing to put aside turf battles, work together in teams, improve their processes, and, above all, put their customers first. After all, their customers were their friends and relatives who would be using what they built in combat. Practically every American was willing to do whatever it took to produce high quality goods and services.

What we learned was that if we put customers first, manufactured what they needed and not what we thought they ought to have, and gave them a product that worked the first time, we would win the war. We learned that when the customer drives the system the chances of success are extremely high. Further, just to produce a large quantity of something is not enough to guarantee success. Also we learned that in order to meet customer needs, accurate and meaningful data must be used to make decisions. Rather than arguing over someone's preference in manufacturing a product, manufacturers should let meaningful data emerge to drive the process. Consequently, products were tested at every point in the manufacturing process. When defects were found in the manufacturing processes, preventive methods were then employed to reduce the defects.

Finally, we learned that when people are involved in improving each process errors and waste are reduced. When people who sincerely care about the customer get involved in continual improvement, the results will be high quality products.

After World War II, the United States realized that it would experience phenomenal growth along with the rest of the world. Therefore, we understood that the best approach would be to produce as many products as could possibly be manufactured. Customers would have to buy what was produced, and they did. The United States had significant resources and, therefore, could build products that were at home and abroad. We built products as fast as we could. Consumers were pleased to own American products. Billions of dollars were spent in designing and manufacturing products and services that consumers were anxious to purchase. Manufacturers began to believe that all they had to do was to invest money in designing new products and consumers would buy them. Top executives in many of leading American corporations began to believe that they knew what was best for the consumers, and they were right during the 1950s through the 1970s.

The idea was to keep designing new products that changed dramatically from year to year and consumers would continue to be fascinated by new designs and purchase these products. The assumption was that people would continue to purchase products frequently and would turn over their purchases on a predictable cycle. Therefore, if the consumers were going to dispose of their products frequently, then the quality of the products was not as important as design and appearance. The problem came when consumer needs changed quickly. And when consumer habits began to change, large organizations had built such a large bureaucracy that they were unable to change quickly enough to meet consumer needs. Further, the management by objectivesystem that most American organizations employed was very effective when a productivity model was needed, since it was driven by meeting objectives. The management by objectivemodel assumed that if all objectives were met, the organization would be successful.

The problems with this model began to emerge when organizations were successful in meeting their production objectives, but were unsuccessful in selling products or sold products that did not work. It became very clear in the 1970s and 1980s that many top executives were out of touch with their customers and furthermore, many were out of touch with their competitors. Large bureaucracies like IBM, Xerox, General Motors, Chrysler, Ford, and Motorola, were so out of touch with their customers that dramatic changes had to be made.

As top management of American business organizations became further removed from the front-lines while building large bureaucratic systems, foreign competitors were using another system of management that focused directly on customer needs and front-line personnel. Rather than using management-by-objectives, international competitors were adopting the principles of Total Quality Management developed by two Americans, Deming and Juran.

When American businesses became so successful in the 1950s through the 1970s, top management took full credit. Many articles were written about how brilliant top management was in designing, developing, and building products. General Motors was so successful that many government officials threatened to break up this gigantic corporation in order to produce competition within the United States. When organizations become so successful, they begin to reward their personnel; however, rather than rewarding all personnel, the large American businesses began to give huge salaries, bonuses, and sizable shares of stock as compensation to top management. Furthermore, large business organizations provided significant perks and allowed their top executives to design their jobs for their convenience.

Almost all of the personnel in the organization knew that their job was only to satisfy the person above them. The primary job of their subordinates was to keep the boss happy and satisfied. The best way to keep him happy was to meet one's objectives. If the boss was responsible for making sure that a product got shipped, employees met that objective. Many workers have reported to us how they often used to ship products that didn't work in order to meet production schedule. Furthermore, since objectives were so important, many companies employed numerous inspectors who also were charged with correcting a problem so that the product passed inspection, but the worker knew that the overall product was inferior. What drove the organization was not the customer, but rather managers.

Personnel who moved to the top of the organization wielded power and demanded respect. To advance, subordinates understood that they had to at least meet their boss's expectations or exceed them.

On the other hand, competitors were using a management model that had significantly contributed to U.S. success in World War II. That management model focused on the customer and the goal was to meet or exceed customer expectations. Rather than organization personnel concentrating on how they could move up the organization ladder by satisfying the boss, the international competitors' personnel knew that advancement was best achieved by working in teams, working in the front-lines, and improving processes so that the product or service would meet or exceed customer expectations. Personnel were taught to keep the customer in mind in making all decisions, and to put quality first and the results would follow.

International competitors understood that it is the customer's convenience that is first priority, rather than the convenient needs of top management.

After many American businesses began to adopt the principles of Total Quality Management, the United States once again established itself as a formidable competitor. In a relatively short period of time, American ingenuity with an effective management system has resurfaced and saved millions of jobs for Americans. Even though many American business organizations are slow to embrace the principles of Total Quality Management, many leading American businesses have prospered. American managers and workers in these organizations that were able to make the dramatic change in the way they do business now have the highest respect.

Changing from MBO (Management by Objectives) to TQM (Total Quality Management) is a significant challenge. Workers must be retrained, and managers must give up significant power. There have been many organizations who have tried to embrace TQM and have failed, primarily because top management fear their loss of control and power. Many top executives believe that their job is to control people and not processes. Many top executives like to think of themselves as excellent judges of others and are effective at motivating and controlling others.

On the other hand, in a TQM culture, leaders focus more on processes and outcomes than on people. If quality is the desired outcome, efforts should be directed to continually improving organizational processes rather than on controlling people.

MANAGING GOVERNMENT TODAY

Prior to the Berlin Wall coming down, the senior author had an opportunity to visit the former Soviet Union. During his visit it became quite apparent that the Soviet Union was going to have a very difficult time surviving. Their primary management approach was "management-by-quotas." The government in the Soviet Union was strictly guided by long-range strategic planning. The Kremlin would meet and decide what was good for all of the Soviet citizens. The top executives, Kremlin leaders, would forecast needs and then instruct manufacturing plants to build a specific quota. It was not a consumer driven economy, but rather top officials deciding what they will build to meet the needs of their people.

Everything then was built according to the plan, and if the plan was wrong, so be it. If the demand for toilet supplies was larger than what the plan called for, then Soviet citizens had to go without. About the only way one could survive was to barter for products in the "underground economy." Government was managed from the top, and there was little the Soviet citizen could do when the top made a mistake.

Soviet citizens working in the factories were all managed under a quota system. Their job was to produce a product according to the quotas. That they usually did. It's a rather simple model: top management does the planning, the workers fill the quotas. Even though most workers filled their quotas, the Soviets were unsuccessful in fulfilling customers' wants and needs. Quality was about the last thing on a Soviet worker's mind. In fact, most Soviets knew that they should not buy any manufactured item, such as a washing machine, that was built in the last three days of the month. Frequently Soviet workers would waste time and build products slowly in the first part of the month and then in the last three or four days would work extremely hard in order to meet their quota.

By contrast, what is interesting in democracy is that, because of capitalism, private organizations compete for customers. Therefore, it's not a matter of ignoring customer needs and wants, but rather how effectively companies under capitalistic rule will compete for customers. When international competition began to take away American business customers, American business responded.

The problem facing government today is the lack of competition that forces government managers to change the way it does business. Even though there is a significant threat coming from Congress and the state legislatures that government needs to rethink the way they do business, most people working in government believe that they can survive the latest onslaught of critics. Top government leaders who have survived the bureaucracy for many years believe that the recent rash of government criticism is only a temporary situation and that the U.S. government will continue with business as usual. Most people working in government are protected by Civil Service, Career Service, and seniority.

Why would these top leaders want to change when for the past 45 years we have built a bureaucracy that was designed to meet the needs of the people at the top? Why should people change when they have finally arrived and are able to enjoy all the perks that come from a top government job? The higher one is in management in government, the more perks one receives and the more things are done for one's convenience. Top government officials enjoy large offices, large staffs, enormous power, control of their time, and usually three or four people to do their work for them.

There are, of course, many exceptions, but, in general, Civil Service and Career Service top managers enjoy the power of controlling people and not processes. Like industry in the 1970s, government officials are so far removed from their customers that the closest resemblance of customer needs comes to them in the form of reports from the front-lines. These reports, however, are compiled by managers who have a significant interest in the outcomes they report. Consequently, there are many statistics reported by lower management that frequently are not accurate, and no one, including auditors, knows how to gather the accurate data in the first place.

It is amazing to note that practically every year government statistics and annual reports show how effective government has been, with the justification that if more money was invested by government, the results would even get better. On the other hand, customer satisfaction with government services declines yearly. The problem is that government workers see their primary customer as Congress and state legislatures. The idea is that if they can satisfy Congress and state legislatures, then government is successful. This is an assumption that is difficult to argue against. Without the support of Congress or the state legislature, a government agency would be practically out of business.

Therefore, most effective bureaucrats understand, just like top management in industry, to keep "the board" happy, and government understands to keep the legislature happy. In the meantime, very few people are listening to the customer. The legislators are supposed to be the spokesperson for the customer, and yet very few members of the legislature understand what is occurring in government agencies. Most legislators respond only to a few horror stories that taxpayers tell them and are highly influenced by the constituency that put them in the office in the first place, primarily big contributors.

Therefore, managing government means making sure that the quotas provided by the Congress and the legislature are fulfilled. However, just like in American industry, achieving quotas doesn't necessarily result in customer satisfaction. This is a difficult reality for top management to accept, whether it be in business or in government.

CHANGING THE WAY WE DO BUSINESS IN GOVERNMENT

Prior to implementing TQM, the Department of Labor and Employment Security became a "pilot" department in Florida. In 1992, the Legislature granted to the Division of Workers' Compensation in the Department of Labor and Employment Security and to selected divisions of the Department of Revenue the authority to act outside of the established personnel and budgeting requirements of the Florida statutes. The following year the legislature granted this increased flexibility status to all divisions within the Florida Department of Revenue, the Department of State, and the Department of Labor and Employment Security.

The grant of flexibility was intended to permit the assessment of the concepts of "right sizing," "productivity investment," and "increased managerial authority" in a government setting. These agencies of government were charged with the authority and responsibility to develop a successful pilot program with measurable and legitimate results.

The Legislature created a Productivity Advisory Group consisting of nine members. The role of this group was to collect baseline data to measure increases in productivity resulting from implementation of programs and procedures. The group consulted with department heads relative to the programs and procedures to be implemented and provided ongoing monitoring.

The goals of the reform effort were

1. to develop better trained, better compensated, more diverse, and more highly motivated associates;

2. to continually review how the agency did business, with extensive employee involvement, to better coordinate service delivery;

3. to maximize revenue and exercise full budget flexibility; and

4. to measure and evaluate efficiency and effectiveness.

A key component of the effort to motivate associates was the monetary incentive reserved for those individuals meeting performance goals. The department paid $10.5 million in productivity bonuses between July 1, 1992 and March 31, 1993. Bonuses averaged $811 per associate. At the same time, by keeping authorized positions vacant and employing other cost avoidance strategies, a total of $44.3 million was "saved."

Unfortunately, the next year the Legislature "discovered" the vacant positions and immediately eliminated them. Their reasoning was that it was obvious that the department no longer needed them if productivity increased without them. Without the funding for the vacant positions, there was considerably less available for bonuses or incentives the following year.

WHAT WE LEARNED

I. The most notable and perhaps most predictable result of the changes was that *money motivates*. When provided with incentives, associates at all levels of our organization significantly increased productivity. Examples of results of monetary incentives included:

• a reduction in turn-around time to issue farm labor contractor licenses from 9 to 5.8 days. Over 137,000 agricultural workers and more than

4,900 farm labor contractors benefited from the more timely issuance of licenses.

- a 49 percent increase in the number of veterans placed in jobs.

- a 10 percent increase in the number of handicapped citizens placed in jobs.

- a 24 percent increase in the number of safety inspections.

- a 16 percent increase in the number of disability determinations for Social Security benefits

II.   There was a direct correlation between pay incentives and increased savings. Table 1 shows these projected savings.

Table 1.   Management's Estimate of Return on Public Investment, July 1, 1992 through June 30, 1993

	Total Cost of Bonuses	Costs Avoided	Net Gain
Department	$17,571,895	$87,777,190	$70,205,295
Source:	Department Pilot MIS.		

III. Individual bonuses can have a negative effect on cooperation and quality. Workers tend to focus only on achieving a bonus and ignoring other aspects of their job. We confirmed the findings of America's leading organizations that people working in teams are the best approach to productivity and quality. We also learned that a financial incentive that is used to motivate associates to increase production has a negative effect on attitudes when withdrawn.

IV. Associates at all levels are willing to work harder, work smarter, and take on more responsibility. We proved some critics wrong who generalize that government workers are "brain dead," and approach government work as an entitlement, not a job where they must win the respect of their customers each day. We found that significant numbers of people were willing to change, to accept daily challenges, and were motivated to provide quality services.

V.   Training was valued and appreciated. The agency-wide pilot followed the precedent set by the Workers' Compensation pilot of establishing an individual training fund for each associate. The department set aside $500 in training funds for each associate. The associate could use these funds to pursue training of their choice beyond that which is offered through the university system tuition free program. The agency specified that this training should increase the associates' knowledge, skills, and abilities so that they are able to enhance performance in their current jobs, or be used to pursue their career paths for further advancement within state government. The individual training funds could be pooled for economy of scale. However, such pooling had to recognize individual staff's wishes and needs.

Over 3000 associates participated in the individual training fund initiative, or approximately 6 out of 10 of the agency's total work force. The average expenditure per associate was around $240. Many associates appeared to respond more favorably to the individual training fund initiative than they did to productivity bonuses. Prior to the pilot, the department's Office of Inspector General consistently cited a lack of associate training as a weakness in its various management reviews of department entities. In particular, associates below managers were infrequently provided training opportunities in the past. In the long term, we anticipate that such training will contribute to increases in productivity and quality.

VI.   Budget flexibility permits more effective management. Budget flexibility allowed department heads to transfer funds and budget authority within the department without prior approval of the executive office of the Governor, provided that the department's comport generally was a legislative intent. Budget flexibility allowed more mobilization of resources. It allowed the Department to transfer rate, to add and delete positions within the department, and to transfer positions within the budget entities without prior approval of the executive office of the Governor.

On the other hand, we learned that even with the increased authority granted to us, we experienced a number of obstacles in exercising budget flexibility. We found that we had many budget partners other than the Legislature—the Governor, federal government, comptroller, auditor general, federal inspectors, and unions all significantly affect the budgetary process. Constraints from these sources forced us to be too conservative.

For example, we did not attempt privatization, even though there are numerous opportunities within the state to test the effects of privatization versus government management. What we learned is that even though the Legislature granted the Department of Labor and Employment Security authority to act outside the established personnel and budgeting requirements, our many personnel and budget partners tend to prohibit many initiatives.

We found that it's not as easy to take risks in government as it is in the private sector. However, budget flexibility has had a positive effect on the agency. It has helped it to be more customer oriented and provided it with the ability to efficiently manage budget resources in a manner which achieves legislative expectations, including maximization of resources at the lowest cost to state taxpayers. We made significant strides towards integrating services and, with the use of personnel and budget flexibility, it has had a positive effect on efficiency and effectiveness.

VII. Increased productivity is not the only answer for effective government. What we learned from our pilot experiment is what American industry learned during the 1970s and 1980s—increased productivity was not the solution to organizations' success. Even though American industry significantly out-produced the rest of the world and continues to do so, many industries fell into disarray. While productivity significantly increased, the demands for American products and services decreased. International competition forced American business leaders to rethink their approach to management.

It isn't productivity, but rather *quality and productivity* that provides a competitive edge. Industry leaders also learned that merely telling employees what to do would not necessarily achieve quality. They learned that quality couldn't be delegated, but rather it was the responsibility of employees at all levels. They learned that it wasn't as easy as dividing up work and assigning tasks, but rather identifying processes, measuring inputs, throughputs, and outputs while working together as teams. Organizations that were willing and able to make significant management changes (Motorola, Ford, Saturn, Federal Express, Olin -St. Marks, AT&T Universal Card, etc.) were able to remain competitive in a global economy.

Like the aforementioned companies, the Department of Labor and Employment Security found that even though productivity significantly increases, it does not necessarily mean that high quality services are provided to consumers. When only productivity is measured, productivity goals may be met even though the ultimate goal of customer satisfaction may not be achieved.

The results of the pilot paralleled similar findings in private industry when productivity without concern for quality was the model. Bonuses increased productivity in American companies throughout the 1950s, 1960s and 1970s without a similar increase in customer satisfaction. Customers showed their dissatisfaction by purchasing quality products from companies that fulfilled their needs.

The customers of government in the 1970s and 1980s demonstrated similar dissatisfaction through angry letters to the editors of newspapers, calls to their legislators and outbursts at public forums. The bonuses awarded in the pilot program did little, if anything to change the perception of taxpayers that government was not working and quality service was nowhere available. Similar problems faced by private industry responded to continual improvement efforts, and there was no reason not to believe that the majority of these same principles would work in government. Government just needed the right principles upon which changes could be implemented. These principles are found in Total Quality Management.

PURPOSE OF THIS BOOK

This is a book about continually improving government processes so that government can be more efficient at meeting and/or exceeding customer expectations. Continual process improvement begins with the assumption that the system, if continually improved, will ultimately work to the benefit of the organization and its customers. Sometimes processes are so broken that they can't be fixed and, therefore, reinventing the process is required.

Our premise is that reinvention should not occur until an organization understands the process and after an attempt at continual improvement has been tried. Too often managers in government come to the conclusion that reinvention is always the final answer before they truly understand the processes. When a function comes under attack by a legislator or a member of the executive branch has a bad experience, or when new management comes into an agency, the easiest and, sad to say, most likely cause of action will be to reinvent what prior managers have left. For years now, government has spent an enormous amount of time and money reinventing processes that very few people understood in the first place.

We believe that reinvention, reengineering, and privatization of government functions should be considered as alternatives to the daily way business gets done in government, however, only after the processes are thoroughly flowcharted and process improvement teams have attempted to improve the existing process. Managers need to know what part of the process isn't working and cannot be improved before they begin to reinvent, reengineer, or privatize.

Understanding inputs into a process, process activities, outputs, and outcomes is the first step towards understanding the way an organization functions. Then an organization can benchmark against other processes and be able to logically conclude whether continual improvement, reinvention, or privatization are required.

The purpose of this book is to describe our efforts to implement Total Quality Management in the Department of Labor and Employment Security in

the State of Florida. The Department had over 7,000 associates and was organized around six Divisions: Administrative Services, Vocational Rehabilitation,
Workers' Compensation, Jobs and Benefits, Unemployment Compensation,
Safety, and the Office of Disability Determination. If the work of these Divisions
was translated into the parameters of Total Quality Management, the Florida
Department of Labor and Employment Security has six core processes: rehabilitation; jobs, benefits, and appeals; prevention, regulation, and protection; collection, analysis, and dissemination of workforce information; revenue collection;
and administrative support.

Throughout this book we refer to the employees of the Department of Labor
and Employment Security as "associates." This reflects the designation we chose
early in our implementation because we wanted to emphasize that, regardless of
rank, title, or position, every person's opinion was as important as another's.
Regardless of where an associate was placed on the organization chart, all ideas
were to be considered important as processes were improved.

Initially, it was a little awkward for some to refer to their co-workers as
"associates" and many made fun of the idea. One or two actually appeared
hostile, stating that this was just another attempt by management to placate them.
This feeling eventually passed, and today "associate" is commonly used.

This book explains exactly what we planned to do, what we did, and the
effects of changing people within a culture that has long been dedicated to
meeting quotas and persuading the powers that control them that they were doing
an exceptional job and needed more money.

Since most leaders thought that whatever they were doing was extremely
important, their goal was to grow government. What better compliment can
people get than to receive more resources for the job they are presently doing?
The theory was a good one: exceed quotas to show that the organization is doing
more than expected, and then develop persuasive materials and presentations to
convince the controlling powers that more could be done if the government
contributed more.

What was forgotten in the bureaucratic process was that people at the top of
the organization were too far removed from their customers to design a system
to meet customer needs. People at the top were constantly worrying about
controlling workers' behavior. Therefore, they developed rules that forced government workers to work within the confines of particular rules. It became our
goal to change this culture to a culture that focused on the customer. Therefore,
the beliefs and principles of Total Quality Management were adopted.

2 FOUNDATIONS OF TOTAL QUALITY MANAGEMENT

"Export anything to a friendly country
except American management."
—W. Edwards Deming

The impact of Total Quality Management on business organizations in the United States is significant. Most companies that have adopted Total Quality Management have been fortunate to record profound results. Federal, state, and local governments have observed the success of many of these companies as they continue to do use Total Quality Management as a system for managing their organizations.

Reported results from articles written in leading business and government publications have been mixed. When most articles discussing TQM report the results of successful companies that have implemented TQM, they also cite a number that have been unsuccessful. We strongly believe that it is not the basic beliefs and principles that fail, but rather management's inability to change their traditional management by objectiveculture to a Quality culture.

TQM has many critics, but no rivals. Most critics look to failed implementation attempts to argue their claims that TQM does not work in organizations. What is interesting is that, with all its critics, seldom does a critic advance a better system of management. The purpose of this chapter is to lay the foundation for TQM and set forth the cornerstones, beliefs, and principles of Total Quality Management.

WHAT IS TOTAL QUALITY MANAGEMENT?

TQM is a management system embracing a set of beliefs and principles designed to empower all associates to continually improve organizational processes with the goal of meeting or exceeding customer expectations.

TQM is a way of managing the organization at all levels, from top to bottom. The focus is on the customer, but the process is driven by the data collected. Organization members work in teams to continually improve processes.

DEMING AND JURAN: THE PROFITS FROM AMERICA

The foundations for Total Quality Management have their roots in two Americans who went to Japan after World War II. Dr. W. Edwards Deming and Joseph M. Juran are both responsible for Japan's recovery after the devastation of World War II.

To understand Deming, it is important to know that he received his Ph.D. in physics from Yale University in 1928. In the business world, however, he distinguished himself as a statistician and worked for Western Electric and later for the U. S. Government until after World War II. During World War II, both Deming and Juran had a significant effect upon American manufacturing. Knowing that quality products were necessary to win the war, statistics became a vital subject since they were used to find the acceptable quality levels (AQL).

The AQL tables prescribed minimum quality levels that were acceptable. Proponents of statistics realized the importance of statistical methodology to obtain quality. In fact, as an outgrowth of World War II, the American Society for Quality Control started in 1945.

Joseph Juran studied electrical engineering and law before he went to work at Western Electric as chief of the inspector control division. In 1954 Juran also went to Japan to lecture on quality management and was the first to deal with the broad aspects of quality management (organization communication, coordination of functions, etc.).

After the war, however, leading management scholars such as Peter Drucker and the infamous General Motors star Alford Sloan influenced major organizations to adopt another approach to management that was widely accepted, management by objectives. Although MBO became the leading management theory in the 1960s and 1970s, the roots of MBO can be traced back to Drucker in his writings in the latter part of the 1940s and the 1950s.

Advocates of quality control such as W. Shewhart, Joseph Juran, W. Edwards Deming, and Armond Feigenbaum were not rejected, however, nor was Total Quality Management embraced by top management. The management-by-objectives approach became far more dominant and accepted by manufacturing leaders. Quality control became more a matter of inspection and detection and not the primary focus of top management.

What is interesting is that all four of the advocates for quality control, Shewhart, Juran, Deming, and Feigenbaum, worked at one time for Western Electric. All four have written extensively on quality control: in 1963 Shewhart wrote *Economic Control of Quality of Manufactured Products;* Feigenbaum wrote *Total Quality Control* in 1961. Perhaps Juran's quality control hand book published in 1951 was the most significant publication and is still recognized as one of the most significant books ever written on the subject.

Of the four authors, Deming and Juran became the most famous, since both of them spent considerable time in Japan assisting Japanese manufacturers in building high quality products. Understanding all four of the writers on quality control requires an understanding of what Deming referred to as "profound knowledge." Profound knowledge emerges from understanding variation and, more specifically, process variance. Since variance is change, the aforementioned authors believed that to understand a process the variation points within each process needed to be identified to achieve quality. As statisticians, they were able to chart the amount of variance in an entire process. When variance was normal, it was thought of as the process being in control. However, when variance was not within the limits of the process, then the process was thought to be out of control.

These quality control advocates suggested that the sources of variations within the process should be investigated when the process was out of control. Statistical data should be used when designing, manufacturing and inspecting quality. American business leaders understood the importance of quality control. However, they only accepted quality control as a step in the process, not one to be applied to the total process.

Consequently, American manufacturers focused on making quality control a specific department within the manufacturing process. Hence, quality control became a function that was applied to the product after it was built, not during the designing and building process. In most American factories the job of the quality control engineers became an inspection and detection function at the end of the line.

They would use statistics to try to weed out the bad products from the good ones. Since American manufacturers dominated the world in products, it was okay for consumers to take their chances in buying American products. American manufacturers realized that they had a built-in market for practically anything they built, and the quality of their products was not vitally important to making profits. Practically all products designed, built, and inspected had consumers waiting impatiently for them. Even when products varied significantly in quality, it was okay. In fact, many industries emerged in America just to repair poorly designed and built products.

Even though American business leaders understood the significance of the total quality control advocates, they refused to let their notions dominate their management approach. Therefore, Deming and Juran went to Japan after World War II to assist Japanese manufacturers in building quality products. Profound knowledge, controlling variation from the design stage to the delivery stage, became the dominant management theme in Japan.

It wasn't until the latter part of the 1970s and the early part of the 1980s that American manufacturers began to realize that they were losing market share and that the management approach they were using may not be in their best interest. In 1980, a television show entitled "If Japan Can, Why Can't We" was aired on a major broadcasting company. This TV program alerted many business leaders, and it caught the attention of the American people. Many business leaders went to Japan to begin studying how they could improve their management methods.

Many Americans had already discovered that products built by our international competitors were better for their pocketbooks than what they could buy in America. The United States was literally forced to rethink how it would manufacture products that would compete with our international competition. Because Deming and Juran had such an impact upon Japanese business leaders, total quality control became the basis of a new management system called Total Quality Management.

To make total quality control work in Japan, Deming and Juran became far more than statisticians and engineers. They used the assumptions that emerged from their study of variance to develop a complete management approach to organizations. Statistical analysis and the study of variance was the foundation of their management approach. However, they became experts in quality leadership, quality teams, the use of technology, the use of data, organizational structure, performance measurement, etc. While American management scholars were writing about management methods to improve productivity, Deming and Juran were focusing management methods to improve quality.

We believe that the management methods advocated by Deming and Juran should be applied in government. In 1992, the Department of Labor and Employment Security in the State of Florida allowed us the opportunity to test the Deming and Juran methods. Their ideas became our foundation for developing a management system for government organizations.

We also were influenced by the work of Phil Crosby, author of *Quality is Free*. Crosby argued that the most effective method of management is to prevent defects. His slogan was "zero defects." Crosby also developed a complete management approach.

In the following pages we will identify the key elements in the management approaches outlined by Deming, Juran, and Crosby. We will use all three approaches in developing what we believe are the cornerstones—the beliefs and principles—of Total Quality Management.

Deming listed fourteen points that he has used with companies in Japan and in America to help them become competitive and successful. When he first started working with the Japanese, he had fewer points—perhaps ten—but as a result of his continued dedication to quality and experience rescuing companies, the list has grown. Although these points were intended for private industry and not for services in government, many apply equally well to government. These fourteen points are presented in a book commended by Dr. Deming, written and explained by Mary Walton in *The Deming Management Method*[1] as follows:

1. *Create constancy of purpose for improvement of product and service.* Dr. Deming suggests a radical new definition of a company's role. Rather than making money, it is to stay in business and provide jobs through innovation, research, constant improvement, and maintenance.

2. *Adopt the new philosophy.* Americans are too tolerant of poor workmanship and sullen service. We need a new religion in which mistakes and negativism are unacceptable.

3. *Cease dependence on mass inspection.* American firms typically inspect a product as it comes off the line or at major stages. Defective products are either thrown out or reworked; both are unnecessarily expensive. In effect, a company is paying workers to make defects and then to correct them. Quality comes not from inspection but from improvement of the process. With instructions, workers can be enlisted in the improvement.

4. *End the practice of awarding business on the basis of price tag alone.* Purchasing departments customarily operate on orders to seek the lowest-priced vendor. Frequently, this leads to supplies of low quality. Instead, they should seek the best quality and work to achieve it with a single supplier for any one item in a long-term relationship.

5. *Improve constantly and forever the system of production and service.* Improvement is not a one-time effort. Management is obligated to continually look for ways to reduce waste and improve quality.

6. *Institute training.* Too often, workers have learned their job from another worker who was never trained properly. They are forced to follow unintelligible instructions. They can't do their jobs because no one tells them how.

7. *Institute leadership.* The job of a supervisor is not to tell people what to do or to punish them, but to lead. Leading consists of helping people do a better job and of learning, by objective methods, who is in need of individual help.

8. *Drive out fear.* Many employees are afraid to ask questions or to take a position, even when they do not understand what the job is or what is right or wrong. People will continue to do things the wrong way, or to not do them at all. The economic loss from fear is appalling. It is necessary for better quality and productivity that people feel secure.

9. *Break down barriers between staff areas.* Often staff areas—departments, units—are competing with each other or have goals that conflict. They do not work as a team so they can solve or foresee problems. Worse, one department's goals may cause trouble for another.

10. *Eliminate slogans, exhortations, and targets for the workforce.* These never helped anybody do a good job. Let people put up their own slogans.

11. *Eliminate numerical quotas.* Quotas take account only of numbers, not quality or methods. They are usually a guarantee of inefficiency and high cost. A person, to hold a job, meets a quota at any cost, without regard to damage to the company.

12. *Remove barriers to pride of workmanship.* People are eager to do a good job and distressed when they can't. Too often, misguided supervisors, faulty equipment, and defective materials stand in the way. These barriers must be removed.

13. *Institute a vigorous program of education and retraining.* Both management and the workforce will have to be educated in the new methods, including teamwork and statistical techniques.

14. *Take action to accomplish this transformation.* It will take a special top management team with a plan of action to carry out the quality mission. Workers can't do it on their own, nor can managers. A critical mass of people in the company must understand the Fourteen Points....

THE *QUALITY CONTROL HANDBOOK*

Joseph Juran's *Quality Control Handbook*[2] covers ten steps to achieving quality within an organization:

1. *Build awareness of the need and opportunity for improvement.* Before a quality improvement program can be successfully launched, managers and administrators need to be convinced that a problem exists. This can be done by acknowledging the loss of customers due to foreign competition, poor records of delivery times, etc.

2. *Set goals for improvement.* Ford Motor set its goal as "Quality is Job One." Some companies decide to be very specific with goals like "We will cut the cost of poor quality by 25 percent within two years." The major reason goals are important is to announce to all that a change is taking placing within the company and that quality is important.

3. *Organize the overall program.* Juran suggests the development of a quality improvement council that actively involves upper management. This group of upper managers guides, supports, and coordinates the overall program. The council helps identify training needs, establishes support for teams, designs recognition plans and plans for publicity.

4. *Provide training.* The implementation of a quality improvement effort assigns new roles to every associate. To be successful requires training in concepts, skills, and tools of continual improvement.

5. *Carry out projects to solve problems.* Juran teaches that all breakthroughs in quality improvement are achieved project-by-project, and in no other way. A project is a problem chosen for a solution and is also a managerial way of life. There is no such thing as an improvement in general.

6. *Report progress.* Reporting progress is critical to ensure that there really is a "meeting of the minds" as to what is happening and what plans are in store for the future. Reports keep managers informed so that they can help the team overcome obstacles.

7. *Give recognition.* There are numerous ways that recognition can be given to project teams including certificates, plaques, and dinners, in addition to the opportunity to report in the office of the ranking local manager.

8. *Communicate results.* Good communication is an essential component of a continual improvement effort. Communication can be enhanced through regular stories in the company's newsletter and local newspapers, posters, and notes on bulletin boards.

9. *Keep score.* Scores can be kept in several ways, including "progress on individual improvement projects, progress on projects collectively and merit rating of individuals with respect to quality improvement." Juran states that there is no debate on revising the merit system to include performance on quality improvement. To do otherwise weakens the emphasis on quality.

10. *Institutionalize the annual improvement process.* Quality improvements need to become a regular component of the manager's job along with supervising, monitoring, etc. Quality efforts should not be viewed as an "add-on" to the other responsibilities of anyone working in the company. No meetings should be held without quality playing an important role in the agenda.

PHIL CROSBY

The author of *Quality is Free*, Philip B. Crosby, is probably best known for the concept of "zero defects" that was popular in the 1960s. Crosby was in charge of quality for the Pershing missile project where this concept was developed. In 1965, he joined ITT as director of quality and then formed his own quality-management consulting firm in 1979. Philip Crosby Associates operates throughout the world now and his book has sold more than a million copies.

Crosby defines quality as conformance to requirements and in defense of the title of his book states that "what costs money are the unquality things—all the actions that involve not doing jobs right the first time."[3] Quality is free when organizations move from detection of mistakes to prevention. Mistakes are caused by one of two things—lack of knowledge or lack of attention. The first can be measured and corrected. The second is an attitude that can be changed by the individual. To achieve this, Crosby lists fourteen steps to quality improvement:

1. *Management Commitment.* Make it clear that management stands on quality, and that the final product will conform to standards at the optimum price.

2. *Quality Improvement Teams.* Representatives from each department will participate on teams because each is a contributor to defect levels.

3. *Quality Measurement.* Quality measurement provides an overview of current and potential nonconformance problems that allows objective evaluation and corrective action. The measurement reports are straightforward and expressed in terms that can be understood and used.

4. *Cost of Quality.* Define and evaluate the cost of quality and explain its use as a management tool. Crosby states that the cost of quality is composed of the costs of scrap, rework, warranty, service (except regular maintenance), inspection labor, engineering charges, purchase order changes, software correction, consumer affairs, audit, quality control labor, test labor, acceptance equipment costs and other costs of doing things wrong. The total expense of these costs should be no more than 2.5 percent of the sales dollar.

5. *Quality Awareness.* It is important that the personal concern for quality be raised by all within the company. This can be accomplished in a number of ways including regular meetings to discuss nonconformance problems, through articles in the company newsletter, etc.

6. *Corrective Action.* The goal of corrective action is to provide a systematic method of resolving forever the problems that are uncovered through previous

action steps. Corrective action is best accomplished when teams work on the most serious problems first—following the Pareto principle.

7. *Zero Defects Planning.* The purpose of this planning by a special quality improvement task team is to list all the individual action steps that must be taken before the zero defects day (see #9) to ensure success. The concept and program of zero defects are explained to all supervisors so that they may explain it to their staff. A time schedule is prepared, functions outlined, and the method of launching the program decided.

8. *Supervisor Training.* The key to a successful quality improvement program is the supervisor. Supervisors need to be knowledgeable and skilled in what to do to carry out their part of the quality improvement program.

9. *Zero Defects Day.* The purpose of zero defects days is to let all employees realize through a personal experience that there has been a change. Zero defects is a new way of life, and accomplishing this requires a personal commitment and understanding that is new to most people.

10. *Goal Setting.* Shortly after zero defects day, the supervisors should meet with their individual workers to determine what kinds of goals they should set for themselves. The goals should be specific and measurable. The goals should be developed by the people themselves rather than by their supervisor, and should be challenging. The goals should be posted by the worker in a conspicuous place.

11. *Error-cause Removal.* Individual employees should communicate to management any obstacles that make it difficult to meet their goals. This is important because one of the most difficult problems employees face is in communicating with management.

12. *Recognition.* People appreciate recognition. Initially, they come to work for the money, but once the salary is established, their concern is for appreciation. Through recognition they realize that management seriously needs and values their help.

13. *Quality Councils.* Quality Councils offer the opportunity for professional quality people to communicate on a regular basis to share their problems, feelings, and experiences with each other.

14. *Do It Over Again.* The purpose of this step is to emphasize that the quality improvement program never ends.

Based on the concepts primarily advanced by Deming, Juran and Crosby, we developed the following model of Total Quality Management. Our model is based on five cornerstones of TQM. These are the essential elements of our theory of Total Quality Management. We believe that if an organization desires to become a quality organization, then it must incorporate into its management method the following tenets of TQM.

TOTAL QUALITY MANAGEMENT CORNERSTONES

1. **A TQM system of management must begin and end with its customers.**

2. **Management decisions are based on fact. Accurate and meaningful data drives decisions.**

3. **Improving processes is an everyday event.**

4. **Partnerships with suppliers, customers, and other organizations that affect the process are required.**

5. **Empowerment, the authority to improve the process, is granted to an associate.**

Our Total Quality Management approach includes these cornerstones in every thought that we advance in this book. Underlying the assumptions, the beliefs and the principles described within this book are the cornerstones. No thought is advanced without taking into consideration the customer, data, process improvement, partnerships, and empowerment. If an organization is not willing to focus on meeting or exceeding customer expectations, not willing to gather, analyze, and make decisions on accurate data, not willing to accept process improvement (no matter how small) as important, not willing to develop partnerships and linkages with their processes, and not willing to empower front-line workers to improve the process, then Total Quality Management is not an appropriate approach for the organization.

On the other hand, however, if it is the highest priority to meet or exceed customer expectation, let data dominate decisions, make incremental changes, develop partnerships with those who link to organization processes, and finally realize the power of empowerment, then TQM is an approach you need to take.

Government leaders will often argue that the cornerstones appear to be appropriate for management in private organizations, but would not be effective in public organizations since the customer for most government leaders is the Legislative and the Executive Branches. The goal has always been to keep them happy. If the Legislative and the Executive Branches are happy, then more resources will be allocated to government. It's often difficult to argue with such a position, since government has grown by leaps and bounds over the past 30 years.

If growth is used as a measure of success, then government is by far the most successful organization in America. The problem is that government is changing, and customers are changing. The consumer now is getting a better product because the consumer is more aware of quality. Because of international competition, the consumer has a lot more options and is using them. Consumers found their power by selecting quality choices. Some might argue, though, that the consumer does not have an option in government. Well, anyone who has followed the voter behavior in the past 10 years realizes that the consumer now understands that they do have options in government. They can control an entire Legislature by public opinion.

The public, just as they did to American automobile manufacturers, is sending a message that is loud and clear. They want a government that's effective, and they want a quality government. We believe that the most effective, maybe the best, method of providing a quality government to taxpayers is to adopt Total Quality Management, and we strongly believe that the cornerstones we have identified here should serve as the foundation for Total Quality Management in government. We believe it's necessary because the consumer/taxpayer is demanding it, but, just as important, TQM is a system that efficiently and effectively delivers what the taxpayers need and want. Further, it is a system that naturally motivates government workers.

We begin our discussion of implementing TQM in a government organization with these cornerstones. Our success stems from using the cornerstones as the foundation for our Total Quality Management initiative.

TOTAL QUALITY MANAGEMENT BELIEFS

A belief is a habit of mind in which trust or confidence is placed. Vital to Total Quality Management is a set of beliefs that is necessary to adopt if an organization elects to implement Total Quality Management. An organization considering TQM should first examine the fundamental tenets underlying TQM. If these beliefs are not embraced by management, then it's difficult to implement a successful TQM initiative.

Many organizations that attempt to implement TQM fail because management failed to adopt a new set of beliefs. It is practically impossible to make TQM work when management hangs on to old top-down, meet-the quota-or-else mentality, and believes that the best way to make production quotas is to tell everyone what to do and if they don't do it, find someone who will do what they are told.

Our TQM initiative is built upon the following beliefs:

Belief No. 1: People Are Untapped Resources

People who work in an organization are the organization's most valuable resource. Traditional organizations have often stated that people are its greatest resource, but believe that "If people would just do what they are told to do" the organization would be effective. In the 1950s through the 1970s, many organizations relied on technology for advancement. The goal was to have technology replace the worker. Technology can replace workers who are hired just to do one task. For example, there used to be many "brain dead" jobs in industry. For eight hours a day, a person would move one part, such as a piece of sheet metal or a door handle or a fender, from one place to the other. No thinking was required. Obviously, it wouldn't be long before technology would replace this person because of the simplistic nature of the job.

Today, because of the advancement of technology and the advancement of modern management systems, workers are seldom hired just to do one specific task. Rather, people are asked to work in teams to use their brains to make improvements in the process. Rather than treating workers like robots, management must find ways to untap their brains so that individual abilities and skills can be maximized. TQM is a management system that allows people to use their brains to improve organizational processes.

If managers believe that the utilization of brains belongs only to top management, then they should not adopt TQM. If, however, they believe that all associates, no matter at what level in the organization, can make a significant contribution, then TQM is an excellent management system. We found that most government workers, even with a lack of financial incentive, appreciated the opportunity to use their brains.

Belief No. 2: People Who Do the Work Are in the Best Position to Improve Organizational Processes

For years, management did the thinking, and the employee did the work. It was management's job to figure out how to improve the system. Consequently, managers would spend their time planning, organizing, directing, and controlling their employees. Managers spent most of their time trying to control people. They believed that if they controlled people, then they were successful managers. On the other hand, in Total Quality Management, the manager's concern is the process, not on controlling people. In fact, there is less need for managers in a TQM organization because workers let the data that is derived from the process control their actions.

Who better knows the job than the individual doing it? Who else sees problems, or potential problems better? They, not their supervisor, or a top executive miles away, are in the best position to improve work. In increasing numbers, state agencies are now asking their top managers to do "work days" in first line jobs so that they can appreciate the actual demands of the job and see why those who actually do the work are the ones who are in the best position to improve the processes.

If a team, formed with members who are closest to and who work on the process, is allowed to meet an hour a week to make improvements, the process would run far more effectively. For a team to be effective, however, they must have accurate data derived from the quality indicators that are measured. If managers can tap the brains of those people closest to the work, then the processes will be successful.

Belief No. 3: Continual Improvement

Traditional management in western culture is largely focused on innovation, or in today's language, "reengineering" or "reinvention." Advocates for innovation management, speak of dramatic large step innovations. We respect this way of thinking,; however, we believe that the most effective way for government to improve is to make continual improvements. We advocate in incremental change, small steps, but over time, very rewarding ones for the organization.

We believe that if government would incorporate the customer as its driving force, rather than the Legislative and Executive Branches, and focus on continual improvement of its processes to meet or exceed customers' expectations, a quality government would evolve. This does not mean the Legislative or Executive Branches can be ignored, but they must be perceived as partners who help interpret the needs and wants of customers—not as a driving force dictating what to do.

The Executive and Legislative Branches of government provide the vision, the mission, and the guiding principles. The workers, through continual improvement of their processes, meet or exceed customer expectations.

Belief No. 4: Values Drive Behavior

Values are what ought to exist in the workplace. Values are concepts that have relative worth and importance to each individual. For society to live cohesively together, they must share values. When people have conflicts, they often result from a difference in values. We believe that an effective organization shares similar values. We believe that these values should be published, role modeled, and used to select people who are entering the organization. For example, government organizations value diversification of its workforce. If an individual does not value diversification, they should understand that working for a government organization may not be appropriate for their background and preferences.

The values serve to notify all associates of proper behavior. Therefore, managers only have to role model the desired values and not spend their time controlling other people's behavior by coming up with their own set of values. Traditional management allows the manager to set values as to what is important and then allows the manager to control others based upon personal values. For an organization to be effective, one set of values must serve as the guiding values. If teams wish to add values to the total organization's values, they may, but the set of values that's adopted by the total organization is the primary set of values that directs behavior in the organization.

Some members of management reject organization values as a whole because many managers would still like to control people using their own value system. Organizations should not tolerate managers who violate the values of the organization. To have "total" quality management, core values are necessary. Managers should not be allowed to designate their own personal values as those of the organization. Values are shared, and people working in the organization are expected to behave according to the values, and that includes everyone from the top executive to the front-line worker.

Belief No. 5: Prevention as Opposed to Detection

We believe the best investment is the one that prevents problems rather than detects mistakes. Too many organizations have quality control divisions whose job it is to inspect end quality. The quality department may send defects back to manufacturing, (who usually complains that if it had been designed right, it could be built right) or the quality department repairs the defects.

Errors are frequently detected in government. Sometimes these errors are detected by customers, sometimes government standards force agencies or departments to count errors, and, of course, they are detected by auditors. According to Al Gore, one out of three individuals working in government is watching the other two. According to Deming and Juran, 85 percent of errors are system errors and only 15 percent can be attributed to worker error. We believe that in government the percentages are much higher, and that 95 percent of errors are system errors and only 5 percent are operator errors. The focus of Total Quality Management is on prevention, and we believe that if government improves its management systems, they can prevent mistakes in the system.

Belief No. 6: Organization-Wide Involvement and Commitment

From top to bottom, everyone in the organization must be involved in Total Quality Management. Obviously, top management believes the TQM initiative, but it's everyone's responsibility to come to work to make continual improvements in the processes. In a TQM organization, brains are not left at the door, but rather brought to work and are required to be used. TQM is not a management method that can be selected for use by specific managers. It is an organization-wide commitment that is required.

For years, managers required loyalty as their primary value. They wanted people who were only loyal to them. Since so many things in organizations were done in secret, loyalty was required. Managers didn't share data, but rather kept it to themselves, interpreted it, and took proper action. The idea was that the manager would look good and get promoted. The subordinates were supposed to make the manager look good and, in turn, the manager would give them raises. Managers built their own teams and expected loyalty.

In a TQM organization, loyalty is to the organization and not to a specific manager. Organization-wide values drive behavior, and the system is an open system where data flows openly and each worker has access to the data.

Leaders must "walk the talk" and demand that quality be the most important component of all work.

THE PRINCIPLES OF TOTAL QUALITY MANAGEMENT

The foundation for Total Quality Management emerged primarily from Deming and Juran. From them, we developed the cornerstones for TQM and then set forth a set of beliefs which we deem necessary for incorporating TQM. Within our framework is a set of principles that guide the management philosophy and approach for a Total Quality Management organization.

Principle #1: Meet or Exceed Customer Expectations

FOCUS: The Customer(s) of Each Process.

The goal of a TQM system is to meet or exceed customer expectations. Rather than being driven by top managers who interpret what the customer needs and wants, the organization is driven by customer focus. The workers who are assigned a given process are responsible for interpreting customer needs and improving their assigned processes. The vision, the mission, the organization's structure, organization's plan, personnel practices, policies, procedures, and the management system (TQM) are the responsibilities of top management.

Principle #2: Manage the Process

FOCUS: On Process Identification and Process Improvement

Efficient and effective organizations are achieved by each process within the organization maximizing process capability. To achieve success organizations should not emphasize the management of functions, nor the management of people, but rather the management of interconnecting processes. The lessons learned from the management of organization in the 1960s and 1970s, that a specific function could be performing well and specific people could be performing well in the organization, yet the total organization couldn't deliver a quality product, should never be forgotten.

A total quality managed organization is only as good as its weakest process. Therefore, each process demands the attention of those personnel assigned to the process, as well as top management.

Principle #3: Data Collection and Analysis Is an Ongoing Activity

FOCUS: On Measurement

Each associate assigned to a process is responsible for collecting and analyzing data that emerges from the study of each activity along with inputs, outputs, and outcomes. Each process, for example, will identify the time, errors, and the amount of rework within a process. It is not the measurement of people, but rather the measurement of quality indicators within the process that leads to continual process improvement.

Principle #4: Decisions Are Data Based

FOCUS: Information Obtained from Data Collection and Analysis to Guide Decision Making

By using Total Quality Management tools, organization members generate meaningful data that is used to make decisions that lead to continual process improvement. Data and information are collected from a variety of both internal and external sources. The collection is a systematic effort that provides valid information to be used by employees to analyze and improve the work processes. Decisions reached within teams and by top management are thus based upon valid data rather than "gut-level."

Principle #5: Process Improvement Requires Supplier/ Customer and Organization Partnerships

FOCUS: On Supplier Quality—What is Received and Customer Quality—What is Delivered

In state government, the "suppliers" include our referral agencies, the vendors that supply services and may include employers who seek individuals that have progressed through the department's processes. Each of these partners has a vital interest in the success of the client's program, and each shares the benefits resulting in quality services. On the other end of the process are customers who receive products. It is critical to continually measure customer's needs and expectations through a variety of ways including surveys, focus groups, etc.

Principle #6: Process Improvement Teams Are Responsible for Continual improvement

FOCUS: On the Use of Teams to Improve Organizational Processes

Teams within TQM are assigned the analysis of the process and are empowered to meet the needs of the customer. They honor the TQM principles and identify and evaluate potential improvement opportunities. They are empowered to implement suggested changes and to verify results.

Principle #7: Organization Communication and Recognition Is a Shared Responsibility

FOCUS: Sharing Organization Information with Individuals and Teams Who Contribute towards Making Process Improvements

Being open and honest regarding organization communication is a requirement for a total quality managed organization. No data, whether it be positive or negative, should be withheld from associates. For an organization to be effective, associates must be trusted and respected. Therefore, it should not be the role of upper management only to tell associates what they need to know, but rather to share information at all levels. To make improvements, associates must understand what is occurring in the process they're assigned, but also in all other processes.

The role of upper management is to assure associates that no matter what data is generated from their work, as long as the data is accurate the data will be treated in a positive manner. If top management doesn't trust their associates and people are punished for delivering bad news regarding quality indicators, then it will be impossible to drive out fear in the organization. If there is fear in the organization, then management is likely to get data that only fits their wants and needs. An organization managed by fear frequently generates data that is designed to make management look good, but the customer goes wanting.

Principle #8: Train All Associates in Total Quality Management

FOCUS: On Training Everyone in the Organization, No Matter What Their Level, in the Organization

Traditional management practices assumed that management knew best. Therefore, management's job was to tell the employees what to do and an employee's job was to do what they were told. Management training was observed, of course, only for managers. In a TQM organization, however, everyone is treated with respect and everyone receives management training since it is everyone's responsibility to work together in managing a process.

Principle #9: Process Performance Is Measured by Quality Indicators, Outputs and Outcomes. Personnel Are Recognized and Rewarded for Their Contributions to Process Improvement and Process Performance

FOCUS: On Developing Management Systems That Yield Quality Outcomes and Reward Individuals Who Work in Teams to Continually Improve Process

Managing performance in a total quality managed organization is not a simple process. It is not a matter of meeting a quota or a goal. Nor is it a matter of just doing an assigned task. Rather, a worker in a TQM organization fulfills many roles and accepts numerous responsibilities. Workers are expected to take ownership of their assigned processes and are empowered to make continual improvements.

Workers do not work in competition with other workers, but rather work in cooperation. Therefore, they are rewarded for their contributions as individuals and team members. Further, performance assessment includes a variety of instruments, including assessments made by customers, suppliers, team members, and management.

Managers use the same instruments as well as evaluations by subordinates.

Principle #10: Leadership Is Transforming a Quality Vision into Action, Creating a Customer Orientation, Letting Data Drive Decisions, Role Modeling Quality Values, Being Highly Visible, and Being Actively Involved.

FOCUS: On Leading by Example, Developing Others, Creating a Quality Culture, Satisfying Customers, Measuring Results, Strategic Quality Planning, Using Human Resources, Maintaining Quality Assurance, and Supporting Team Work

An effective TQM leader must be out in front. Leaders must make it clear that meeting or exceeding customer expectations is the driving force and that associates should look to the customer for direction. It is not the leaders' interpretation of what the customer needs and wants, but rather data that is derived from customer analysis which motivates process improvements. TQM leaders aim at process control, not controlling people. TQM leaders manage the process, not people. They set forth the vision, help construct the mission, develop a culture so all associates can practice the values, and recognize associates who contribute towards making continual improvements. TQM leaders respect people, have high expectations of them, and enable associates to attain quality work and a high level of performance. TQM leaders have high energy and energize others.

To achieve a quality government, we need to change our principles of management. For years, organizations followed the management productivity principles of planning, organizing, directing, and controlling. Management did the planning and the controlling while the employees did what they were told to do. Management was supposed to listen to employees, but management made the decisions. Even today, most managers think their job is to plan the work of their subordinates, organize their work, direct or motivate them, and control them. The concept is a simple one—management knows best. If employees follow the plan, fit into the organization, are motivated to achieve success, and don't deviate too much from the "best employee model," the organization will be a success.

What we found is that the old scientific management model works well when the goal is productivity; however, it has its limitations when we're trying to meet or exceed customer expectations. Today organizations no longer want an employee "who doesn't think." Employees who can come to work every day, know their processes, document the process, and use their brains to improve the process are desirable.

In Total Quality Management, the management label doesn't imply the traditional view of a management that does the planning, organizing, directing, and controlling, but rather a management that takes on a new perspective and includes the following principles:

1. The process is managed.

2. The process goal is to meet or exceed customer expectation.

3. The process is data driven.

4. The process is thoroughly measured.

5. People work in teams.

Management's role is not to plan the work and control the employee, nor to motivate the employee. The system or process, if done correctly, is in itself motivational. Once the process is in place, there is no need for a grandiose plan nor a major innovation, but rather continual improvement of the process. In order to accomplish this, the five principles identified above should be followed. To make these principles work, managers need to:

1. Communicate constantly,

2. Train people,

3. Focus on total performance, and

4. Lead by example.

The total quality principles of management do not make the distinction between management and the associate (employee—previously explained). What they encompass are ways to get associates involved in every aspect of improving the process they work on. These principles are designed to empower the individual, to tap their brain, and use their full potential in the workplace.

IMPLEMENTING TOTAL QUALITY MANAGEMENT

Changing an organization from a functional organization to a process improvement organization is indeed a significant challenge. For years government organizations were designed around functions. In fact, as government grew, they divided the organizations into more and more functions. This organization leads to a very comfortable work environment where challenges to improve are ignored. Once the function is outlined, rules are developed, and policies implemented, there is little need for creative thinking.

Trying to untap the brains of front-line workers is one of the most difficult challenges facing today's government organization. The question is, how do we get government personnel to make continual improvements in the processes they manage on a daily basis? In this chapter, the foundations, beliefs, and principles we believe critical to the successful implementation of TQM were outlined. The next chapter, "Designing a TQM High Performance Organization," discusses how we successfully applied TQM.

NOTES

1. Walton, Mary. *The Deming Management Method.* New York: Perigee Books, 1986.

2. Juran, Joseph M. *Juran's Quality Control Handbook.* New York: McGraw-Hill, 1988.

3. Crosby, Philip B. *Quality is Free.* New York: Penguin Books, 1980.

4. Feigenbaum, Arnold V. *Total Quality Control.* New York: McGraw-Hill, 1961.

3 DESIGNING A TQM HIGH PERFORMANCE ORGANIZATION

In September 1993, the National Performance Review, sponsored by Vice President Al Gore, published a document which clearly outlined what government should do to develop a new customer service contract with the American people. The goal was to develop a new guarantee of effective, efficient, and responsive government that puts customers first and demonstrates to the American people that their tax dollars will be treated with respect for the hard work that earned them.

The National Performance Review looked to see how successful organizations—business, city and state governments, and organizations of the federal government—had made savings and efficiencies. They concluded that successful organizations had several things in common. They

- cut red tape—shifted from a system based on accountability for following the rules, to one where employees are accountable for achieving results.

- put the customer first—listened to them, restructured basic operations to meet their needs, and used market dynamics such as competition and customer choice to create incentives for success.

- empower employees to get results—decentralized authority and empowered those who work on the front lines to make more of their own decisions and solve more of their own problems.

- get back to basics—abandoned the obsolete, eliminated duplication, and ended special interests' privileges.

The report suggested the following steps to cut red tape:

1. Streamline the budget process.

2. Decentralize personnel policies.

3. Streamline procurement.

4. Reorient the Inspectors Generals.

5. Eliminate regulatory overkill.

6. Empower state and local governments.

To put customers first, it suggested the following steps:

1. Give customers a voice—and a choice.

2. Make service organizations compete.

3. Create market dynamics.

4. Use market mechanisms to solve problems.

It suggested the following steps to empower employees to get results:

1. Decentralize decision-making power.

2. Hold all employees accountable for results.

3. Give workers the tools they need to do their jobs.

4. Enhance the quality of work life.

5. Form a labor-management partnership.

To cut back to basics, the report suggested the following steps:

1. Eliminate what is unnecessary.

2. Collect what is due the government.

3. Invest in greater productivity.

4. Re-engineer programs to cut costs. [1]

The Report of the National Performance Review could not have occurred at a more appropriate time for what we were trying to achieve in the Department of Labor and Employment Security in the State of Florida. It assisted us in reinforcing what we were trying to achieve in our department, and, furthermore, it clearly described the need for change.

VISION

Our first step towards designing a high performance workplace was to clearly describe what we wanted to create. A vision is a statement that describes the desired state of the organization, what it should become. We started with the question: What do we really want to create? A vision is an object of one's imagination, and our goal was to describe how we would manage the organization based solely on the beliefs and principles of Total Quality Management.

We wanted to create a workplace that embraced the TQM cornerstones, accepted the beliefs, and practiced the principles of Total Quality Management.

OUR TQM VISION

Our vision emerged from the cornerstones of Total Quality Management. We wanted an organization that focused on the customer. The goal was clear: To meet or exceed customer expectations; where we managed by fact and made decisions based on accurate and meaningful data; where process improvement was an everyday event and incremental change became the role of each associate in the workplace; where partnerships evolved, including between suppliers and customers, so that workers could do the right thing the first time; and, finally, where every worker was empowered to work as a member of a team to scientifically improve the way we conduct our business.

Our next step was to develop our mission.

TQM MISSION

To develop our mission we answered the question: Why do we exist? Our purpose was to implement the beliefs and principles of Total Quality Management in the Department of Labor and Employment Security.

TQM STRATEGIC PLAN

To create our vision and to achieve our mission, we developed a TQM strategic plan. Our plan included a strategy, a series of planned activities designed to implement TQM throughout the organization. Our overall goal was to have all organization associates using TQM beliefs and principles in managing the organization.

The purpose of the rest of this chapter is to set forth the steps we initiated in our strategic plan. In this chapter, we will only describe the steps we initiated to fulfill our mission. In the latter part of the book, we will present the tactics we used in the actual implementation of our strategy.

We believe that the strategic plan outlined in this chapter is an effective strategy to follow for any organization that desires to implement TQM. The steps outlined herein provide an excellent framework for implementing TQM, and at the same time recognize that reactions to each step will vary significantly, depending upon the culture of the organization. This chapter sets forth a model to follow in implementing TQM in the organization.

We place our model in the context of a logical time sequence. We realize that each organization differs significantly and that the steps and time sequence will vary significantly. We believe, however, that in the course of implementing TQM into an organization, at some time each of the steps we recommend must be fulfilled. We realize up front that planning and decision-making are two separate functions: Planning what to do, and deciding when it actually is done are not always the same.

Implementing TQM is both an art and a science. The speed at which TQM is implemented is directly affected by many organization variables. Some organizations have a past management philosophy and practice, such as management by objectives, that is so entrenched it is almost impossible to move the organization in another direction. Managers, particularly top management, find it very difficult to embrace TQM, since they have achieved personal success in a "top-down" organizational culture. It is very difficult for people who have spent their organization careers meeting the goals and objectives outlined by their supervisors to change to a management system that focuses on the customer, is driven by factual data, pays attention to partners, and empowers subordinates to work in teams while making process improvements. Acceptance of TQM will be dramatically different in each organization.

We present the following TQM strategic plan as only a model to follow and not a prescription on how to do it. Later chapters on TQM implementation cover how associates reacted to our plan and the tactics we needed to employ to make our plan work.

FIRST SIX MONTHS

Creating Awareness—Seminars

Goal: *To expose organization members to the cornerstones, beliefs, and principles of Total Quality Management.*

During the first six months, the senior author conducted more than 30 "Introduction to Total Quality Management" seminars. The first seminars were offered to the directors and bureau chiefs, followed by seminars for anyone in the organization who wanted to receive exposure to TQM. This seminar set forth the following beliefs:

Belief #1— We believe that people are untapped resources.

Belief #2— We believe people who do the work are in the best position to improve organizational processes.

Belief #3— We believe in continual improvement.

Belief #4— *We believe values influence behavior.*

Belief #5— *We believe in prevention as opposed to detection.*

Belief #6— *We believe in organization-wide involvement and commitment.*

At the conclusion of discussion of the beliefs, we covered the Principles:

Principle #1— *Our goal is to meet or exceed customer expectations.*

Principle #2— *We manage the process—each process is important.*

Principle #3— *Data collection and analysis is an ongoing activity.*

Principle #4— *Our decisions are data based.*

Principle #5— *Process improvement requires supplier/ customer/partnerships.*

Principle #6— *Process improvement teams are responsible for continual improvement.*

Principle #7— *Organization communication and recognition are shared responsibilities.*

Principle #8— *We train all associates in the principles of Total Quality Management.*

Principle #9— *We measure process performance by quality indicators, outputs and outcomes. Personnel are recognized and rewarded for their contributions to process improvement and process performance.*

Principle #10— *Leadership is transformational.*

Create Awareness—Reading Material

The first step in creating awareness is to select a few appropriate reading materials for organization members. We recommend two books: Walton, Mary. *The Deming Management Method.* New York: Perigee, 1986; Imai, Masaki. *Kaizen: The Key to Japan's Competitive Success.* New York: Free Press, 1986.

Further, we recommend that the organization develop its own booklet presenting its TQM philosophy. A copy of the booklet that we used in the Department of Labor and Employment Security can be obtained by writing the Total Quality Coordinator, Florida Department of Labor and Employment Security, Hartman Building, Suite 303, 2012 Capital Circle SE, Tallahassee, FL 32399, or fax a request to (904) 488-8930.

Flowchart Core Processes

Goal: To gain a better grasp of what is managed in the organization and to have a clear picture of all processes including customer and suppliers.

Each division in the organization should flowchart its core processes. Core processes focus on how work gets done in the organization. Process goals are aimed at meeting or exceeding customer expectations. Since the goal is to change people's thinking from being functional thinkers to process thinkers, flowcharting the core processes accomplishes two important objectives. First, flowcharts will provide organization members a clear picture of how work gets done, and second, organization members will realize that they are customers of customers and that meeting functional objectives does not necessarily mean that the organization is successful in meeting customer needs.

Mapping core processes serves many purposes. First, top management clearly begins to understand how work gets done. Second, organization members realize how one process affects another and how the results of one process affect the results of another. Third, organization members will understand that allocating work according to the division of labor is not the most effective method for achieving organizational success.

Form Teams to Improve Processes

Goal: To identify process improvement teams and empower them to make continual improvements.

Once the core processes are completed, it becomes readily apparent that many processes are natural for a TQM team. Volunteers who would like to serve on process improvement teams should be solicited. Their job is to improve the process, and they should be given the following outline to guide their team:

1. Identify the core processes to be examined and improved.

2. Empower process improvement teams.

3. Schedule team meetings.

4. Flowchart the process.

5. Identify customer expectations.

6. Collect the data.

7. Analyze the data.

8. Follow the PDCA cycle (Plan, Do, Check, Act).

9. Document the improvements.

10. Improve again.

Although each team will likely have a different perception as to what each step means in the process, the outline will provide a framework to those members of the organization who accept the beliefs and principles of Total Quality Management and are eager to get started. About one-third of the people working in the organization generally are not satisfied with the present way work gets done and will jump at the opportunity of being empowered to make changes.

Even though we believe that these teams will soon be requesting training on process improvement, it is in the best interest of the organization to allow them to get started. If organization members accept the beliefs of TQM and desire to practice the principles, they are well on their way to becoming effective members on a continual process improvement team.

Communication and Recognition

Goal: To send messages to the entire organization that process improvement teams are functioning and to recognize team members who step forward and take the risk of applying the beliefs and principles of TQM.

Teams should be expected to make the results of their work highly visible. For example, flowcharts should be posted, quality indicators should be identified, and quality data collected should be posted so that all team members and managers have access to team information. It should be clear that the team "manages by fact" in process performance, rather than just following directives given by management.

When teams begin to function, management should recognize activities and feature team participation in the organization's newsletters. Any improvement deserves the recognition of all associates in the organization. Process improvement teams that meet or exceed customer expectations deserve attention and newsprint.

Team leaders and managers who support TQM also deserve recognition. They should be recognized along with the teams they support in articles appearing in the organization's newsletter. The primary objective of organization newsletters should be to promote and communicate quality.

Leadership

Goal: To stress the importance of leadership in the successful implementation of Total Quality Management and to have leaders who truly do "walk the talk."

TQM leaders are out in front. They know that quality cannot be delegated. They need to be highly visible and "walk the talk." They must make it clear that they strongly embrace TQM and share the vision of the organization becoming a system that is driven by customer focus and accurate and meaningful data in the hands of associates who are empowered to make process changes that allow them to do their work right the first time. Much of their time is invested in assisting teams in making continual improvements and providing recognition to teams willing to work towards improving organizational processes.

Leaders demonstrate daily their commitment to the vision and mission of the organization. They work to drive out fear and empower front-line associates to do the right thing the first time. They role model departmental values.

Establishing Top Management Team Values

Goal: To establish values that will drive top management behavior as TQM begins growing in the organization.

Soon after departmental leaders adopt the cornerstones of TQM beliefs and principles, they should agree on a set of values that guides them in working as a team. These values developed by departmental leaders should not be published immediately. These are the values that they have agreed to role model for the purpose of working together in creating a TQM organization. A formal set of values that will be distributed to the entire organization will be developed with associates representing all levels in the organization.

Establishing a Mission

Goal: To point in the right direction—customer focus.

Top management should work as a team to establish the mission of the organization. The mission describes the purpose of the organization and focuses primarily on how the organization meets customer needs. The mission provides a clear statement on why the organization exists and its primary focus.

TQM Planning Team

Goal: To help direct and implement TQM in the early stages.

Shortly after associates become aware of Total Quality Management and see that top management is committed to implementing TQM, a number of people will emerge who are deeply committed to the initiative. Some will be in top management positions, however, extremely bright and talented associates at lower levels will show interest in becoming more involved. TQM leaders should tap these resources so that these people can be actively involved in making TQM a reality.

One of the most effective ways that they can contribute is to become a member of the TQM planning team. This will be a team of TQM leaders representing all levels of management who are willing to do their assigned jobs as well as whatever else is necessary to implement TQM.

One of the most effective planning tools is the SWOT analysis. This analysis requires answering the following questions:

1. What are the strengths within the organization relative to TQM?

2. What are the weaknesses preventing the implementation of TQM?

3. What opportunities are available to promote TQM?

4. What threats are perceived that may impede progress towards implementing TQM?

The TQM planning team meets regularly to assess TQM progress and to recommend a plan of action.

SECOND SIX MONTHS

In the second six months of implementing TQM in an organization, we recommend continuing to do everything that was done in the first six months while also implementing the following strategy:

Establish a Quality Council

Goal: *To guide the Total Quality Management initiative.*

The Quality Council is made up of top organization leaders, members representing middle management and members representing the front-line. The purpose of the Quality Council is to formalize the TQM process and recommend actions that advance the TQM initiative. We recommend that the council does the following:

A. Develop a mission.

B. Set forth the organization's values.

C. Sponsor process improvement teams.

D. Develop criteria for rewarding process improvement teams and instructions to be given to process improvement teams for their presentation to the Quality Council.

E. Develop criteria for a TQM leadership award.

F. Develop quality principles.

G. Review the training program and suggest improvements.

H. Encourage teams to appear before the Quality Council.

I. Sponsor a quality forum—honor the best teams and leaders.

We have only included some of the more significant steps a quality council should take in this outline. Obviously the Quality Council will do much more. In later chapters, we will describe in detail how our Quality Council functioned within the Department of Labor and Employment Security in the State of Florida.

Training

Goal: *To train all associates in the basics of Total Quality Management.*

There are significant differences of opinion regarding when to start training in an organization that's attempting to implement TQM. One extreme position suggests that no TQM initiative should begin until all organization members receive basic TQM training. On the other hand, another strategy advocates that TQM is a simple and logical process and organization members can meet the challenges that confront them without participating in extensive training.

Tracking Teams

Goal: *To chart progress regarding continual improvement teams.*

Begin tracking teams by identifying all teams that are making process improvements. There are a number of different ways to track, including the use of commercially available software packages such as Paradox. Even a simple spreadsheet can be developed. The major objectives are to insure awareness of what teams are functioning (by department or division), which associates are team members, how often they are meeting, what training they have received and where they are in their work. Tracking enables identification of teams that may be having some difficulty or are not making the progress they should. Tracking also identifies when a team is nearing completion of their improvements so that meetings of the Quality Council may be scheduled to recognize and reward team members.

Benchmarking

Goal: *To compare process results with the best organizations.*

Benchmarking is a process of comparing internal organization processes with the best organizations. The best organizations that are recognized as the leaders in the field are targeted for benchmarking. Process performances are compared against the best. Since government, particularly state governments, have many processes that are duplicated throughout the state, there are many opportunities to compare. There are often many excuses why one process doesn't compare to another, e.g., it's a larger state or the culture of the state is different.

Even though there are not absolute comparisons available, there is adequate information to make judgments on the effectiveness of the processes. Benchmarking is an effective process for getting the organization members to look beyond their own boundaries.

SECOND YEAR

In the second year everything proceeds as it did in the first year, but with the following additions.

Initiate Process Improvement Guides

Goal: *To empower those individuals who have demonstrated special interest in quality by designating them as process*

improvement guides to help teams by providing technical assistance.

Teams often experience significant difficulty in getting started and keeping their momentum. In our first year, we thought that facilitators would be sufficient. However, we realized that teams encountered significant obstacles that required more than just a facilitator. It required individuals who worked with top management and process improvement teams to eliminate barriers that impeded their progress. A number of associates were especially interested in TQM, were active on several teams, and wanted to have more training and experience in quality concepts. We called together a "class" of these individuals early in the second year and provided them with a special five-day intensive seminar on TQM. Upon completion of the seminar they were designated as Process Improvement Guides (PIGs) and were given the responsibility to help team members in the group process by (1) observing and evaluating how the team was functioning, (2) providing training as needed in team dynamics, the teachings of the quality improvement "gurus," (3) helping select appropriate "tools" for teams to use, and (4) helping the teams prepare presentations for the Quality Council. The concept of the process improvement guide was a highly successful one, and by the end of the second year there were several hundred PIGs operating around the state.

Organization Surveys

Goal: To assess TQM progress.

We used an organization-wide survey to assess our progress. The survey focused on a number of significant topics, including:

1. Opportunity to participate in TQM activities, including teams;

2. Awareness of TQM training opportunities in a timely manner;

3. Encouragement to participate in TQM by supervisor;

4. Awareness of TQM tools; and

5. Feeling of empowerment.

Establish TQM Project Teams

Goal: To address a specific management-selected problem.

On occasion, a special project team may be formed to address a special "one-time" need. These differ from "process" teams that in theory never complete their mission, for there are always improvements that can be made in any process. For example, in anticipation of specific issues that might confront the organization, we empowered the following teams listed below. Special project teams may need to be created during the first or second year of implementation.

1. Measuring and performance.

2. Development of a TQM survey.

3. Development of a TQM strategic plan team.

4. Quality data team.

Leadership Development

Goal: To identify and recognize leaders of the TQM initiative.

In the second year, many managers may still be "anti-TQM," and some will even be downright hostile. They may be unwilling to accept a new paradigm. They still believe that management is controlling people and maintain the attitude, "IF people would only do what I tell them to do we would be a successful organization..."

We believe the best strategy at this stage in the TQM initiative is to ignore them unless they are just openly hostile and to focus on supportive managers who actually lead the TQM initiative. Leaders who support the TQM initiative should be encouraged to take on more responsibility, and if possible, should be recognized for their efforts by an increase in pay.

In many government organizations, increases are across the board and it's difficult to accept that managers who are not supporting the TQM initiative are also given raises. However, reclassifying some leaders will provide them with a financial recognition. Furthermore, leaders can be encouraged to attend conferences and to represent the organization at professional meetings. Our approach was to invest in those who invest their time and effort in our organization. Managers who are working against TQM should not be rewarded by participation in the few perks that go with government jobs.

In the third year, TQM may become mandatory in your organization; and then if managers refuse to support TQM, then we suggest that they be demoted.

In the first couple of years, we recommend that people should be patient with managers. People gravitate towards TQM at various paces, and we have observed many managers who fought TQM in the beginning of the initiative do a reversal and become excellent TQM leaders. TQM leaders understand and promote what Deming refers to as the "constancy of purpose." Their development is key to a TQM initiative.

Move Towards Eliminating Quotas and Standards as the Only Goals

Goal: To eliminate quotas and standards.

Perhaps the most challenging obstacle to overcome in implementing TQM is the long history of federal and state governments trying to manage from the top with quotas and standards. Like clockwork, both federal and state governments spend an enormous amount of time each year determining what the new quotas and standards will be for the following year. If quotas and standards continue to be the driving force behind the government management system, ineffective bureaucracies will continue.

On the other hand, a TQM organization can place the quotas and standards into a proper perspective. While not totally ignoring these requirements, we found that, with the proper execution of TQM, the quotas and standards are easily met by effective process improvement; and where the quotas and standards were not met in the first year, we found on further analysis that the quotas and standards had never been met for the past 10 to 15 years. We also found that in organizations where quotas and standards were met each year, customer satisfaction was very low, front-line service providers were extremely unhappy, and there was significant turnover.

Take Action to Drive Out Fear

Goal: To eliminate fear in the workplace.

This is another challenge to overcome. In the first year of implementing TQM it is practically impossible to eliminate fear. Many people are afraid that they will lose their jobs if TQM is implemented. In fact, people frequently say that, "If they eliminated the errors in this organization, what would I do?" Also, after they have looked at a flowchart and see the amount of rework that has to be done, they will realize that if the process was done right the first time, it would require fewer people.

For front-liners, it's often the fear of losing their job. For managers, it is the fear of losing their job; and in many cases, the fear of losing power and control over people. We addressed this issue by making a claim that there was plenty of work to be done in the organization; and if their job was eliminated, we would find them another one in the organization.

One of the most effective methods for driving out fear is to increase the knowledge and skills of workers. Fear comes from the loss of something important, such as a job or power. What reduces fear is the self-image individuals have regarding their professional knowledge and skills. Treating all organization members as professionals, investing in their education, and improving their skills is a major step forward in driving out fear. Once the organization members know the organization is serious about putting the customer first and that you allow accurate and meaningful data will drive decisions in the organization, they will gradually begin to build their trust in the organization.

Driving out fear is a slow incremental process. Managers will try to sabotage TQM efforts by constantly reminding teams that they can go ahead and meet but they better meet standards and achieve their quotas. Usually managers who are against the TQM initiative will wait for the team to experience some difficulty and then sit back, laugh and say, "See, I told you so. They can't work together."

Building trust often requires taking two steps forward and one step back. Fear disappears only by practicing the principles of Total Quality Management. When the focus is on correcting the system and not correcting people, fear in the organization will dissipate.

THIRD YEAR

The implementation process should continue as it did in the first two years.

Apply for a Total Quality Management Award

Goal: To have the organization evaluated against criteria used to measure a Total Quality Managed organization.

For example, if the organization were to be evaluated using the Baldridge Award criteria, the following criteria would be used by examiners:

1. Customer driven quality.

2. Leadership.

3. Continual improvement.

4. Employee participation and development.

5. Fast response.

6. Design, quality, and prevention.

7. Long-range outlook.

8. Management by fact.

9. Partnership development.

10. Corporate responsibility and citizenship.

Applying for the award in itself is extremely valuable. It is a lengthy and difficult process and requires organization members to make a significant investment in time and effort. The application process itself has many positive outcomes. First, the members who participate in filling out the application learn a lot about their organization. Second, it renews TQM spirit within the organization since organization members will conclude that their organization has a long way to go in becoming a Total Quality Managed organization. And, finally, obvious weaknesses emerge that need immediate attention.

Once the application is reviewed, and if the organization is selected as one of the organizations to be visited, a renewed spirit for TQM will again emerge. Preparing for a visit from award examiners is exciting and, of course, the visit by the examiners is a significant challenge. Even more rewarding is the examiners' evaluation after they have completed their visit. Of course, anyone interested in TQM within the organization looks forward to their written critique.

Establish Internal Examiner Team

Goal: To develop members of the organization as internal examiners.

After the organization is reviewed by a TQM award organization, people who participated in writing the application and who participated in the review process are chosen to form a team. This team will evaluate processes within their own organization as well as other divisions. Their assistance is invaluable. They can help their division as well as other divisions in the organization to implement TQM.

Develop Relationships with Organization Partners

Goal: To establish relationships with outside organizations whose processes directly affect the organization's processes.

Successful TQM implementation often depends upon others whose processes impact upon those of the organization. It is essential that steps be taken to involve them in the organization's efforts to improve processes. For example, in the Department of Labor and Employment Security, we began to develop relationships with the Department of Management Services and the Comptroller's Office. Both of these organizations directly affected the time it took to complete our processes and both had a significant effect on all our error rates.

Organizational Alignment

Goal: To realign the organization to support the TQM initiative.

After the organization identifies its core processes and teams are in place to make continual improvement of these processes, it is obvious that significant changes in the way that the organization is structured are necessary. The best strategy is to identify and improve processes first and then align the organization accordingly. Many organizations are often too quick to respond to organizational change by restructuring or reinventing the organization. It's best to first understand how the organization actually works and then focus on realignment as a continual improvement process rather than a reinvention process.

Too many organizations make the mistake of focusing on structure because it's easy to change from the top and then expect continual improvement. We have found that focusing on organizational structure too soon can become a diversion to TQM. Such as focus allows autocratic managers- an opportunity to concentrate on ways to control people rather than on improving processes.

Rather than starting out to flatten the organization as an initial objective, focus on continual improvement, and then realign the organization according to the natural flow of work. We have found that if the organization is realigned according to natural process flow, the end result will be a flattened organization. There will be less need for top management control of people, less need for managers, and less distance between the top and the front-lines.

Advanced Training

When more than 50 percent of organization members have graduated from initial TQM courses, most of the graduates want further education. They will want to become more sophisticated in their knowledge and skills. Therefore, we suggest offering the following courses:

1. An in-depth study of Deming and Juran.

2. Advanced TQM tools.

3. Statistical process control.

4. The psychology of working in teams.

5. Advanced facilitation skills.

6. Advanced presentation skills.

7. House of Quality—Customer focus.

8. Process improvement and the use of technology.

9. Measuring performance in a TQM organization.

10. Advanced leadership.

INSTITUTIONALIZE TQM

As TQM becomes a habit and not something done to satisfy management, it will become the organization plan. In the first year and second year of TQM implementation, the traditional methods of top-down planning will likely occur. Slowly, TQM as a management philosophy and methodology will work into the traditional management approach. Rather than having a top-down management plan, the organization will eventually have a customer-driven plan. The organization's goals become the customer-driven goals developed by front-liners.

When the planning department begins focusing on goals developed by front-liners to serve their customers, the planning document will be easy to develop since planning specialists will be obtaining data from the front-lines to identify organizational goals that can be easily measured. Furthermore, the importance of discussing the TQM approach becomes less necessary. The discussions about TQM as a subject become passé and the important subjects provide answers to the following question: How do we improve our processes to meet and/or exceed customer expectations?

NOTES

1. *Creating a Government That Works Better and Costs Less.* Executive Summary, the Report of the National Performance Review, Chaired by Vice President Al Gore, September 7, 1993.

4 CUSTOMER FOCUS

"If you're not listening to the customer,
you'd better be listening to someone who is."
—*Karl Albrecht,* **Service in America**

One of the most difficult challenges for today's worker is to shift from a management by objective mentality to a customer-driven mentality. Americans have led the world in productivity improvement for years and continue to do so. Productivity improvement is a relatively easy concept to understand. One sets an objective and achieves it. Management sets the objectives and employees, if they do what they are told to do, will achieve the objective. It's a relatively simple system. It is based on the concept that management knows best. Effective employees are defined as those who do what they are told. Effective employees are retained; others are let go. The overall goal for every organization is to meet or exceed objectives. All of the objectives are to be clear, have specific dates, and numbers.

In the fifties, sixties, and seventies, the American automobile industry stood out as the ultimate model of management. First, the automobile industry prided themselves in hiring the best college graduates. Competition for Ivy League graduates was practically a war. And, of course, the competition within the industry was very secret. The best brains in America got together each morning with one objective: Sell more cars than the competition. Their approach would be to do market research, design an automobile that sold well, manufacture cars by a division of labor (assigning each individual a task), have a quality division to inspect each car and make corrections, and then tell a sales force how to sell products. The management concept appeared to be a rational one. Management does the thinking, workers do the work. After all, the best and the brightest knew what the customer wanted.

Furthermore, management systems were designed to reduce work to a specific activity so simple that one could be "brain dead" and still do the job. The automobile industry calculated that they would be successful if top management merely listened to marketing, told the engineers what to design, manufacturing how to build it, and sales how to sell it .

They were right for some time. However, another management system which was not solely based on the four historically accepted principles of planning, organizing, directing, and controlling would have a devastating impact on the automobile industry. International competitors had developed and followed principles and beliefs contrary to the long accepted American management principles. International competitors based their principles upon contrary beliefs. First, they replaced the concept that only management knows best with the concept that all associates are a resource and can make a significant contribution to the organization. Second, international competitors were not just interested in innovation but rather in continual improvement. They had learned when a company only values and prizes innovation, the average worker is left out of the process; ninety-nine percent of the workers are left out of the process. Rather than just innovation, they had each worker who they highly respected come to work every day with the assignment of making improvements in the process. International competitors strongly believed in people and their ability to improve the quality of their products and services.

They used a management system now defined as Total Quality Management. It begins not by putting management first, but puts the customer first. The goal is to meet or exceed customer expectations, not necessarily to meet or exceed objectives. The American automobile industry year after year was successful in meeting its productivity objectives. American cars were built faster than those of international competitors. The problem was that when America's top automobile executives were telling people the kind of cars they needed and how long they ought to last, they were out of tune with what American customers really wanted. Consequently, Chrysler almost went broke and Ford and General Motors knew they were in for a long-term battle to win America and foreign customers alike back.

What the American automobile industry slowly learned to understand was that they had to change their management system. It was no longer enough to meet management's numerical objectives; building a product that either met or exceeded customer expectations was required.

GOVERNMENT CUSTOMERS

Federal, state, county, and city governments across America are in a similar situation to what the automobile industry faced in the eighties. For years the government agencies have been extremely productive. One hardly ever reads a government report that does not show how successful the organization is in achieving its objectives. Furthermore, you frequently hear top executives in government frequently describe their organizations as "one of the best" or even "the best" in the nation. When confronted with a question of how they can make that statement, they will rattle off statistics claiming that the cited numbers make them number one. When it is demonstrated to them that other state organizations are better in that statistic, they immediately will claim that state can't be used as comparison because it is, of course, different than theirs.

Like the automobile industry, the government is very productive. It rehabilitates more people, finds more people jobs, improves safety in the workplace, builds more roads, arrests more people, fines more people, builds more prisons, arrests more speeders, enrolls more students in our schools, hires more teachers, builds more buildings, inspects more facilities, gives out more Social Security checks, has more welfare programs, and collects more taxes. The concept gets old, and every division of government wants more. If more resources are provided to government, it increases numerical objectives. It's an unending cycle that creates an ever larger government bureaucracy.

The problem is, like the automobile industry, meeting or exceeding the numerical objective set by top management is not the answer. When the automobile industry executives first began to learn that what they thought was best for the customer wasn't what the customer wanted, they first went through a period of denial, and then began to blame each other at the top, causing a reshuffling of top executives, finally coming to grips with the real problem: the customer was not driving the process, but rather the thinking of top executives was driving the process.

Most government executives understand today they can no longer deny that they are out of tune with their customers. However, most believe that reshuffling government administrations at the top is the answer. Many would argue that, yes, government is out of tune with society, but that's only because the people at the top refuse to change and are not listening to their customers. Top government officials still believe that the best people to interpret what the customer needs are the people at the top of the organization. Many top executives in government believe that if they could only hire better people and pay people more, government would once again be effective. First of all, government does hire many qualified and able people; and second, government salaries, although not competitive at the top and middle levels of organizations, are very competitive in many areas of our country. It's not the people that make government ineffective, but rather it's the managerial system. Joseph Juran, one of the original "gurus" of customer satisfaction, observed that most of the inefficiency in an organization is the result of faulty systems through which the work must be done, and not the fault of the worker. Juran believed that a full 85 percent of problems can be corrected only by revisions and improvements in the processes.

Government is not customer-driven. It is top management driven. It still uses the old management by objective approach. People at the top set the overall objective, the organizations are supposed to align themselves with the objective and each month, quarter and year provide the government the statistics that show the objective was achieved. In all probability, more than 90 percent of the objectives were achieved last year in all governments whether it be federal, state, county, or city. If that's the case, then why are so many customers dissatisfied with government services? Why do people resent going in to get their license plates; why do so many people resent going in to get an unemployment check; why do so many people resent asking for help in job rehabilitation, etc.? The point is, why do so many people know and feel that if they've got to deal with a division of government, it's going to be an unpleasant experience?

Government has lost sight of its customers. The phone call requests at any government telephone receptionist station will demonstrate how many people receive the "run around" when they deal with government. One has to feel sorry for all of the callers. Most people have been in the same position when dealing with government. Even most intellectual organizations, (colleges and universities, where supposedly both the person calling and the person receiving are part of an intellectual elite) can't seem to communicate with each other on who to call. Finally, the representative from the university quits in frustration and gives the caller another number, with the only objective of getting the caller off their back. Government customers stand in long lines, only to be told that they don't have the proper documents. During a recent switch to a new computer system, an agency decided to "rope off" half the available terminals for customer use to keep the mainframe from being overloaded. No one bothered to make a sign explaining why half the terminals were unavailable. It appeared that the agency purchased too many terminals and did not know what to do with them. Lines formed at the available terminals. Government customers stood in long lines and watched government employees chat, laugh, and take breaks right in front of them.

THE TRAPPED CUSTOMER

Many government customers feel like they are just trapped. They would like to remove themselves from the trap; however, they can't because they need the government service. We have observed people stand in unemployment lines who just lost their jobs and are looking at a three- to four-hour wait to get their unemployment check. Little do they know that after they finish the paperwork for their unemployment benefits, they must to go to another government agency to prove that they are looking for a job. At a second office, they had to fill out the same forms one more time. Consequently, it often takes days to get an unemployment check. The first day entails waiting to be signed up for unemployment and the second entails signing up for Job Services (of course, Job Services is in another building, generally 10 miles away).

TOP DOWN MANAGEMENT MENTALITY

In our study the attitude of government top management was often one of "We're doing the best we can with the resources we have," when confronted with the trapped customer. The easy answer was "If we only had more resources, we would be able to serve the customer more effectively." Top management denied the real problem, "The Management System." Practically all decisions regarding the way customers were treated were made levels away from the actual interaction between the front-line staff member and the customer.

Furthermore, dividing the labor and the task made sense to government officials. With two divisions, one to provide an unemployment benefit and the other to provide Job Services, government officials thought they could be effective. After all, both were separate tasks. This is exactly the problem; top management only sees the tasks to be completed and therefore plans and organizes around a division of labor. Of course, each division means a larger bureaucracy, higher pay to those who leave the division, and more power to the division directors. Government is set up and managed the same way cars used to be built. Top management sets the objectives, does the planning and the organizing, tells the customer what they should get and how they should get it, and tells government employees how to behave. And when the system doesn't work, they have to either blame the other executives and therefore have a reshuffling at the top, reorganize the system (a common solution), or hope someone buys the excuse that if the top executives could only hire better people, the system would work.

The reality is that top down management driven systems are doomed to failure whether it be in private industry or in government. We must move away from the mentality that government customers are "trapped" and therefore accept the treatment they receive. It is our contention that government can no longer operate with this attitude. It's time we put the customer first. The customer must come first. It's a time to shift away from trying to tell customers what they need, what they want, and how they will receive it to *starting* with them. Customers, after all, are the people served by government, and they, not just government employees, should benefit from government services.

CUSTOMER-DRIVEN DECISIONS

It doesn't take any observer of government management systems very long to conclude that the management system is designed for management's convenience and not for the convenience of customers. Customers frequently have to fill out duplicate forms for duplicate divisions because management wants it. Government employees fill out more forms and spend more time trying to figure out what management wants than what their customer wants. These employees are not stupid. They realize that their supervisors complete the forms that grant pay raises and future promotions. The customer plays absolutely no role in pay raises or promotions, so why should anyone pay any attention to them? The smartest move is to deliver exactly what management wants—properly filled out forms and good paperwork.

Decisions at the top are often made on the pretense that customers will benefit by such decisions. However, top management is often so far removed from what's happening in the front-lines, they make the wrong decisions. Furthermore, they train all their employees to look to the top for the answers. Consequently, the United States government has built huge bureaucracies. And it appears that the larger the bureaucracy, the less the organization is customer-driven. It's a very simple scenario. People at the top of government, the most removed from the customer, make the decisions and the people below them are expected to carry out the decisions. After all, the people making the higher salaries know what's best for the customer. They often have the most years "in service" to the agency and are paid to do the deep thinking. Employees further down deliver the services thought up at the top.

Not only can government bureaucracies be criticized for idiotic thinking, an example of it in private industry is IBM, one of America's best organizations, where they did exactly what government is presently doing and built a bureaucracy that became insensitive to customer needs. After years of building on a foundation of being customer oriented, IBM made the same mistake as the automobile industry: top executives became too far removed from their customers. While IBM customers were moving away from IBM's bread and butter industry, mainframe computers, the top executives denied reality and continued to tell their employees what to do. When IBM's customers were moving away from buying mainframes, management at first thought that their marketing people were not doing an effective job, and therefore began to reshuffle the marketing department. Since IBM was like the government (didn't want to fire their people), it was truly a reshuffling act. Even though the market for mainframe computers was changing, marketing still had to accept the blame. After reshuffling marketing didn't work, they reshuffled their executives. That, too, met with defeat.

Finally, IBM had to deal with the reality that was difficult to swallow. They, too, like the federal government, had built a bureaucracy that made it difficult for them to maintain close relationships with their customers. They realized that if they were going to continue with their success, they were going to have to make a significant change in the way they did business. IBM was willing to make that change and move from a top-down management driven system to a customer-driven management system. The customer must drive the process. Consequently, IBM, for the first time in its history, had to lay off thousands of people. What IBM realized was that it built a management system just for the sake of the people at the top. They realized they didn't need to cut salaries, but rather cut people. IBM still invests in their people; however, one of the best corporations in America had to make radical changes in the way they do business in order to survive. If the U. S. government is to earn the respect of the American people, it must make radical changes.

The radical change begins by starting with what the customer needs and wants. It is data that is obtained from the front-lines that must drive decision-making in the organization. Furthermore, customer-driven decisions are made by the workers closest to the work.

WE ALL WORK FOR CUSTOMERS

Each government worker, whether they are on the front-line or happen to be the President of the United States, should come to work every day with the attitude of improving customer service. What kind of government service do customers want? The answer: Quality. For each customer, quality is defined a little bit differently. However, generally speaking, customers want respect. Customers want government workers to respect them as people, show concern for their time, have their forms be accurate and reliable, and receive the benefit of services. Customers should feel that they "came to the right place" and would recommend the services to others.

All government workers should feel the same way. They should feel that they are working in the right place, a place that respects them, cares for them, and that the total organization processes information accurately and reliably. It is a total organization that is required for giving quality to customers.

GOVERNMENT'S NO. 1 GOAL: TO MEET OR EXCEED CUSTOMER EXPECTATIONS

Not long ago a government worker expressed, "Let's cut out all of this customer crap, customers have choices and people wanting government services don't have a choice." Obviously, this is not healthy attitude. It suggests that customers will take what is provided and if they don't like it, that's tough. Also missing from his logic is that government customers do have choices. On the surface, government customers appear to be trapped, but in reality they have the power to change the system. First of all, they have the power to complain—which probably does little good—but sometimes these complaints can irritate even the front-liners. And when there are enough complaints, government might decide that it's best to privatize government services. Recent government surveys demonstrate that most Americans are not satisfied with government. Even though all the data suggests that government is extremely productive, most American taxpayers feel that they do not have a quality government. One need only look back to the elections in the Fall of 1994, when citizens expressed their dissatisfaction with government by removing many seasoned political leaders. One common complaint heard throughout the land was that government had become too big, too intrusive, and was not interested in meeting the needs of its citizens.

To attain a quality government, the focus must shift to the customer. Each time government representatives interact with a customer, their goal should be to meet or exceed the customer's expectations. Customers should not be thought of as being trapped, but rather as an opportunity for government workers to make the customer happy they received quality service and proud of the way "their" government works.

WHAT ABOUT ALL THE GOVERNMENT CUSTOMERS WHO DON'T WANT GOVERNMENT SERVICES?

Not everyone who comes into contact with government appreciates government intervention into their lives. Not all government organizations are like Education, Health and Welfare, Rehabilitation, Job Services, and Waste Management, etc., where their customers come to them. Government often goes to the customer, and often the customer is not very happy. Even when the customer goes to government for help, the answer is sometimes "No." Customer intervention into lives of the citizens is not always appreciated. For example, the speeder who just received a ticket, the thief sentenced to 10 years in prison, the person who's just been told that they didn't pay enough income tax, or the CEO who is just cited for polluting the environment are not happy customers. Therefore, some would argue that Total Quality Management is not applicable to many government operations. On the contrary, Total Quality Management is most applicable.

The goal is to meet or exceed customer expectations. The person speeding down the road at excessive speed was not happy when the policeman arrested him for speeding; however, the person arrested realizes that government just exceeded his expectations. He expected not to get caught because he thought that the "lazy police officer was probably drinking coffee and eating doughnuts." He quickly understood that a quality police system exists when the officer treated him with the highest respect, accurately and pleasantly explained to the speeder what had occurred, graciously wrote out a ticket, and professionally dealt with the customer. When the arrested person leaves, they know that they just dealt with a quality police officer.

Not all situations are so simple as the one described above. There are customers who are irate and insult the police officers. Officers know that they are in control of the situation, not just because of the power given to them by the badge, but in their own ability to deal with irate customers. And when the customer goes beyond the limits of normal behavior, the officer politely exceeds the customer's expectations by handcuffing the customer and taking him off to jail. The difference is that the officer is well trained in the art of the arrest. The arrest is made without injury to either the customer or the officer. Thousands of dollars are spent in training the officer before a first arrest. The officer is aware of the law's many facets and knows when an arrest can be made and the circumstances that must precede the arrest. The arrest will stand up in court and will not be a waste of tax dollars. Furthermore, the officer is aware that not every infraction of the law will always result in an arrest. There are special circumstances when an arrest would be wrong, and the officer knows the difference. Officers are paid sufficiently well so that a career police force exists that is a quality one.

If a government's customers must go to jail or prison, then it's government's job to meet or exceed their expectations. For some going to jail, it is a very scary moment. They expect to be treated poorly, to perhaps be assaulted. Obviously, in this case, government needs to exceed their expectations. Government must protect their Civil Rights and respect them as people. On the other hand, some customers going to prison may think it's a lark and their expectations are three meals a day and a roof over their head. In this case, government just might meet their expectations. On the other hand, if the goal is to rehabilitate prisoners, then government should exceed their expectations.

The goal of each government worker is to provide services that meet or exceed customer expectations. However, customer expectations are not defined by those at the top. Each situation is different and each government worker should be empowered to determine the best, most effective method of dealing with the customer.

THE ROLE OF MANAGEMENT

Managers who are afraid of losing their power and grip over workers immediately retaliate at the suggestion that the person providing the service be empowered to decide on the best approach to each customer by arguing that this will only create chaos. The trouble with management is that since they think they know what's best, they tell front-line workers how to deal with customers. However, management doesn't know best and will be continually shifting the goal. One day management suggests that processes should be speeded up. Therefore, workers are told that customers are not being handled fast enough. Therefore, the front-lines spend less time with the customer. A month later managers claim that there are too many errors. Now all the front-liners worry about making errors. The process gets slower. A month later, the manager gets a complaint and worries about how customers are treated. Now the front-liners are asked to focus on being nice to people.

The focus of TQM is on targets. The target, for example, might be for police officers to improve safety in areas they manage. Since no one police officer can be in charge of improving safety in that particular environment, offices would have to work together as a team. Their target would be to improve safety—make it safer for everyone in that area. The problem today is that officers are given an objective, for example, to give so many tickets in a particular area. Therefore, their objective is to make a specific amount of arrests in a particular time. What's interesting is that they achieve their objective, but the accident rates go up. Thus the objective needs to be changed and targets provided. A target is an objective without a date and time. The target for officers should be to improve the safety of their area, along with other team members. And they, along with their teammates, can set certain objectives. When police officers are given a target to improve safety, the police officers' perspective enlarges. They may be more concerned about signs in the area, cleanliness of the area, accident areas that have other causes, for example, over-growth of trees. Police officers today claim that they don't have any right to make improvements in other areas that may cause accidents in their area. What government must do is empower these police officers to work as a team to work on all of the problems that cause accidents in their area.

The assumption in Total Quality Management is that a team armed with data and empowered to improve the process is in the best position to meet or exceed customer expectations. The role of management should be to help teams to understand the target, and the role of the team is to improve the process so that everyone works together on the target. For example, targets can be as follows: (1) workplace safety, (2) prisoner rehabilitation, (3) education, (4) healthy people, and (5) educated workforce—quality workforce.

Each target can have a benchmark that is defined as the best process. Each process has baseline data. At a minimum, every process needs to collect baseline data.

What then is the role of management? The primary role of management is to support front-liners. The primary role of managers is to identify the process that they manage and help team members improve that process. Each process can be thought of as having a supplier and a customer. In the following chapter, we will get into detail on managing processes. In this chapter we are dealing only with the customer of the process. What managers will fully understand after they implement Total Quality Management is that they are more in control of the process than they've ever been in the past. Their situation is more in control than ever. They will have less control over how individuals manage the customers, but will have more control over how the total process operates. The role of the manager will be to not to manage individual personalities and individual performances, but rather to manage the process.

Managers know that the goal of the team they put together is to meet or exceed the customers' expectations. Their job is to help the team members gather data so that individuals can put forth their best effort in providing quality service for the customer. Therefore, measurement of the process through its effects on customers is one of the primary drivers of managerial action. By collecting objective data, managers can deal objectively with situations and not just with their whim for that particular day, week, or month. Workers must feel that they work for the organization and that their job is to improve the process, and that the management role is supporting them. The management role isn't telling people how to behave, but rather how to function as teams in improving the process.

EMPOWERMENT

Empowerment is defined as "power delegated downward to make key policy decisions previously made at a higher level." Simply, it is the ability to "stop the line" when a problem is found, to abort the installation of a new computer if an error is detected, or to resolve "on the spot" a problem a customer is having. When a salesperson can make an immediate refund, or when a waiter can issue a certificate for a meal without asking the manager, they have empowerment.

It is the right given to the person to improve the process and provide services to the benefit of the customer. It provides the opportunity for each person providing the service to make decisions that benefit the customer. In the traditional system, the manager would tell the employee how to behave. In the age of empowerment, employees are allowed to make decisions, are given every opportunity to do what they think is right the first time in dealing with the customer.

Some managers go around the office telling others how dissatisfied they are with the way one of their employees handled a situation with a customer. This is not beneficial to anyone. First of all, it's after the fact; the customer has already been hurt by their experience if the manager is correct. Second, other employees listen and say to themselves that they will not make that mistake. Therefore, employees spend their time trying to avoid mistakes rather than doing what's right for the customer. And finally, the manager doesn't know that the employee was wrong in the first place. All the manager knew was that he didn't like the way the front-liner behaved. That's why people should not be empowered to make decisions to the best benefit of the customer unless a Total Quality Management system is in place. At a minimum, baseline data that's meaningful to the front-liner should be collected, and associates need to meet at least once a week in teams in order to discuss the baseline data so that each team member can help improve the process.

Managers who think they know it all and know what's best for the customer find it extremely difficult to move to a TQM system. They often have many excuses that if only they could pay more or if only top management would only listen to them, things would be better. These Machiavellian-type managers think they know what's best for the employee and what's best for the customer. There were a lot of these Machiavellian managers in the automobile industry, computer industry, etc. (and there still are many Machiavellian managers in industry). Not every organization has been successful in moving towards a customer-driven organization.

Empowerment can only come when organizations learn to manage by fact and share the facts with teams. Armed with facts and meaningful data, people can provide quality service.

KNOWING THE EXTERNAL CUSTOMER

To know the external customer, targets must first be understood (e.g., highway safety, educated workforce, people with disabilities, etc.). Second, customers' wants and needs should be understood. Third, a management system that empowers service for providers with the resources to meet customers' wants and needs must exist. Once customers have been targeted, they should be impressed with services. Customers may be impressed with how much the IRS knows about their finances, how well the FBI captures someone, how effectively a teacher teaches, how much a prison guard knows about and cares about prisoners, how well human services can protect child welfare, etc. It goes on and on.

What government needs to do is define its targets and then empower teams to continually improve processes that move toward targets.

Knowing the customer means collecting data. What data should be collected? Data collection should be determined by the front-lines when dealing with external customers. Front-line associates need to determine what the customer expects and what the organizational requirements are. Practically every process must deal at a minimum with the following expectations: Was the customer treated with respect; did the customer get what he came for; did the customer get what he came for in a timely manner; was the data given by the customer and taken by the front-liner accurately; was the service processed in a timely manner?

Knowing customers means knowing their expectations. Since government has so many different types of customers and deals with such varied personalities (i.e., some customers may be mentally ill), front-line servers must understand the expectations far more than even top management. The problem is that front-liners often understand the expectations, but top management, who doesn't understand the expectations, are the ones giving the orders. Whether one is a police officer, a human service counselor, an employment interviewer, a rehabilitation counselor, an IRS agent, a teacher, a transportation representative, a judge, an environmentalist, a janitor, administrator, etc., one needs to know the expectations of the people served. The job is to improve processes so that customers are amazed at how efficiently and effectively everything works.

CUSTOMER SURVEYS ARE NOT ENOUGH

Practically all government agencies do customer surveys. The surveys may not always be familiar, for some government agencies are not practicing TQM. One government worker who was being interviewed for a position in our department was asked if his agency ever conducted customer satisfaction surveys. The worker replied that it certainly did. When asked how the surveys were taken, he replied that they "counted the screams" in the waiting room. He was being serious. Customers of that agency were so angry because of the poor service that they actually screamed obscenities at the receptionist. "We keep the Prozac handy for our workers," he told us.

In other agencies, government is effective at measuring customer attitudes towards service. They let the customer respond to closed- and open-ended questions. They get demographic data and allow the customer to rate and rank services. The problem with the typical government survey is that very few people pay attention to it; and, secondly, even when they do, it does little good. Most of the surveys are conducted by top management and the information is sent to top management. Many organizations will try to rank order different offices for customer service. In this case there is always a No. 1 office, and there is also always a bottom office. In the office ranked at the top, the manager takes full credit. In the office ranked at the bottom, there are many excuses for why it is at the bottom; and in most cases it's due to the diversification of the clients served or the diversification of the people hired. In any event the excuses generally hold up, for very few managers have ever been dismissed from government for providing poor service. Individuals who work for these poor managers might be terminated, but not the manager.

For surveys to be effective, they need to be designed and conducted by the people who provide the services. All top management needs to know is that there is a team functioning to improve the quality of their services and that the team is measuring their efforts daily, weekly, and monthly.

Front-line teams continually reevaluate expectations of customers in light of the data they collect. For customer process improvement to occur, baseline data needs to be collected.

Frequently, managers misuse teams to specifically collect data and take corrective action. For example, managers will set up a project team and give them the project of measuring customer satisfaction. Although there is sometimes a need in a Total Quality Management organization for a project team, which is often referred to as a "committee," to study a special problem, the primary need is for process improvement teams. These are the people who work daily on the process, and processes are far more complicated than someone just studying one particular part of the problem. That's why it is important to have customer-driven process teams who study the effects of their process. Front-liners are the people who deal directly with the customer and are in the best position to determine expectations and the most effective way to meet or exceed customer expectations.

After being appointed Secretary of Labor and Employment Security in the State of Florida, Frank Scruggs used one of the authors to facilitate front-line meetings. He wanted to learn from the front-line what needed to get done. The front-liners were the first to tell him that customers waste time by being forced to go to two different Divisions, filling out similar forms twice in order to get their benefits. For years top management attempted to keep the division between receiving unemployment compensation and getting a job. Secretary Scruggs put the customer first and brought together the two divisions in order to provide a one-stop service. It took approximately three years to achieve what Secretary Scruggs wanted to achieve. Management of both divisions went along with the change kicking and screaming. Even today, after the processes have been implemented, people who worked in one division or another complain. They wish it was like it used to be. It used to be more convenient for them to have it separate.

What's interesting is that the front-line knew what the customer expected and what the customer could achieve if only the organization put the customer first.

Armed with baseline data, front-line teams can then begin to set their own objectives. Customer-driven objectives where dates and times are attached are what are often called "quality objectives." For example, it may be an objective of a front-line team that no customer waits longer than 15 minutes. In the Jacksonville office of the Department of Labor and Employment Security, when the wait time becomes more than 15 minutes, managers immediately become additional front-line interviewers. This same office, that used to have lines that went completely around the building before the manager implemented process improvement teams, now has a record of serving the customer within 15 minutes, and, furthermore, has the lowest error rate of any office in the state. Morale in this office is extremely high. In one case, they exceeded a customer's expectation to the point where it produced dissatisfaction for the customer. The customer had been a previous customer four years ago when he was laid-off and was back again to get unemployment benefits. He remembered the previous visit and inserted enough quarters to be in the Unemployment Compensation Office for four hours. When he got out in less then 15 minutes, he became upset because he had just put in enough quarters for four hours, and he had just "lost" all that money. The Jacksonville representative offered him a seat if he would like to sit and read so that he could get his money's worth. The man laughed and walked out the door.

By empowering teams to determine customer expectations and to improve processes that either meet or exceed them, effective and efficient service can be provided for the target population. Success cannot be achieved by having bureaucrats in the top level of organizations tell the front-liners that they know what the customer wants, that they know how to treat customers, and that they will determine what is good service.

EXAMPLE OF A SURVEY DEVELOPED BY FRONT-LINE ASSOCIATES

The following survey is an actual survey developed by a team examining customer satisfaction in their local office. Homestead, Florida experienced a direct hit from Hurricane Andrew in August, 1992. A small farming community southwest of Miami, its customers are a diverse community of Hispanics, Haitians and others. The survey was written in English, Spanish and Creole.

> **"The Keys to Success"**
> **The Department of Labor and Employment Security**
> **Jobs and Benefits Division**
> Tell us exactly how you feel about our service. We are commit
> ted to your total satisfaction because <u>WE CARE</u>.
> 1. Our professional staff is trained to be courteous and respect-
>   ful. How would you rate us?
>   Excellent ( ) Good ( ) Fair ( ) Poor ( )
> 2. Were the written and oral instructions clear?
>   Yes ( ) No ( )
> 3. How would you rate the overall services of this office?
>   Excellent ( ) Good ( ) Fair ( ) Poor ( )
> 4. How can we improve our service?

EXCEEDING CUSTOMER EXPECTATIONS

A basic principle of quality improvement is that people closest to the process are the most likely to understand the process and to be able to improve the process. These people are also closest to their customer and interact with the customer. People closest to the customer are also the most likely to understand the customer's expectations better than any, and thus have the responsibility for defining expectations. The team of associates empowered with improving the process has the following responsibilities:

1. To define customer expectations.

2. To identify quality indicators in the processes that directly affect customer outcomes.

3. To identify procedural processes.

4. To define how to measure quality indicators.

5. To define methods for obtaining feedback concerning customer service (interviews, surveys, focus groups, customer councils, suggestion system, complaint system).

6. To identify customer expectations relative to front-line behavior (i.e., to make the customer feel as though the front-line associate was courteous, respectful).

7. To identify customer's expectations relative to timeliness of service.

8. To identify front-line associates' perceptions made by customer (i.e., was the front-liner helpful, responsive, knowledgeable?).

9. To identify procedures (i.e., were the forms clear and understandable?).

10. To identify the customer's perception of the facility (i.e., was the facility clean, and comfortable, and did it give the appearance that it was a professional organization?).

11. To collect baseline data on all quality indicators.

(Quality indicators are what is necessary to know from customers so that their expectations can be met or exceeded. The team should distinguish between customer types when doing its surveys. Some customers may be very upset because the results of the service provided were not in their favor. Every effort should be made to identify what is important to the customer. Without knowing what's important to the customer, it's difficult to meet or exceed their expectations.)

12. To display quality indicators to all members of the team, to know what's being measured, and, more importantly, to make it available to the team so that they can make improvements in the process.

The framework for developing customer-driven quality begins with understanding the customer, the customer's requirement, and obtaining customer input. The team can approach these questions from either a positive or a negative question. For example, a negative question might be, "What does not meet customer expectations?" The second step in establishing a framework is to develop measurements. It is necessary to establish baselines and collect baseline data that are consistent and have a common language. The measurements always go back to the question, "What is important to the customer?" In the third step, this data is used to increase the response to customer needs. It is important to remember that front-line associates form in process improvement teams to improve the process to meet customer expectations.

DEVELOPING THE CUSTOMER SURVEY AND IMPROVING THE PROCESS

1. Identify the customer.

2. Define customer expectations.

3. Validate customer expectations.

4. Decide what data will be collected.

5. Determine the times at which data will be collected.

6. Select the sample.

7. Select the method for data analysis.

8. Determine how data collected will be distributed and displayed.

9. Select questions for survey.

10. Pretest questions.

11. Collect data.

12. Analyze data.

13. Graphically display data.

14. Select areas where improvement is needed.

15. Plan methods for improvement.

16. Test methods of improvement. (Do.)

17. Check methods of improvement. (Test.)

18. Act on improvements. (Implement.)

19. Conduct surveys—ongoing assessment.

IMPROVING FRONT-LINE CUSTOMER BEHAVIOR

Traditional management practice has been to tell the front-liners how to behave. Millions of dollars have been spent on training front-liners on how to behave. Generally after management gets a number of complaints, government organizations hire outside consultants to come in and teach front-liners what to do. Traditionally, they teach the front-liners to not lose their temper, not to argue with the customer, be positive, listen, look for areas of agreement, ask customers what they want, be polite, thank the customer, call the customer by name, allow the customer to blow off steam, provide a caring demeanor, etc.

Total Quality Management advocates that with an effective system that empowers people, they will automatically care. What is important is that people shouldn't be taught to act as if they care, but rather a management system that allows people to care should be developed. Therefore, empower teams to design their own training. If the team feels that they need training in the area of how to perform customer service, they should receive it. It shouldn't be just management "telling them" they need it. Improving front-line behavior should be a direct result of the team first seeing that there is a need for it and, secondly, being empowered to design the type of training they need. When the data shows that the customer is dissatisfied with the personal behavior of associates, the team will request training. Some teams may automatically feel that there is a problem with personal service, and most do, and will do that even ahead of the data. The important thing is that the team sees that there is a need for it and is committed to improving personal behavior.

5 DATA-DRIVEN IMPROVEMENT

"Facts do not cease to exist because they are ignored"
—Aldous Huxley

When we began our implementation of Total Quality Management in Florida, it became apparent that teams would need an overview of the quality tools that would help them with problem solving. Individuals in our agency were a unique group, with some having a great deal of formal education, including graduate study, and others possessing a high school degree or its equivalent. Teams were composed of employment interviewers, rehabilitation counselors, safety specialists, unemployment representatives—many of whom completed masters, or even doctorate, degrees in their professional area. Yet, many team members were also secretaries, clerks and others who never attended college. Each was a valued member of their team, but came with various skills, knowledge and abilities. To provide meaningful training to this diverse team would prove to be a challenge.

We began by contacting the chairman of the statistics department at Florida State University, who also happened to be a very strong believer in TQM. Dr. Duane Meeter, an active member of the Tallahassee Quality Council, met with us and agreed to present an overview of seven quality tools for our associates in the headquarters office. A series of seminars was held for team members to present an orientation to flowcharts, histograms, cause-and-effect charts, Pareto charts, scatter diagrams, run charts and control charts. These seven tools, in addition to a brief discussion of check sheets, met the immediate needs of team members in the headquarters office.

As a result of these initial presentations, a training manual, *Continual Improvement Tools—an Overview,* was developed to continue offering the orientation to associates in Tallahassee. Three associates offered to serve as instructors, and a series of seminars was held throughout the state using this manual. The training proved popular, and continual improvement tools later became a component of the department's training modules. A great deal of credit for the

75

development of our tools training manual goes to Dr. Meeter. Without his assistance we would not have made the progress we have in our quality improvements.

A first glance at the tools manual might lead one to question the level at which the subject is presented. There are few references to statistics, with the exception of the section addressing control charts. Each tool is presented in a relatively light, non threatening manner. We found that most of the associates "enrolled" in this training had been out of school for many years and were not too sure of their ability to understand mathematics. Some were rather fearful of the concept of using "tools" that required algebra or even "arithmetic," much less statistics. In the seminars, we were able to alleviate their fears and, by beginning with flowcharts, we did not even have to mention numbers right away. In fact, we found that the majority of teams were able to function very well with a good understanding of flowcharts, Pareto charts, cause-and-effect diagrams, and histograms. A review of the eighty-five teams that presented to the Quality Council in FY 94 revealed that all made use of these relatively simple tools. On occasion, we found a team member who was really into statistics and "just had to work" on a control chart for the team. Team members generally humored that member and gave in.

In this chapter, we provide an overview of the tools just as we presented them to our associates. We believe it is important that this information be presented in this chapter so that those who wish to begin their effort may do so now, with the understanding that there is a wealth of books on TQM tools that are available and ready for consultation.

When we presented tools, we began with an overhead that listed the following:

- All work is composed of processes.

- The goal of each process is to meet or exceed customer expectations.

- All processes involve actions which can be improved.

- Gradual, unending improvements combine to produce lasting results.

- Improvement requires understanding of a process.

- People closest to a process are most likely to understand it.

- People who understand a process can improve it.

- Measurement of each process is essential

- Graphic problem-solving is best with processes charted.

- Decisions to improve the process are data-based.

- Understanding a few basic continual improvement tools facilitates problem solving.

- People empowered with the proper tools can make changes.

During the first part of the training, emphasis was placed on the need to base decisions on valid and timely data, vs., "gut level" feelings or hunches. Too often, decisions in government are made by the seat of a director's pants. In many cases, a justification for this approach may be found in the director's lack of faith in government statistics. Unfortunately, they are often right, for our experience has been that often the "facts" generated by mainframe computers are questionable. Recall the cliché "garbage in, garbage out," that seems to hold more validity with government statistics than anywhere else. As a result of this mistrust of data, one team began addressing the improvement in the department's numbers, and continues to suggest improvements to this day.

The lack of faith in numbers generated in the field but stored on the mainframe in Tallahassee provided more awareness of the need for team members to gather their own numbers. This is an extension of the principle that people who are closest to a process are most likely to understand the process. People who are closest to the source of the data should be the ones gathering and analyzing the data. The power of personal computers rivals that of mainframes when the numbers remain small, as they do near the source. It is preferable for associates to gather data on the front lines where they know what data will be helpful in their assessment for the need for improvement. For example, a team in unemployment compensation considered several tools when they began to analyze the time spent by customers in unemployment lines. Starting with a check sheet, they developed Pareto charts showing the worst day for applicants was Mondays. Before they gathered the data, they did have a "gut feeling" this was true, but they had no actual numbers to prove their suspicions. Flowcharting the process, they were able to identify the steps in the process, and with a cause-and-effect diagram they began developing solutions.

In the tools training, associates were given a diagram (page 78) outlining what tools should be used in different stages of their deliberations.

Participants appreciated this simple diagram to help them select the proper tool to use at a given stage in the process. This also helped them understand the relationship between the tools and the fact that some tools can serve different purposes during the steps in quality improvement.

WHAT TOOL SHOULD WE USE?

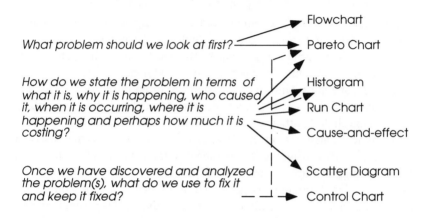

FLOWCHARTS

One of the most popular tools in our agency proved to be flowcharts. Once participants understood the real value of this tool, they were off and running. We explained the purpose of flowcharts as follows:

- Flowcharts graphically represent the flow of work.

- Flowcharts can be used to document the "actual" way a process works vs. the "official" way it is supposed to work vs. the "ideal" way it might work.

- Flowcharts show where there may be problems, delays, or omissions in the process.

We stressed that team members should use common sense and not get excited about the proper box that should be used. Some people became quite intense when they began the process of flowcharting. It was not uncommon for members of a team to break into heated discussions about whether a box or a diamond shaped symbol should be used to define a step. Some members bought green, plastic IBM Flowcharting templates used by computer programmers with 26 defined shapes (including ones for transmittal tape, punched tape, and magnetic tape operations). Other team members invested in computer software that produced dazzling displays for their team.

One of our trainers demonstrated one easy way to flowchart by using a pad of those little yellow "note stickers" and a flip chart. He used the note pads as a square to define an activity and then turned them slightly to make a diamond shaped box for decision points. He further demonstrated the fact that flowcharts are never final by adding, deleting, and changing the note pads on the flip chart to reflect new thinking by the team. The idea was to stress that the whole concept of a flowchart was that it was a tool to be used by the team, and not something with its inherent rules and regulations governing use.

We even suggested that teams make up their own boxes or symbols as long as they provided a "key" for their interpretation by the quality council. A few teams took us up on the offer, demonstrating that we were all free to use flowcharting to help, not to hinder the process of improvement.

Other tips that we offered included:

- Flowcharts are fluid, often changed and never final. Keep this in before making a "pretty" chart, or before investing in an expensive computer program.

- Even if the process is "working" now does not mean that it cannot be improved.

- All of the team should be involved; one person, because of rank or stature, should not influence the team's analysis of the process.

- Try using large sheets of paper posted on the wall for all to see. Consider placing the draft flowcharts in a hallway where others, not necessarily members of the team, can view the work and comment.

- Ask questions:

    Are there any "loops?" Why?

    Does each step add value? Could a step be eliminated?

    Where are the delays? Why?

    Where are the measurements taken? Why?

    Where should the measurements be taken?

    Where do customer complaints originate?

    Where do most of the errors occur?

    Where are workers identifying problems with the process?

    How can the process be improved?

During the training provided to associates, the instructors often completed the section on flowcharting by asking the group if they had a process that they would like to flowchart with the instructor's guidance at that moment. Often very difficult processes were suggested, for example, the reimbursement of travel expenses. Other times, participants often expressed humor with their requests for an example of flowcharts. On one occasion, a group helped chart the purchase of a six-pack, another making coffee, and still another a husband selecting a gift for his wife in an intimate apparel shop. Without exception, each was charted, and the participants realized how very valuable flowcharting was to understand a process, and, as importantly, that it can be fun.

CAUSE-AND-EFFECT DIAGRAMS

The next tool presented in the training seminars was that of the "Cause-and-effect" diagram, also known as the Ishikawa diagram or the "fish-bone" diagram. This is a great tool not just to use, but to teach because groups have so much fun using it. The tool is used to identify all possible causes of a given problem, and like the flowchart, makes no use of statistics. Participants in training begin to see that quality improvements can be made without getting bogged down in mathematical formulas or statistical tables.

The cause-and-effect diagram represents the relationship between an effect (problem) and its potential causes. It is used when the team needs to identify, explore and display all of the possible causes of a specific problem or condition. The team brainstorms the possible causes to minimize the chance of overlooking one or more causes. Most problems have multiple causes, often interacting with each other. A typical cause-and-effect diagram developed by teams in Florida's Jobs and Benefits division follows.

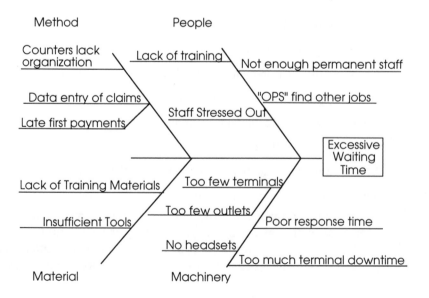

Dr. Kaoru Ishikawa, undoubtedly one of the world's experts on cause-and-effect diagrams, invented the concept in 1943 when he was teaching a group of engineers how to analyze problems. In his book *Guide to Quality Control*, Dr. Ishikawa provides reasons why his diagram is helpful to teams:

- Preparing a cause-and-effect diagram is educational in itself. Many new associates can learn a great deal about their jobs just by participating in the preparation of the diagram.

- A cause-and-effect diagram is a guide for discussion. Preparation of the diagram will tend to keep team members on task.

- The causes of problems are sought actively. There is a plan to seek out the causes of problems.

- A cause-and-effect diagram demonstrates the level of technology. When a cause-and-effect diagram is prepared thoroughly, it means those doing it know quite a bit about the process.

- A cause-and-effect diagram can be used for any problem (i.e., quality matters, safety, work attendance, or any kind of personnel problem).

Cause-and-effect diagrams can become very complex, especially in government bureaucracies with the labyrinth of policies and regulations. When one adds the dimension of politics, budgets, etc., the diagrams can become very complicated. A complex diagram does confirm a team's dedication, however, for a very simple diagram may indicate only a superficial analysis or too generalized an approach.

PARETO CHARTS

Pareto charts graphically identify the major causes of a problem. The old adage "if you're hunting ducks, go where the ducks are" helps explain the uses for the Pareto. Teams in our program routinely used this tool, along with the flowchart, as they began their analysis of problems. Not only is the chart relatively easy to construct—thus a popular choice—but it helps teams focus on what is important. Teams begin to understand the need for meaningful and accurate data as they develop their analysis. Often, team members are not familiar with the kinds of data that should be collected and analyzed. The gathering of data and preparation of Pareto charts gives them a good introduction that is not threatening. There are no statistical formulas, and the results are immediate. Shown on page 82 is a simple Pareto chart that was developed by the West Palm Beach Appeals Team in charting what reasons customers had to make a telephone call to their office.

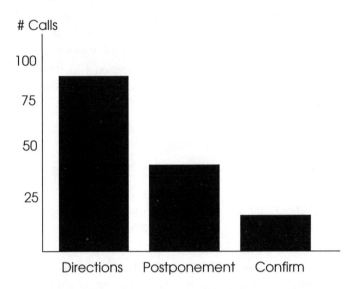

This chart is a simplification of the chart prepared by the team. Actually, they found seventeen different reasons why the calls were coming into their switchboard. The primary cause, however, was that customers needed directions to the hearing site. In fact, calls for directions "were 80% more frequent than the next highest category." The team developed a quick and easy solution to this problem—including road maps to the hearing site with the notice. A second Pareto chart prepared after the maps were included showed a tremendous drop in the number of calls asking for directions. Not an earth-shaking idea, or improvement for that matter, but it was a real improvement for customers!

HISTOGRAMS

Histograms are charts that show where most of the data is concentrated, and can be used to estimate the percentage of cases below or above specific points. Construction of the histogram is a little more complicated than the Pareto chart. In our training sessions on continual improvement tools, we presented an example to the class with a blank handout that they completed with the instructor. The following steps to construct a histogram were presented with the instructions that future sets of data could be "plugged into" the same outline.

Steps to Complete a Histogram

#1. *Collect the data.*

Example: 51, 53, 44, 48, 57, 41, 55, 22, 53, 63, 45, 39

34, 43, 65, 59, 62, 73, 43, 66, 49, 61, 59, 78

44, 41, 15, 33, 57, 34, 71, 27, 39, 49, 53, 47

46, 57, 43, 67, 46, 53, 35, 35, 44, 35, 48, 75

46, 42, 62, 49, 65, 33, 42, 55, 51, 48, 49, 67

#2. *Count the number of data points.*

Example: The above collection has 60 data points. We use the capital letter "**N**" to designate this number. Thus, **N=60.**

#3. *Determine the Range (the largest number minus the smallest).*

Example:

Largest =	78
Smallest =	15
Range =	63

#4. *Select Interval Length where the # of intervals (K) depends upon the # of observations (N).*

N	K
< 30	Try a scatter diagram instead
30-50	6-8
51-100	8-11
101-250	11-16

Example: We have 60 observations (data points), thus an interval of 8-11 is appropriate. We will pick the number 9.

#5. *Calculate the cell width with a simple formula:*

Cell Width	=	Range/#of Intervals (or Cells)
	=	63/9
	=	7

In our example, we were lucky to have a range of exactly 63 and a "9" for our number of Intervals. That will not always be the case, and it will need to be rounded off when the answer is a decimal. If the range were 76, for instance, the cell width would be 9.5714. This would be rounded off more conveniently to "10."

Now that we have our Cell Width, we can proceed to list our cell boundaries. We take our lowest number, and then make certain that there are a total of 7 numbers in the first interval. Therefore, the first will be:

15   16   17   18   19   20   21

Thus, our first interval will be from **15 through 21.** The second interval will be from **22 through 28.** It is important to notice that the intervals are **mutually exclusive.** In other words, we do not have one interval from 15 through 21 and the next interval from 21 through 27. If we did this, what interval would we use for the number 21? It could fit into two intervals.

#6. *Construct a frequency table.*

Example:

Interval #	Interval Length	Frequency	Total
1	15-21	x	1
2	22-28	xx	2
3	29-35	xxxxx xx	7
4	36-42	xxxxx x	6
5	43-49	xxxxx xxxxx xxxxx xxx	18
6	50-56	xxxxx xxx	8
7	57-63	xxxxx xxxx	9
8	64-70	xxxxx	5
9	71-77	xxx	3
10	78-84	x	1

There is a "hidden" histogram in the table above? Look at the "x's." It might help to turn the page sideways.

#8. Draw the histogram.

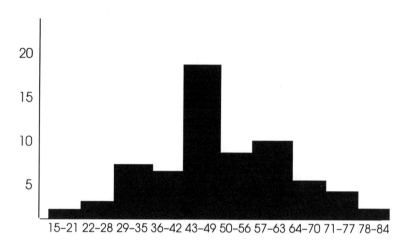

15–21 22–28 29–35 36–42 43–49 50–56 57–63 64–70 71–77 78–84

Questions to Ask:

1. Does the spread fall into specifications? In other words, are there any data points that fall outside acceptable limits?

2. Is the distribution symmetrical or skewed (lopsided)? The above example falls into a roughly "normal" distribution, with almost an equal number of measurements above and below the average. Other histograms may show more measurements on one side or the other, and be "skewed" to the right or left. In the training presented to team members, a histogram showing the number of years state employees had in the Florida retirement system was used as an example. In the district offices, the histogram was regularly "skewed to the left" because there were far more "newer" workers in entry level positions. When the exercise was done in the headquarters' office, the opposite was true with the histogram "skewed to the right" reflecting the many years of service upper management associates had in their retirement account.

3. How much variability is present? A large variability may indicate a wide range of performance.

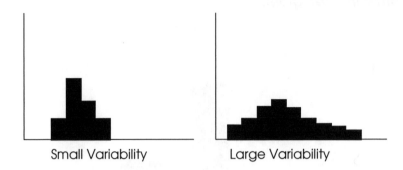

Small Variability   Large Variability

4. Is there more than one peak? Could data be coming from more than one source? In Florida state government, there was a period in the late 1960s and early 1970s when hiring was increased. Histograms prepared in training classes on "years in service" occasionally reflect this occurrence with two peaks.

5. Are there any orphans? An isolated bar or data could indicate an unusual case that should be investigated.

SCATTER DIAGRAMS

Scatter diagrams are used to investigate the possibility of an association or relationship between two variables. Correlation does not necessarily imply causation, in that two variables which appear to be related may both be driven by a third variable. On the other hand, lack of correlation between two related variables might be due to large measurement errors, or to the fact that one variable is restricted to lie in a narrow range. This restriction might occur because it is a key process variable or because the sampling plan did not target extreme conditions.

A fairly typical scatter diagram is shown on page 87. In this scatter diagram, it is apparent that there is a relationship between the two variables—the "longer" a customer must wait for an interview correlates negatively with the number of placements the office reports. We would expect that to be the case (a "gut-level" assessment), but now the actual data confirming the belief.

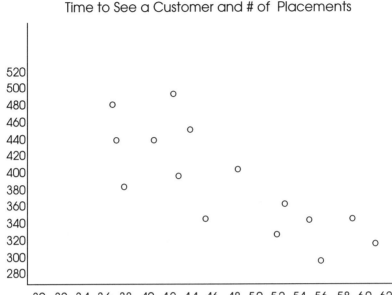

Time to See a Customer and # of Placements

Vertical axis represents # of placements. Horizontal axis represents # minutes taken to interview a new customer.

RUN CHARTS

Run charts are very helpful in identifying trends or cycles and can be used to spot unusual observations. Control charts, the next tool to be discussed, are run charts with control limits and tests for patterns added. Run charts are not difficult to construct. The following one on page 88 shows the number of customers filing an unemployment compensation claim in one of our offices. It demonstrated the need to consider ways of "evening out" the flow of customers. Those coming in on Monday's overpowered the available help and often had to wait as long as two hours to discuss their needs. After the team suggested appointments on Tuesdays, the flow evened out.

When the average is calculated (31 above) for the five day period and drawn as a horizontal center line, it is easy to see the need to address the Monday "problems."

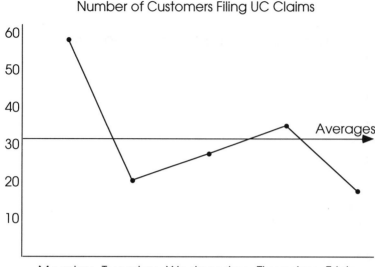

Number of Customers Filing UC Claims

CONTROL CHARTS

The control chart is the last tool that we included in our initial training. For many associates, it proved to be the most challenging in view of the statistics involved. The control chart is a run chart that makes use of statistical formulas to define upper control limits (UCL) and lower control limits (LCL). The control chart identifies when a process is out of control so that the cause can be analyzed. When the process is in control, no effort is made to adjust the process. The UCL and the LCL are determined by examining the results of the process by taking samples and using a series of statistical formulas. The goal of the control chart is a simple one—to signal when a process is in or out of control.

Even the best of processes will not produce 100 percent "ideal" results. There will always be some variability. If in control, the variances will stay within the control limits. The outcomes vary without setting a trend or a cycle of any kind. The reasons for the variables are small and numerous, but of no concern because they fall within the control limits. The only way to impact on these minor variances is to change the system (with a new process, perhaps).

When a process is out of control, with extreme variances falling above or below the control limits, it is apparent that the process is unstable due to some rather large cause. Perhaps there was a change in policy, or a new vendor has been hired (one not familiar with quality). Perhaps associates are angry at management, or are just "burned-out," caring little about quality. In any event, a process out of control is one in need of attention.

Just because a process is in control does not mean that it represents one that will meet customer needs. It only means that results are consistent. They may be consistently bad. To address meeting customer needs requires that specifications (upper and lower) be developed, which can be more restrictive than control limits if a genuine quality service is desired.

There are two basic types of control chart. The continuous (variables) control chart is used when data samples are measured (waiting time in lines, dimensions, etc.). The discrete (attributes) control chart is used when samples are counted (number of calls per hour, typographical errors, late payments, etc.). Most of the data analyzed in teams within our agency fell into the variables category, and the following pages present the steps taken to develop a continuous control chart.

In our training on control charts, we provided a complete example that was introduced as follows:

1. Control charts demonstrate vividly that there is variability in every process. About one-half of the data points will tend to be above the mean and the other half below. Dr. Deming notes that variation can be minimized by "improving constantly and forever the system of production and service."

2. A process is out of control if one or more data points fall outside the control limits.

3. A process is out of control if the data contains unpredictable values, trends or cycles, e.g., if there are two points out of three very close to the upper control limit (or lower control limit). The same may be said if there are nine or more data points falling in succession either above or below the mean.

An Example of the Use of Control Charts: Days Required to See an Orthopedic Surgeon

Step 1. Gather the Data

	Jan	Feb	Mar	Apr	May	Jun
	52	55	54	51	46	49
	46	47	48	50	60	53
# Days	45	57	53	47	57	47
	61	55	54	52	51	54
	55	53	57	47	57	54
Average ($\overline{X}$)	51.8	53.4	53.2	49.4	54.2	51.4
Range (R)	16	10	9	5	14	7
Number of Samples	5	5	5	5	5	5

Step 2. Analysis

a. Calculate the "Process Average"—the "average" of the averages in Step One—Answer: Process Average ($\overline{\overline{X}}$) 52.233

b. Calculate the Average of the Ranges—Answer: Average Range ($\overline{R}$) 10.167

Step 3. Calculation of Control Limits

a. Calculate the UCL for the Mean.

   $$UCL - Mean \quad = \overline{\overline{X}} + A2 \bullet \overline{R}$$
   $$= 52.233 + (.58) \bullet 10.167$$
   $$= 52.233 + 5.897$$
   $$= 58.130$$

b. Calculate the LCL for the Mean.

   $$LCL - Mean \quad = \overline{\overline{X}} - A2 \bullet \overline{R}$$
   $$= 52.233 - (.58) \bullet 10.167$$
   $$= 52.233 - 5.897$$
   $$= 46.336$$

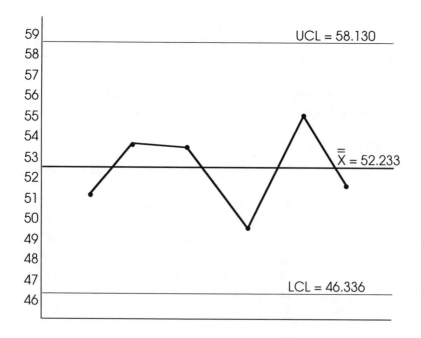

c. Draw the control chart for the Mean.

d. Calculate the UCL for the Range.

$$UC - Range = D4 \cdot \overline{R}$$
$$= (2.11) \cdot 10.167$$
$$= 21.452$$

e. Calculate the LCL for the Range.

$$LCL - Range = D3 \cdot \overline{R}$$
$$= (0) \cdot 10.167$$
$$= 0$$

f. Draw the control chart for the Range.

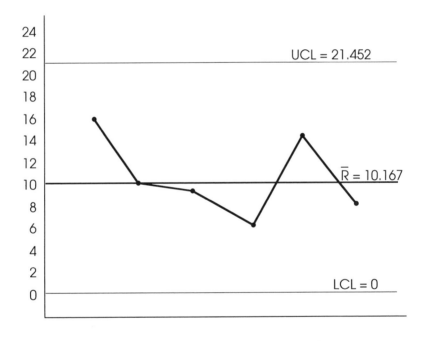

As participants in the training worked on the development of their control charts, using the above format, they soon discovered the need for information relating to the values for "A2," "D4," and "D3." A table was provided in the training manual for these values:

Table of Factors

Number of Observations in Subgroup (n)	Factors for X Chart A2	Factors for R Chart D3	D4
2	1.880	0.00	3.268
3	1.023	0.00	2.574
4	0.729	0.00	2.282
5	0.577	0.00	2.114
6	0.483	0.00	2.004
7	0.419	0.076	1.924
8	0.373	0.136	1.864
9	0.337	0.184	1.816
10	0.308	0.223	1.777

The use and understanding of these seven tools helped teams study the causes of problems in the delivery of services. Furthermore, the actual improvements were validated through the use of these same tools after improvements were made. It is anticipated that additional tools will be studied and used as teams become more sophisticated.

6

CONTINUAL PROCESS IMPROVEMENT

"Insanity: Doing the same things, the same way,
and expecting to see a difference."
—Roger Milliken

Chapter 4 identified the external customer as the target, the ultimate and final destination. Meeting or exceeding the external customers' expectations is the goal. The best strategy to achieve this goal is to embrace the values, beliefs, and principles of Total Quality Management. Government organizations will be more efficient and effective if they shift from traditional management beliefs, approaches, and techniques to Total Quality Management. Government will become successful if its organizations shift from organizing around functions to organizing around processes, shift from using the principles of division of labor to the principles of team work and continual process improvement; shift from focusing only on output (production) to outcomes (customer satisfaction and society benefit); and finally shift from individual competition and incentives to team incentives and recognition.

American business leaders and, for the most part, the average American worker, still deny the approach and benefits of Total Quality Management, even though business organizations show their markets drastically reduced by foreign competitors primarily due to the advancement of Total Quality Management in other countries. For many reasons, even though the tenets of TQM are relatively easy to comprehend, TQM acceptance has been a difficult struggle in the United States. Very few Americans find TQM easy to embrace after their initial exposure. Perhaps the primary reason for denying its benefits is because it flies in the face of past U.S. management beliefs, assumptions, and practices. It often takes American managers and workers months and even years to accept and embrace Total Quality Management in American organizations.

When we embraced TQM as our management approach in our pilot program, our focus continued to be on satisfying the federal government and the state

Legislature, but we took on a more important goal—to meet or exceed the expectations of the "real" customers. Rather than organizing around functions, we organized the Department around processes. Rather than managing functions, we managed processes. We shifted from functional management to process management.

PROCESS MANAGEMENT

Process management starts with the external customer. However, it realizes that if external customer needs are to be met, the organization must meet the needs and the expectations of internal customers. Therefore, TQM focuses on the way work gets done throughout the organization. The focus is on the organization of people, procedures, equipment, and work activities for the purpose of process optimization.

PROCESS DEFINED

A process is a series of interrelated activities that results in an output. At a minimum, each process has a supplier, a processor, and a customer. It has at least two or more sequential steps, has a beginning (input), an ending (output), and a benefit for the customer (output).

PROCESS IMPROVEMENT

For government organizations to be effective, they must improve their processes. They must improve the way they do business. Rather than take up the position that the people at the top of the bureaucracy know what the customer wants, know how the work should be done, and know how every worker should behave in performing customer service, government organizations are going to have to change. Government needs to change from top down management making bureaucratic rules, to starting with their customers and empowering front-line workers to not only meet the needs of their customers, but interpret better methods for meeting and exceeding their customer's expectations. Rather than government looking to constantly reinvent the way it does business, government should focus on process improvement. Each day, each week, each month, each year government needs to continually improve its processes.

Rather than assigning specific job tasks to workers, it should be the workers' responsibility to improve the process to which they have been assigned. For example, the Department of Labor and Employment Security is responsible for paying travel expenses of associates. Before TQM, the travel vouchers would come into the department and each person who worked in travel was given a specific number of travel vouchers to process that day. Once the vouchers were given to the associates, then it was their responsibility to see that the vouchers were processed. As complaints mounted in the field, with many associates waiting as much as two months to receive their travel checks, we went to the Travel Manager and were told that they could do better if they had more people. We gave them more people. Again, the reimbursements fell six or seven weeks late. We found out the answer wasn't more people, but rather that we needed to improve the process.

SCIENTIFIC MANAGEMENT VERSUS PROCESS IMPROVEMENT

In scientific management, workers were assigned tasks by management who knew best. In process improvements, the worker is assigned a process and their job is to improve it. Their job is to use their brains to make the process more effective.

In scientific management, the target was management: keep top management satisfied. In process improvement, the target is the internal or external customer.

The goal in scientific management is to meet numerical goals; whereas, the goal in process improvement is to meet or exceed customer expectations.

The objective in scientific management is for workers to do what they are assigned. It is the end towards which effort is directed. In process improvement the objective is continual improvement of the processes.

In scientific management the outcome was how many, how many errors, how many defects, etc. The worker knew how to improve the processes, but wasn't allowed to. The outcome in process improvement is quality, customer satisfaction, less frustration for the workers, an opportunity for workers to improve while they improve the processes, worker control over their work, focus on prevention, and personal growth.

The output in scientific management is the result of individual effort; workers only knew what they did and what their output was. In process improvement, the output is the result of a team effort which is measured and the results shared with each other.

In scientific management, the input was whatever was provided to workers who performed specific assigned tasks. In process improvement, workers can evaluate suppliers, know the quality of the product or service received from suppliers, work with them to improve their quality and are empowered to accept or reject what they receive.

BECOMING A PROCESS THINKER

Organizations develop over years a culture that fosters specific behaviors. In some organizations, employees are so dominated by bureaucratic managers that the employees wait until they are told what to do. Whatever thinking employees do, it revolves only around their task. Some organizations might be a little more advanced, in that employees may be comfortable in asking the manager what to do if they are not clear about their task. A third level of bureaucracy might maintain a culture of participation where one may recommend something to the manager and with his or her approval, can take action. Some are even a bit more advanced, allowing workers to take action on their own and then advising the manager what they have done. All of these cultures are management driven and force the employee to become task oriented (do something, whether it is right the first time or not).

Training an employee only to be a task thinker does not yield high quality. Then employees only focus on their task and do not use their brain power to contribute to making improvements that ultimately benefit the internal as well as external customers.

To maximize quality and productivity in government, associates should be trained to be process thinkers and be able to act on their own or as a team member to make decisions that contribute towards improving the process. Process thinkers understand that they are not just assigned a task, but rather are accountable and responsible for the entire process to which they are assigned.

A process thinker is empowered. The process thinker is empowered to collect and analyze data relative to process inputs, reject poor quality inputs, make changes in process activities that improve the quality of the process output while keeping in mind the ultimate user of the output, the customers. The most effective method of developing a culture where process thinkers thrive is for the organization to implement the following process improvement sequence.

THE PROCESS IMPROVEMENT SEQUENCE

The following sequence of activities begins by identifying core processes, which are defined as those interrelated steps that begin with an activity (input) and result in an output. The core processes are the primary reason why the organization exists. For example, American industry recognized in the 1980s that they could not provide quality products and services by dividing functions and tasks, but could by accepting the fact that building a product was a design to production process. American industry realized that to build a better product and to save costs, they had to do more upstream thinking that focused on preventing downstream problems, and the most effective way to achieve success was by managing the entire process rather than functions.

Step 1: Identifying Core Processes

When the Bureau of Financial Management changed from focusing only on work (which was defined as a set of tasks performed by people to meet an objective, measured by time taken, and result) to process management, it identified its core processes as vendor payments, travel, payroll, financial reporting, reconciliations, revenue management, and grant reporting. The bureau chief was responsible for these processes and accountable for results.

In the past, the bureau chief reacted to day-to-day problems and focused on solutions. It was similar to the Wackenole game where the player uses a hammer to knock down the next wooden nail to pop up, testing his or her eye-hand coordination.

By shifting to process management, the bureau chief lost some power over directing the task of others, but gained control of the organization not by understanding what each person was doing that day or that worrying about a person doing what they are supposed to do, but by understanding, knowing, and measuring process inputs and outputs.

To improve the quality of the organization, the bureau chief understood that she had to empower people closest to the work to figure out the best way to achieve quality.

Another example occurred in the Division of Vocational Rehabilitation where it identified the mission of the core process as gaining employment and increased independence for people with disabilities. Vocational Rehabilitation identified six processes within their core process. This is shown in the following diagram:

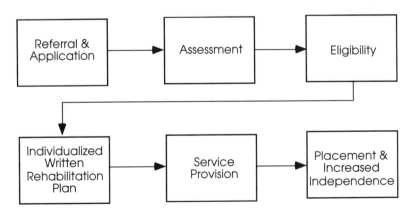

As a result of this process, the outcome was increased independence for the customer of VR.

The division then identified key processes in the administration that supported their primary core process. This included information systems, case consultation, budget, program evaluation, training, quality assurance, contracts, and planning.

The most effective way to identify core processes is to have the management team flowchart the way work gets done in your organization. One can start with suppliers or one can start with customers and work backwards. The flowchart does not have to be all encompassing, that is have every detail, but rather, graphically display how work gets done. The flowchart provides a picture of the organization and allows everyone to begin thinking about processes and not the traditional way or organizing: division of tasks.

Step 2: Empowering Process Improvement Teams

Once core processes are defined and broken down into sub-processes people who work in those processes should be asked to become members of a process improvement team. Our approach in the Department of Labor and Employment Security was to ask for volunteers. We felt that if we could put together a team of three to twelve people, who had a positive attitude towards making improvements, we would be more successful. Our approach was to allow participation of workers with a desire and willingness to accept the responsibility for improving the process, rather than telling people that they had to be part of a team. Our experience has shown that if a team member didn't want to participate, they were more destructive.

Orientation sessions, consisting of an overview of the continual improvement process, were scheduled for all potential team members. Many of those attending these introductory sessions admitted that they were asked to attend by their supervisors. They were pleased to learn that from that point forward their participation was completely voluntary. Some did not wish to consider joining a team, at least in the early implementation stage. In fact, the junior author was "booted out" of one office, more or less. He was told that the people working in that particular office already had more than "they could say grace over," that the office already offered good services, that TQM was a fading fad, and that given the fact that they were career service (protected) workers there was nothing anyone could do to them. We left them alone, but within a year we found that they were actively involved in teams. They looked around at the other offices in their division and saw that they were the only ones not pursuing quality, and they stood out because of it.

After the TQM overview, volunteers were asked to come to a meeting sponsored by the manager and were given the assignment to improve the process of how work gets done. Each team had a team sponsor who was generally a manager willing to provide back-up and support to the team. In most cases, however, the team sponsor did not attend meetings. Each team was empowered to select its leader if they thought one was needed. The team sponsor's job was to make sure that each team member felt empowered to change the process. They were given the authority and responsibility, and were empowered to take actions that would improve the process.

The sponsor also helped ensure that teams were given the opportunity to meet regularly. It is not unusual to find that offices serving the public are busy ones. Customers arrive before offices open in the morning and keep coming all day. It is easy to fall into the trap of not being able "to find time" for quality. Once managers realize that process improvements create additional time by streamlining and eliminating unnecessary steps this concern fades away. On occasion, we told the story about the woodcutter who had no time to sharpen his saw.

Step 3: Team Meetings

At the initial team meeting, the sponsor empowered the team and provided them a process improvement guide. A process improvement guide can be a written description of the steps the team should follow in organizing and implementing quality improvements. Or it can be a person who is trained to help teams through each step of the process improvement sequence. In the following chapter, we will describe in detail the role of process improvement guides.

Generally, a time for process improvement meetings is assigned and in the beginning it is usually one hour per week. In the early meetings, the team focuses on their mission. They generally identify the purpose of their team, and what their values ought to be. The team adopts TQM beliefs and principles and finally takes ownership of the process.

Step 4: Process Mapping

To understand their processes, the team should flowchart the way they presently do work. A flowchart is a graphical sequence of how work flows. At this stage, as team members begin to understand exactly how work flows, they tend to immediately want to make changes. However, the team should go slowly. Their first objective is to understand the current work flows. It immediately becomes obvious to them once they flowchart their process that there are redundancies and obvious steps that should not be performed or could be performed more effectively if changes were made.

Step 5: Identify Customer Expectations

The team should visualize what the customer wants as a result of their work. The team should establish their commitments to the customer. If necessary, they may want to conduct in-depth interviews, set up focus groups, do face-to-face discussions, use telephone interviews, or mail surveys to their customers. We found that, at a minimum, customers want prompt service (responsiveness); promised service that is dependable and accurate (reliability); and assurance that the service provided is carried out by knowledgeable, "process interested" personnel. Finally, customers want to communicate with personnel who are caring, have a positive attitude towards them, who are willing to give personal attention to them, and who convey a deep understanding of their problems.

Process improvement teams must understand that they work for the customer. Total quality managers must understand that they, too, work for the customers. They work to support the team and must be willing to give up their power of daily directing individual workers. Total Quality Management managers lose power over individuals, but gain control over the process. Each process has a customer, and the goal is to meet or exceed customer expectations.

When we analyzed our customers in the jobs and benefits process, we knew that their expectation was to receive an unemployment check in a timely manner. However, we wanted to exceed their expectations by immediately helping them to get another job. We were also interested in helping them get the training that was available to meet their needs. With the goal of exceeding their expectations, we put the customer first and designed our processes to meet his or her needs.

Step 6: Data Collection

Each team needs to collect meaningful data about their process. This is often a very difficult task for people working in government. The term "data" in government leads people to think of "database" and has almost become synonymous with the collection of numbers that appear on information system reports. What is interesting is that with all the data collected in government, very little of it is used for process improvement.

To collect meaningful data, the team will need to at least understand the number of activities in the process, the number of steps, the number of customer contacts, cycle time, backlog delays, missing information, input errors, and output errors.

One must remember, however, that teams may be uncomfortable in collecting this data. Many never will have done this and may feel that they are not "qualified" and that the task should be left to the "experts" in the state capital. This feeling is actually encouraged by the expert bean counters who conduct research and who provide overviews of their work in the orientation sessions new associates all attend. The guardians of the data (i.e., mainframe statisticians) do not wish to relinquish their control very readily and may scare new staff by emphasizing the need for "representative samples," etc. An understanding of how good data can be obtained with simple tools usually puts team members at ease.

Sometimes Total Quality Management is defined as "management by fact." The team needs to understand that collecting facts is part of their job. Sometimes facts prove to be embarrassing, and that's why the need to practice the value of open and honest communication is important. Sometimes processes aren't as good as previously thought. People need to learn to accept the truth, to accept the facts as they are. The job is to continually improve the process, and ignoring and hiding facts just so management can look good will not yield a quality government. What's interesting is that associates in the "field" offices often know that the "facts" are often based on bad data and are sometimes fabricated to make the office look good to outsiders. Living in this make-believe world keeps the paychecks coming in and outsiders "off their backs," but there is little pride in the work accomplished. Once everyone learns that it is best to accept real facts, even if embarrassing in the short-term, services will actually improve as processes are improved.

Step 7. Data Analysis

Once data is analyzed, there are many opportunities for improvement. There are ways to add value to the workplace, e.g., by increasing the work of a government service to an external customer. It adds value from their perspective. However, there is work that's necessary to keep the organization functioning effectively, but has no value to the external customers. Further, the team will realize that there is unnecessary work, and that is work that does not add value. These are tasks that are unnecessary in the process, e.g., generating reports that no one reads.

Data may show that the process demands a lot of re-work activities. These are activities that become necessary only because something wasn't done right the first time. In government, it has been argued that re-work is acceptable since every time the process is out of control, government is able to add more people. Bureaucrats are constantly going to the Legislature and the Congress asking for more money so that they can secure more people and technology to meet customer needs.

Since there is never a bottom line (that is a point in which the organization either changes its processes or goes broke, e.g., Chrysler Corporation), government continues with its traditional management approach. The function of government, it appears, is to unload the tax dollars as they arrive in the state capital and spend them as quickly as possible before another truck arrives.

Step 8: Plan, Do, Check, Act

The plan, do, check, and act process focuses on "What are we going to do?" Once a course of action is determined, experiment with the change in the process (pilot test to see the effects of the plan). Next, check out the results of the test to see if the plan has a positive effect on the process. Finally, if the results are good, take action, institutionalize the change.

One of the tools that helps in the PDCA cycle is "imagineering." This tool requires the team to visualize how the process could work perfectly, i.e., a process with no problems, no errors, no duplication, no complexity, and no waste.

The data collected in the previous step should indicate to the team where the process breaks down. For example, a significant percentage of the work in the process may be re-work such as finding and fixing errors, making errors, interruptions, inspections, responding to customer complaints, etc. A certain percentage of work may not be necessary at all because either it doesn't add any value to the customer or no one in the process needs the result of this work; such as generating reports, working on the wrong things, preparing reports that no one reads (now housed in libraries across the state)—tasks that produce output but that no one wants or needs.

There are many opportunities for improvement where the team can begin working on the right things that make the process more effective. The team attempts to answer the question, what needs improvement? They focus on what they should stop doing and start doing, and on what they don't track and should be tracking.

They also answer the "what can be eliminated" questions, what can be combined to make the process simpler and easier? What can be rearranged? Or they can answer the questions of how can the process be improved? Where can the process be improved? What parts of the process need to be improved? When should the process be improved? Why is a specific activity done in the process? How long does it take to do the process?

Another way to determine what to do is to answer the question, does a particular activity add value to the service in the eyes of the customer? Is the activity critical to the process? Does the activity overlap with other activities? Is the activity redundant?

Process improvement teams will not always make dramatic breakthroughs but should be pleased with small incremental changes. Many of the best process improvements are relatively small changes. For example, a team in vocational rehabilitation came up with a short guidebook listing the most frequently used computer codes. Before the process improvement, secretaries and counselors would spend hours looking up codes to input into the mainframe terminals. With the guide listing the most frequently used codes, much time was saved. The team was very proud of this accomplishment.

Likewise, total quality leaders should appreciate small incremental improvements and not look to teams to constantly produce short-term and dramatic results. The process improvement team should focus on customer needs and priorities, reduce cycle time, eliminate nonvalue-added activities, simplify the process, and innovate incrementally.

Step 9: Document Improvements

The purpose of documenting improvements is to report on the effects of changes made in the process. One of the most effective methods is to graphically compare the process before and after changes were made. Frequently, teams show a flowchart before action was taken and then a chart after improvements were implemented. Also, they graphically display before and after process time, process errors, process re-work, customer surveys, process simplification, process inputs, process outputs, etc.

The data displayed provides a basis for appraising process performance. The graphs should focus on measurements that are meaningful and important to process improvement. They should also be relevant and show the results of quality indicators. The data displayed should be accurate and, finally, the team needs to display all relevant data that they will continue to collect on a weekly or monthly basis to ensure that the process is under control.

If there is a significant variation in the process, then the team needs to account for the variation. If the variation is caused by a random event, then the team will know that it's not as a result of the process. However, if the team identifies the significant variation and the results point to a special cause, then the team needs to analyze the special cause and re-institute the plan, do, check, and act cycle.

Graphically displaying quality measurements reinforces and demonstrates a commitment to quality improvements. It increases quality awareness among associates and keeps all associates informed and interested, and enables them to take corrective action. Furthermore, it allows the team to benchmark its processes against other similar processes. The data that the team collects can be considered baseline data for their process. If the team can find another similar process which they can compare, then they can establish themselves as the benchmark; or if the other process is more effective, then it becomes the benchmark. For example, in Unemployment Compensation, the benchmark for error rate in the State of

Florida is set by the Jacksonville office. It has an error rate of less than 1 percent. Another office in another part of the state has an error rate as high as 16 percent. The benchmark for the state then is Jacksonville, and the other process has a long ways to go in order to improve their process in the payment of claims.

In the Department of Labor and Employment Security in the State of Florida, we've established benchmarks throughout the state. What is interesting is that there are very few benchmarks in state government. One would think that many of the states all perform similar processes and that benchmarks would be more readily available.

Step 10: Improve Again

The job of every associate is to use brain power to improve organizational processes. Therefore, process improvement is a never-ending task. In a rapidly changing environment, customer needs change, technology produces change, policies change, etc. The job of everyone who works in an organization is to monitor processes, react to change, and prevent problems by continually improving processes. No matter how good a process is, change is required.

Therefore, leaders in government organizations must empower personnel assigned to the process to manage the process.

PROCESS IMPROVEMENT CHECKLIST

1. Process identified.
2. Process owners identified.
3. Process owners accept responsibility.
4. Customer defined and measured.
5. Supplier defined and measured.
6. Process flowcharted.
7. Quality indicators measured—key indicators tracked.
8. Measurements graphically displayed.
9. Accurate and reliable data collected.
10. Data analyzed.
11. Plan, do, check, act.
12. Process monitored.
13. Quality improvements documented.
14. Process simplified.
15. Customer satisfied.

7

PROCESS
IMPROVEMENT
TEAMS

*"Isn't it logical? If you work together, you should end
up with something better than if you work apart?"*
—W. Edwards Deming

In the preceding chapters, we set forth a framework for continual improvement in organizations. In a quality organization, the focus is on the customer, the process, and the tools which facilitate process improvement. Since data is readily available in a quality organization, people can now be trusted, no matter what their position in the organization.

Furthermore, in a quality organization, everyone understands their goal: to meet or exceed customer expectations. In traditional organizations, lower echelon workers were to do what they were told or make every attempt to understand the next signal from management. On the contrary, in a quality organization, workers look to their customer for direction and changes are directed not from management, but from meaningful data workers collect.

WORKING IN PROCESS IMPROVEMENT TEAMS

We believe that to become and to maintain a quality organization, process improvement teams provide the best strategy. First, teams provide the best methodology for using the intelligence of each worker. By each worker participating on a process improvement team, the organization will be able to tap worker insights and gain their perspective on how the process might be improved. Second, teams are more effective in gathering and analyzing facts. When working in teams, people have a stronger desire to accurately and reliably collect data, whereas managers in government often send data up the organization channel without a sense of ownership, accuracy or reliability. Third, in modern organizations, teams have replaced the hierarchy. In team-based organizations,

105

there are fewer levels of management. Finally, there is collective wisdom in teams. Rarely does one person have sufficient knowledge and/or experience in any specific process to understand everything that goes on. Not only are teams able to generate more ideas, they provide checks and balances that allow creativity, while at the same time check radical suggestions.

DEFINITION OF PROCESS IMPROVEMENT TEAM

A simple definition of "team" is a small group of individuals with a purpose, generally to complete a task. The reason the team assembled is because team members or a team sponsor thought it was in their best interest and that of the organization. It is important to understand that the group (the whole group) becomes *more* than the sum of its individual members. In other words, the team can do better working together than each individual working separately.

A process improvement team is defined as a group of individuals who accept the beliefs and principles of Total Quality Management, accept the ownership of a specific process, and unite together for the purpose of improving their process. Process teams are composed of volunteers, usually from the same organization, who meet regularly to identify problems related to a process and who select ways to improve the process.

On occasion, it is useful to have "project" teams. Project teams are formed by management to address a specific management-selected problem. Membership is based upon individual expertise and experience. A project team functions as long as it is needed to solve assigned problems and is discontinued once the problem is resolved.

"Team Guidelines" were provided to associates in the Department of Labor and Employment Security to assist in the formation of teams. These guidelines were not to be rigidly enforced, but rather to serve and assist the teams as they began. These included the following:

Membership: Teams are usually composed of 6-12 people who do related work. Membership may be for a set period of time, and rotated among all associates in the work group, or indefinitely for a set group of associates. Team members often select a "name" for their team that identifies them as a special group working on process improvement. This encourages identification and membership, friendliness, and a sense of team cohesion.

Leadership: May be provided by an elected leader within the group and rotated among group members, if so desired. The team leader communicates the progress of the team to management, coordinates with the team facilitator, helps design training needed by the team, and prepares the meeting agendas and objectives in order to keep records of what is accomplished. The team leader establishes the date, time and place for the meetings, and guides the team through the problem-solving process encouraging full participation, openness and trust by all members

Facilitation: Is provided by an individual who has received training in facilitation skills. The facilitator's role is to help guide the group and to keep them on target without having the responsibility of recommending change. At times, the facilitator may be a coach (serving as a resource person) or as a coordinator (linking with other teams or with management).

Sponsorship: May be provided by a member of the management team. The primary responsibility of this individual is to make certain the team receives all the support, resources, and recognition they need to perform.

Effective quality organizations link their processes and then empower teams composed of members closest to the process to make continual improvements. An example of how processes are linked is shown in the illustration below. The vocational rehabilitation program has as its foundation a core rehabilitation process composed of six processes. Every customer who is eventually placed into employment progresses through each of the six processes (i.e., referral, initial interview, eligibility determination, individualized written rehabilitation plan, provision of services, and finally placement and follow-up).

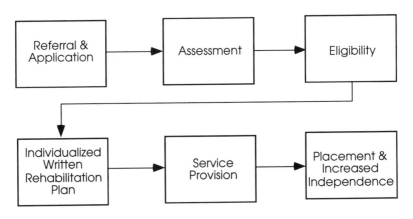

The six teams suggested improvements in the process they worked on, communicating regularly with the teams addressing other processes. For example, one team examining the individualized written rehabilitation plan was able to develop an improvement that used the department's mainframe computer to eliminate much of the "paperwork" associated with the planning process. A series of "pull down" menus, similar to those found in Microsoft's Windows 95 program, now assists counselors and their customers in the planning process.

Each of these process improvement teams focused on inputs, activities, outputs, and outcomes.

CROSS-FUNCTIONAL TEAMS AND PROJECT TEAMS

Two other types of teams are frequently used in quality organizations. The first is defined as a cross-functional team. This team comes together because organization members see the need to break down the barriers between functions. When organizations first get involved in Total Quality Management, they will often use cross-functional teams to break the barriers between departments.

If an organization is designed around, structured by, and follows the principles of Total Quality Management, fewer cross-functional teams are needed. Members of teams would automatically involve members of other departments in their process. Furthermore, as the organization becomes extremely effective, all of the barriers between departments will be broken, and in fact, the ideal TQM organization would reorganize completely around processes. However, cross-functional teams are needed to make the transition from the traditional productivity organization to a quality organization.

An example of a cross-functional team in the Department of Labor and Employment Security was the vendor payment team. Even though vendor payment can be flowcharted as a specific process and is identified with one bureau within Administrative Services, many of the functions required of vendor payments are performed outside the bureau. Therefore, Vendor Payments developed a cross-functional team composed of members from the divisions they served.

A second type of team is defined as a project team. A project team is often referred to in government as a committee. Project teams are generally formed by management because they have a task that requires a lot of information and many points of view. Or in some cases, management believes that they can gain commitment and buy-in from associates by allowing the associates to have input up front. In most cases, management reserves the right to make final decisions.

In traditional organizations, the project team is put together by management to gather data and make suggestions. Generally, management thought of this benevolent act as "management by participation." What it turned out to be was often that the employees did the participation and management made the decisions. However, in a quality organization, project teams can play a significant role. As managers become more open and trusting of their associates, they often have more respect for project teams. Furthermore, leaders in quality organizations aren't as likely to just delegate the participation to the project team, but rather be a member or take the lead themselves.

EMPOWERING INDIVIDUALS

To move away from the traditional management concept of knowing what the employee ought to do and telling them what to do, a new concept in organizational literature called "empowerment" must be embraced. To empower means to give unto another the right to act on one's behalf. In traditional organizations, power was granted to managers so that they could act on behalf of the person above them in completing a task. In a quality organization, power is not a concept that is only identified with management. Rather, power is granted to all associates.

Workers are now given the power to improve their processes, to take action to improve the way they do their work. When something is wrong or an opportunity exists for improvement, individuals in quality organizations are expected to do the right thing. They do not have to accept poor quality work from their suppliers, nor do they have to continually do their work in an illogical manner, nor do they have to pass on poor quality work resulting from their process, etc. They are empowered to come to work every day and use their brains and skills to make the organization more effective.

EMPOWERING PROCESS IMPROVEMENT TEAMS

Perhaps the most difficult challenge to changing to a Total Quality Management organization is to get managers to truly accept the benefits of empowering process improvement teams. It is very difficult for managers to release their employees, to allow employees to exercise their own judgment regarding work and how it gets done. So when managers are first approached with the concept of empowerment, most resist the concept. Many managers often believe that turning over the processes to the workers is not only irrational, but will seriously affect output.

When we first asked our managers to empower work teams, most of them lacked personal involvement and frequently would threaten the work team by telling them that they could meet for an hour a week only if productivity didn't go down. Most government managers resisted the concept of empowerment so much that many tried to make sure that empowerment failed. They would sabotage teams by forcing the teams to bring all decisions to them before any action could be taken. In other words, most managers would try to sabotage their process improvement teams by making them management-by-participation teams. In other words, workers participate and management decides.

Furthermore, teams do not always function very well in the beginning. Managers would often be amused by the inability of workers to work together in teams. When the team had disagreements, the managers would often side with some of the team members who were very reluctant to be on the team in the first place. Managers frequently approached the concept of empowerment as a gift to their employees, and at the same time made it clear to the teams that they could take the empowerment gift back.

Empowerment is not a gift. It is not something a manager gives to associates and then takes it away. Empowerment is an organizational strategy. People are empowered because it is in the best interest of the organization. The organization's leaders should take action to remove all obstacles and barriers that prevent empowerment. Effective managers become effective leaders. Effective leaders are involved in all of the processes they lead. They know the process better than anyone. They know when to get involved with their teams and when to allow their teams to work on their own. Effective leaders allow facilitators to facilitate meetings and realize that appointed leaders are not always the ones that ought to lead process improvement. Consequently, effective leaders empower others. They empower teams not to go off and do whatever they think the organization should do, but rather to focus on their assigned processes, and thus their empowerment falls within the boundaries of their process.

Empowering process improvement teams is the power granted to a group of people who either have been assigned to a process or have volunteered to improve a particular process to exercise judgment, to take responsibility, and to take action with the intent of making process improvements that benefit the customer and the organization. The following questions served as the test for one organization: Is it good for the customer? Is it good for the organization? Is it ethical? Is it consistent with our beliefs? Is the team willing to take accountability for their actions? When people in the organization believe they are empowered, they believe their knowledge is valued; their job expertise appreciated; they can solve problems with accurate and reliable data available to them; they can improve a process rather than just putting "band aids" on situations; they receive quality training not just for specific tasks, but for quality improvement and professional growth; everyone takes the responsibility for doing it right the first time; everyone is encouraged to question the way they work; everyone takes the attitude that continued improvement is part of their daily job; everyone is trusted, respected and recognized as a valuable asset; and finally everyone can break down barriers that prevent them from doing the work right the first time.

IMPLEMENTING PROCESS IMPROVEMENT TEAMS

The first step towards implementing process improvement teams is to have top management flowchart the core processes of their organization. The flow chart indicates how the work is processed in the organization. The core process flowchart does not show all the details, but rather breaks down the organizational processes so that everyone in the organization can see how work flows. For example, the diagram below illustrates the core processes in the Department of Revenue, State of Florida:

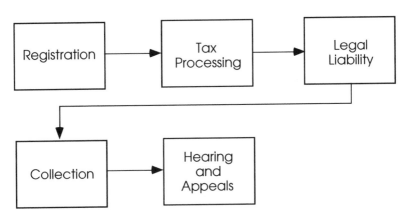

The Department of Revenue had identified five major, interrelated key processes that spanned the administration of thirty-one taxes and fees. Key process teams were established to analyze and define each major process, to document the flow, identify customers, establish measures, evaluate performance and improve the process.

The second step in implementing process improvement teams is to identify sub-processes within the core processes. This is generally easy to do since sub-processes can be identified first by documenting their inputs and their outputs. A good example can be illustrated in the Division of Vocational Rehabilitation (see page 112).

A well organized TQM implementation plan would identify teams for each of the processes. Ideally, everyone working within a process would volunteer to become a member of a process improvement team. In reality, however, many managers and associates will have difficulty in making a change from being a functional organization to a process organization. Further, managers at all levels frequently oppose the general notion of empowering teams. Even though managers will gain more control of their processes, they resent the fact that they may lose control of people.

Therefore, when we implemented process improvement teams, we asked for volunteers. We did not want managers and individuals who were opposed to Total Quality Management to be in a position to sabotage the process. Even though we were losing brain power from a lot of workers and managers, we believed it was in the best interest of the organization to let those who accepted

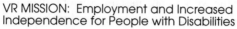

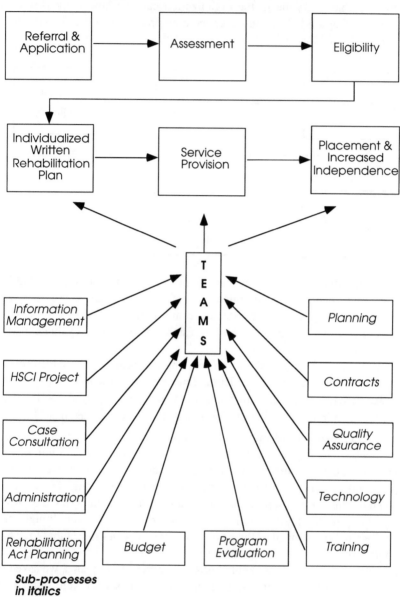

the beliefs and principles of TQM to start the process. We let those managers and workers who wanted to work independently and use the traditional management practices to continue. As we got more and more successful with TQM, more and more people joined our TQM initiative.

The third step in implementing process improvement teams is training, which is discussed in detail in Chapter 9.

In step four, each team should select its own leader. In most cases, it was not the manager. The manager's role early in the process was to empower teams, get out of the team's way, and mostly play a supporting role. The elected team leader generally was one of their members who understood Total Quality Management beliefs and principles and had the primary responsibility of planning and scheduling meetings. Their job was to keep the team focused and to see that they followed the process improvement steps.

In step five, we provided the process improvement team with a facilitator. The facilitator is generally a person who is "outside" of the process. Their job is to assist the team in the application of the process improvement steps and the TQM tools. Facilitators have specific training on how to keep the team focused and moving towards their goals. Furthermore, the facilitator makes sure team members are involved and can make a contribution to improving their processes. Facilitators do not schedule, conduct the meeting, or maintain team records. Their role is primarily to facilitate communication in the team.

Process Improvement Guides were appointed in step six. As our organization began to experience small successes, we realized that there was one important element missing from each team. Even though we had over 85 teams make presentations to the Quality Council in the first year, teams appeared to be frustrated. Even though many of the team members had received training and most had very effective leaders and facilitators, they were still frustrated. We realized we needed to give the teams more help, so we decided that we were going to train Process Improvement Guides. Even though the acronym came out to be PIG, members of the organization quickly embraced it, and we became the "PIGs."

Over 125 people volunteered for our first PIG seminar, 225 in the second, and over 200 in the third. These were people who wanted to know more about Total Quality Management than just what was being offered in our TQM courses, and, further, they wanted to be change agents. They were to be more than just team facilitators, but rather support the Total Quality Management initiative. Some thought of themselves as internal consultants because their role was to make sure that teams got started when people on the front lines wanted to volunteer and to make sure that each team was successful.

Each PIG was empowered to do the right thing for the organization. If they ran across barriers and obstacles that they couldn't handle, then they were to call the Secretary or the Deputy Secretary. Since we knew that not too many would likely call the Secretary or the Deputy Secretary, we knew that they needed a support group. Therefore, we set up Process Improvement Guide teams in seven areas of the state. The PIGs were given the responsibility of removing barriers to team success in the organization.

Process Improvement Guides were selected primarily because of their interest in Total Quality Management and not because of their position. The first requirement was that they must volunteer; and the second requirement was that they must feel that they can contribute extra time towards changing the entire organization. We had volunteers from the front-line to top management.

The PIGs had taken all of the TQM courses and were already skilled as facilitators. Their primary role was to facilitate change, to help the organization move from traditional management to Total Quality Management. They were expected to develop the TQM culture by role modeling organization values, by being TQM leaders (knowing TQM beliefs and principles and influencing others to accept them), by helping the organization communicate its direction, and by giving recognition to those dedicated to continual improvement.

After we trained about 200 Process Improvement Guides, the growth of continual process improvement teams, particularly in the field, was phenomenal. We were able to intervene in divisions and districts where the front-line people wanted to participate in TQM, but were not allowed to by their management. Now, the front-line had a voice in the organization. They had people with whom they could communicate and would support their efforts. Furthermore, with PIG teams in each of the seven areas of the state, we were able to keep the momentum and enthusiasm generated at the PIG seminar going.

PROCESS IMPROVEMENT TEAM MEETINGS

Phase I—Initial Meeting

When there are enough volunteers from a specific sub-process, one of the associates or even a manager will call a team meeting. All the management and associates know at this time is that top management is committed to improving processes and that to do it, teams need to be developed within the process. The initial meeting is extremely difficult, particularly if a Process Improvement Guide is not available to assist.

In addition, the initial meeting is more difficult because it is unlikely that any of the team members have had any training. All the members know is that they are frustrated with the way they are presently working and would like to find a better way. Some members think they already know a better way, and therefore, can't wait to get their two cents' worth in on how they can solve all the problems within their process.

Also, since most members reject the notion at first of measuring their entire processes because they fear the results, there is a reluctance to gather data. Even though members later become convinced the data is important, they don't see how they can presently gather data and still do their present job.

The meeting will be successful if all that can be achieved is that team members recognize that by working together they can make some improvements. It would be a bonus if members felt good about working with each other and valued the ideas that each other offered. The meeting can also be considered a success when members come to the realization that there is power in working in teams as opposed to just working individually.

The probability of achieving the above in the initial meeting is not good. More likely, the initial meeting will be one of complaints and solutions. Members will criticize the present system and immediately have a solution. Many members will feel that if everyone would perform as expected under the existing system, things would be much better. They are looking for quick solutions.

Phase II

In the second phase, which may be at the second meeting, the team members should try to identify the mission of their process. For example, their mission might be to reduce errors and improve processing time, or to return unemployed workers to work. The mission is the purpose of the team, and it answers the question of "Why are we meeting?" Frequently, the mission doesn't take the team very long to decide. Some teams, however, get into a discussion on how the mission should be stated. Also, the members still want to get to the solution part of the process because as they discuss the mission, other comments will be made. Frequently, team members begin to blame problems on others within the team. Even though the mission is an important phase within the team development, many members will wonder why they are doing it in the first place since it's so obvious.

If the team is successful at defining their mission quickly in the second meeting, then the team can move to the third phase of establishing team values. Values are what ought to be in instilled in the team. They guide the behavior of team members. Each team should have its own set of values even though the organization may have already published its values. If team values can be identified in the second meeting, then each of the team members can be asked to volunteer to select one of the values identified by the team and come to the next meeting with a definition. For example, the team may value communication and now it needs to be defined. A member may come back with a definition of openness, honesty, and integrity. Or a team might suggest that they value learning, which they may define as personal growth.

A good example of how one team defined their values, developed in addition to those values defined for their division, is found in a team in unemployment compensation that addressed customer waiting time. Their values were listed in their report right below their division's values.

Division Values

- Striving for Excellence (Total Quality Management)

- Maintaining High Ethical Standards in Conduct and Performance

- Planning for the Future

- Establishing Open, Honest Communication

- Creating One Seamless Department

- Caring for People

- Using of Technology Effectively

Team Values

- Establishing Respect for One Another

- Recognizing Every Member's Contribution is Equally Important

- Developing Sense of Pride in Accomplishments

- Maintaining a Sense of Humor

- Sharing Recognition

Phase III

Values are the desirable state of how people want to relate to each other. It's what everyone desires in the workplace. Therefore, a complete discussion followed with a description of each value is necessary for effective teams. Since the team is spending so much time on mission and values and there will be a lot of disgruntled members in that they will want to get on with it. This is a time when they need to be reminded that at this point they are trying to build a team for long-term process improvement and not to do "it" immediately. At the end of the third meeting, there may be a recognition of the need to flowchart the process at the next meeting.

Phase IV

In phase four, which may take as few as three meetings or as many as five or more, the leader opens the team meeting with a discussion of flowcharting. It may be wise at this point to invite one of the flowchart trainers to attend the meeting and explain to the members that a flowchart provides a map of their process. It helps everyone to understand the total process, identify suppliers and customers, and identify barriers, unnecessary tasks and duplication of effort.

At this point, members will start committing to process improvement. Within every group, there may be two or three people who are excited about doing a flowchart. From a majority of the members, however, there may still be resistance. The team should do the skeleton flowchart. Immediately, there will be debate. Often, teams will waste time arguing about whether a step belongs in a box, diamond-shape, circle, or other shape symbol. The important thing is to get the actual step down on paper, regardless of the shape of the symbol. We have advised some teams to use the "Post-It Notes" to construct their first charts. They can turn the sticky paper 45 degrees to make it a diamond (decision) shape and can modify the flowchart easily on a flip chart before transferring it to paper. Most teams do not agree with the original flowchart. Some team members love personal computers and rush out to purchase software to make flowcharting easier. Often these team members will become so motivated that they will want to do the flowchart themselves and bring it back to the next meeting and present it the way it is. Don't take away from their enthusiasm. Let them do it. However, don't delegate the responsibility for the flowchart to any particular member. The team must take ownership of the flowchart. They all must agree that that's the way things work.

Phase V

The flowchart is still the focus of the team as phase five begins. Numerous arguments may evolve. People will actually get angry with each other. At this point, the team may even want to quit because there is such a lack of agreement. Furthermore, there are still some members who could care less about the flowchart. They still want to get on with blaming others and hoping that someone will listen to their solutions.

When the arguments begin, the team should not forget about the values they set out earlier. The team should always be reminded of their mission and the values that they chose. Some members may not live up to the values and may elect to quit. Also at this time people that didn't volunteer to be a member of the team may want to join the team because they see the other team members reflecting on their work, and they now want to become involved. Some teams post their flowcharts outside the break room and ask other associates, who are not team members, to comment on the chart. Often, comments are penciled in throughout the flowchart by these "outsiders."

Phase VI

The flowchart becomes more meaningful for all of the members. They now see a starting point and an ending point. They now are beginning to get an accurate perception of what they do. At this meeting, they may begin to focus on their suppliers and their customers. Suppliers provide input to the process and the customer receives the output. Every process in the organization has a supplier and a customer. Depending upon the process, it's best to start with either a supplier or a customer. If the process has an internal customer, analysis of inputs serves as the starting point. If the process serves an external customer, analysis of customer expectations serves as the starting point. At the end of this meeting, the team is asked to prepare for the next meeting by focusing on one or the other.

Phase VII

At this meeting, if the focus is on the supplier, the question put to the group is: Does the supplier meet our expectations? Put another way, "What do you need from your supplier to do your job effectively?" Initially, there will be nothing but complaints. However, after a lengthy discussion, team members will come to the realization that they need to gather data. It is at this point they should be introduced to the Total Quality Management tools found in Chapter 6.

If the team members have already had the tool classes, they can proceed to collect data. However, if most of the members are not familiar with TQM tools, then it's best to bring in a trainer who teach them the tools by using examples in their process.

Phase VIII

The agenda for this meeting depends on the team's knowledge and about TQM tools. It may take three or four meetings just to get the team to the point where they can use the tools. Once they have a working knowledge of the tools, they can begin collecting data. They may want to begin at first with just collecting data on inputs they receive. They might identify suppliers, what they supply, and how it meets expectations. They become the customer. They may want to find out how many errors are made by suppliers, how many corrections have to be made, how much rework is required, and if the supplier improves their process, how they would do it.

Phase IX

In phase nine, which may take as many as fifteen or more meetings, the focus is on activities within the process, the work that is done. At this point using the tool "Imagineering," where people imagine how the process would work if everything worked perfectly, might be appropriate. An imaginative flowchart, sometimes called the "Ideal" flowchart, is compared with the real flowchart. The comparison should show where the bottlenecks might occur, where unnecessary tasks are performed that shouldn't be, where there is duplication, where additional tasks may be necessary, and where data should be collected.

Phase X

The teams need to understand the customer and need to know their expectations so that members can meet or exceed them. Members can begin collecting data by developing a customer survey, conducting interviews by telephone or in person, or having focus groups. The primary goal is to develop questions that when answered will provide information about customer expectations and satisfaction.

The team needs to know if customers are experiencing problems and the significance of their problems. Begin data collection by:

1. Identifying the information needed from customer.

2. Determining a sample, a selective group or the entire group of customers.

3. Deciding what kind of instrument to use: personal interviews, phone interviews, or mail questionnaires.

4. Developing the questions designed to secure required information.

5. Reviewing questions to see that they will not be misunderstood or are too difficult or unclear.

6. Compiling the questions into a format.

7. Field testing the questionnaire.

8. From the field test questionnaire, constructing how data will be displayed, what type of graphs will be used, and how statistics will be compiled. Displaying data is just as important as field testing questions. The answers to the survey have got to be meaningful to the team and displayed so that the team can identify opportunities for improvement.

9. Revising the questionnaire or interview questions.

10. Sending out surveys or beginning the process of interviewing the customer. If a focus group is used, prescribed questions should be used that have been previously tested in a smaller focus group.

11. Compiling survey response data and displaying the responses so that it's meaningful to all team members.

12. Analyzing data. Through the use of graphs and charts, display all of the data collected to provide a picture of the entire process.

Now the team is ready to make quality improvements. Since the team is empowered to work through their supplier to change the process, and to make changes in the process that improve timeliness, accuracy, etc., the team now can begin making improvements to meet or exceed customer expectations.

Phase XI

Through the use of TQM tools, the team can begin to easily identify the most serious problems or opportunities for improvement. For example, customers may expect a reduction in waiting time, or internal customers (associates) may ask for a reduction in the number of errors that suppliers make. These internal customers may ask for a streamlined process. Members should always keep in mind the Pareto principle which suggests that 80 percent of the trouble comes from 20 percent of the problems.

Further the team should keep in mind Dr. Joseph M. Juran's conclusion that at least 85 percent of the problem in a process can be corrected by changing systems and less than 15 percent are under a worker's control. The goal of the team at this point is to identify problems and begin changing the process to solve the problems.

There are three of tools that teams can use in order to improve team work: brainstorming, nominal group technique, and multivoting. A brief description of each follows.

Brainstorming: Brainstorming is an activity that encourages creative thinking by allowing team members to express any idea that comes to them without fear of criticism. Each member is free to offer ideas, often by taking a turn in sequence if that is the desire of the team. If the team elects to offer ideas in sequence, it is called "structured" brainstorming, while in "unstructured" brainstorming, members express ideas whenever they come to mind. The disadvantage of unstructured brainstorming is that some members may dominate the discussion and those less aggressive may not express their ideas. Ideas are not discussed as they are presented, but merely listed on a flip chart. Discussing the ideas as they are presented can kill creativity. A brainstorming session should not take a great deal of time, usually less than 15 minutes.

Nominal Group Technique (NGT): The Nominal Group Technique is often used along with brainstorming. The major purpose of the NGT is to insure that every member of the team has an equal voice. Recall in "unstructured" brainstorming the concern that the most vocal, often management, can dominate. The NGT addresses this domination, and can be used alone or with brainstorming. The process can be best explained in a series of steps:

1. Everyone on the team expresses what they think is the most important (either vocally or in writing). If the team members do not write down their suggestions, someone needs to place their ideas on a flip chart as they are suggested. If the suggestions are written down, they should be collected upon completion by the recorder.

2. The recorder writes down all the idea statements where the entire team can see them. The recorder looks for duplication, or similar ideas and collapses them. Every idea has a "letter" placed in front of it by the recorder.

3. Team members are asked to write down the letters corresponding to the suggestions submitted. For example, if eight ideas were suggested, all team members would write down "A," through "H" on their paper. Scoring is then produced by assigning numbers. With eight ideas, the top score would be "8" representing the best idea, and a "1" would be assigned the worst.

4. Team members then vote individually. The flip chart might list the following eight suggestions:

    A. Higher salaries

    B. More training

    C. Better personnel rules

    D. More sick leave

    E. More vacation time

    F. Longer breaks

    G. Better medical insurance

    H. Flexible working hours

    Each team member would end up with a set of numbers corresponding to their assessment of the relative worth of each idea. Their papers might look like this:

    A. 8

    B. 2

C. 4

D. 1

E. 7

F. 6

G. 3

H. 5

The recorder then totals all the responses from the team members. Perhaps, this would result in the following:

A. 8, 7, 8, 6, 7, 5, 6, 7 = 54

B. 3, 4, 3, 2, 5, 6, 4, 8 = 35

C. 8, 5, 2, 1, 6, 7, 2, 3 = 34

D. 4, 8, 6, 2, 4, 1, 6, 5 = 36

E. 1, 4, 7, 3, 8, 7, 2, 5 = 37

F. 1, 1, 6, 3, 8, 1, 5, 4 = 29

G. 8, 7, 3, 6, 4, 1, 7, 5 = 41

H. 1, 2, 5, 2, 3, 2, 4, 3 = 22

The item with the highest ranking ("A" with a vote of 54) is the one that is most important to the team. It might not be the same as the individual who was most vocal, but it is far more democratic. "Higher salaries" is far more important than is "Flexible working hours" in this team's assessment. The team may then discuss the relative importance of the ideas and come to yet another conclusion.

Multivoting: It is readily apparent that the Nominal Group Technique is very useful when the number of ideas (or problems) is relatively small (perhaps ten or less). But what happens should a team come up with a large number of problems (perhaps a hundred or more!)? Multivoting is a method to reduce large numbers to a more manageable level. Multivoting is exactly what it sounds like, multiple voting. A series of "rounds" or "elections" is held. On the first round, every member can vote once for every problem, but they usually select the ones they see most important. After the vote, the team decides the "cutoff" number of votes where those problems falling below are no longer considered. The team thus has fewer choices in the second round. The cutoff number should not be too high, perhaps ensuring that no more than half of the original problems (ideas) are eliminated. Votes may be taken in subsequent rounds, ever narrowing the number of problems to be eliminated. Eventually, the number may be reduced to five or ten concerns, problems, or ideas to consider.

The goal of this eleventh meeting is to identify the root causes of problems and verify the causes with data. The three tools described above can facilitate this goal.

Phase XII

At this stage, the team decides on a plan for improvement. They begin to implement the plan, do, check, act cycle. By analyzing the data, they suggest changes in the system that they feel are appropriate. At this stage, the team is learning to "manage by fact" and not by intuition. The team learns to trust their data and to start trusting the process. They identify improvement opportunities and then predict what tasks do not add value, what tasks they may add, what errors can be reduced by changing the system, and what changes they could make that would eliminate duplication.

Phase XIII

During the meetings in Phase Thirteen, the team makes changes in the processes to test their predictions. They now finally find out if they have been empowered. For example, one team began rejecting inputs that had more than one error. Under their old system, they would get on the telephone and make corrections themselves in the documents they received. This took considerable time and required hours of rework. After notification that they were going to reject documents with more than one error, there was an outcry from their suppliers. The suppliers' director called the supervisor responsible for their process and asked that this rule not go into effect. In this case, the supervisor was completely informed and in agreement with the process team and therefore stood his ground. Team members at that point knew that they were an empowered team.

This is not always the case. Some teams spend considerable time identifying the problems, but are not empowered to fix them. Some managers feel as though they are losing control over people and actually work against the team. These managers look for reasons why the process improvement team should be removed.

Also, teams will find out if there are other major road blocks to their success. For example, the team will find out that they don't have resources to fix the problems identified. They may need a piece of equipment that would be extremely helpful to them, but there are no resources available to purchase the equipment. They also may find that there is a lack of time allowed to them to significantly reduce errors. And also, not all teams live their values. Some team members may begin focusing on personalities within the team and find that they have serious conflict. Therefore, they are unable to cooperate and work together. These conflicts can often prevent teams from testing an excellent suggestion.

Piloting a suggestion is an important step, and it is often at this time a number of barriers will emerge. The team should be persistent and follow through on their pilot project.

Phase XIV

The team begins checking the results of their pilot in this phase. They check to see if improvements are effective and if improvements meet customer expectations. They find out if changes did eliminate time, reduce duplication, reduce errors, etc. If their plan is effective, they institutionalize the plan. The plan now becomes a permanent part of the process. They document the results and continue to track the process. Most teams at this stage write up the results of their work and expect to be recognized for their contribution to the organization.

Teams may then make a presentation to the Quality Council, who will award them with a plaque. The process and criteria used by the Quality Council are outlined in our chapter on communications and recognition.

Phase XV

The team starts the plan, do, check, act cycle again. Continual process improvement is a never-ending process requiring renewed commitment to start the process of planning all over again.

QUALITY MEETINGS

The most effective method of listening to employees is to have effective meetings. Teams are the heart and soul, the engine and the transmission, the sail and the rudder of the TQM initiative. Team members working together with their collective knowledge of the process are in the best position to identify problems and to propose solutions. By assuming this heavy responsibility to "fix" the process, team members in turn have the responsibility to take their work seriously. Team members should want to attend all meetings and participate in all team activities. Working together, they have an opportunity to implement solutions and to share in the glory when the process is improved.

RESOLVING CONFLICT

The most effective way to resolve conflicts in teams is to show respect for others by first acknowledging that the conflict exists. Second, conflicts should be defined specifically. Try to keep the conflict from being a personality problem and make it a process problem. Those who focus on managing personalities will always be in the middle of a conflict. Personalities differ significantly, and one can spend considerable time trying to alter a person's personality.

Therefore, focus on the process and not the personality. If the two or three people who are in conflict focus not on personality differences but on opinions regarding the process, then progress will be achieved in resolving the problem. Make sure that each person is allowed to state an opinion. If people talk about personalities as the source of their conflict, then lead them away from personality differences to their opinion about the process. Don't give them advice on what they can do, but rather let them understand where their differences are regarding what needs to be done.

Be very open and admit mistakes. Generally, if it's a problem due to faulty analysis about data or the process, then the conflict can easily be resolved. If the people in conflict are arguing over beliefs such as conservative vs. liberal or type of clothes one is wearing or personal habits, then the conflicts are not easily resolved. Therefore, the focus must shift to a conflict that is meaningful and once resolved, will be helpful to the team progressing towards its goal of improving the process.

EVALUATING TEAMS

Each team needs to evaluate its own effectiveness from time to time. Therefore, team members should be surveyed periodically. A suggested format that can be used follows:

	Strongly Agree	Agree	No Opinion	Disagree	Strongly Disagree	Total
	1	2	3	4	5	
1. Team members are committed to continual process improvement.						
2. Members practice the values agreed to by the team.						
3. The team is committed to meeting and exceeding customer expectations.						

4. The team is supportive
   of all members.
5. All team members
   contribute.
6. There is an effective
   agenda for all meetings.
7. The team does an
   effective job in identifying problems.
8. The team does an
   effective job in analyzing
   and solving problems.
9. Records are kept of each
   meeting and are helpful.
10. The team does an effective
    job of informing
    management on their progress.

Team data on the above surveys should be collected periodically and the results should be provided to the team. When a question has received three or above, a discussion of this item should be scheduled at the next meeting.

TEAM PRESENTATIONS

When teams complete their problem identification and solution process, they are ready to present to management their findings and proposed solutions. While each division in our pilot study developed their own procedures for teams to follow "on the road to the Quality Council presentation," most asked teams to present first to their regional quality council. Review at this first level is intended to help teams polish their work and presentation. Suggestions for improvement center on effective use of visuals, content of charts, handouts, etc.

Upon completion of review at the region level, teams progress to the second level—presentation to their division's quality council. This presentation is usually made at the state office headquarters in Tallahassee, and is considered a "dress rehearsal" for the final presentation. At this second level, final suggestions for improvements are made, and the team is asked to attend the next meeting of the Quality Council to present their report.

Team members can attend a special one-day seminar entitled "Presentation Skills" if they wish. This brief training covers the essentials of quality presentations and helps the team:

- Examine their audience and tailor the content and tone of the presentation accordingly.

- Prepare their presentation.

- Make effective use of visuals using consistent formatting.

- Use enthusiasm and humor.

- Practice their presentation.

TRACKING TEAMS

The amount of paperwork in government is unbelievable. People who do not work in government may think that they know how much paper is consumed by government, but they do not. Only those who have been inside can fully appreciate the fact that no one really ever knows how much time and money is consumed by the mountains of memorandums, forms, and reports generated daily throughout the system. Government has probably been responsible for more trees lost than all the forest fires added together since the beginning of time.

During our pilot project, a major objective in our implementation of quality was to insure that we did not add to the paper created by our agency. Thus, we required the absolute minimum of reports, memorandums and written policies. Nevertheless, it is important to track team activities for several reasons, including:

- to identify team progress,

- to help teams when training needs surface,

- to determine when a facilitator or Process Improvement Guide is needed,

- to improve communication between teams addressing similar improvements, and

- to identify when recognition is needed.

We began tracking teams using a simple Microsoft spreadsheet application known as "Excel." An uncomplicated report was generated by the database function that included the names of every team, team members, their mission, and where they were in the process. The reports generated were helpful to team members, facilitators, Process Improvement Guides and managers. Team members were able to continue their work with a minimum of reporting. In most cases, all that was asked of them was a copy of the minutes of their last meeting and records that were maintained by the team leader or Process Improvement Guide.

As implementation progressed, our reporting became somewhat more sophisticated with the development of reports generated by a relational database application known, such as Paradox by Borland International. This enhancement of our tracking system allowed us to generate reports that included:

Team Name

Division

Bureau

Office Address

Office Manager

Names of Members

Team Leader

Team Facilitator

Team Sponsor

Record of Training Completed (with date completed)

Overview & Communication Skills

Teams

Tools

Facilitation/Leadership

Customer Service

Presentation Skills

Other

Status—Stages Completed

Mission

Values

Vision

Goals

Process Selected

Customer Survey

Flowchart

Measurements

Analysis (Pareto, etc.)

Solution Matrix

Action Plan

Pilot

Check Results

Presentation to District Quality Council: (date)

Presentation to Division Quality Council: (date)

Presentation to Department Quality Council: (date)

Award

The reports generated by Paradox, using the above data, enabled us to meet our objectives in tracking team activities: to identify team progress, to help teams when training needs surfaced, to determine when a facilitator or Process Improvement Guide was needed, to improve communication between teams addressing similar improvements, and to identify when recognition was needed. This was accomplished with a minimum of paperwork and time. The tracking system follows a TQM principle in that it is constantly changing with continual improvements. Tomorrow's reports will be even better.

TQM ACTION REGISTER

Another mechanism that proved to be exceptionally useful in tracking was the "TQM Action Register." This simple form helped us keep current with action items—who had responsibility, the due date, and the current status. The register was first used by the Quality Council, but later worked its way throughout the department.

PROCESS IMPROVEMENT GUIDES

Perhaps one of our best ideas was the development of "Process Improvement Guides" to assist teams as they began their process improvements. These guides, referred to as "PIGs," were all volunteers who embraced TQM as they learned more about continual improvement. Their role was defined as follows: a Process Improvement Guide is an individual who has been selected to provide technical assistance to quality improvement teams as an "outside" consultant. Their job is to help team members in the group process by observing and evaluating how the team functions. They also provide training as needed in quality improvement tools, team dynamics, the teachings of quality improvement "gurus," including Dr. Deming, and help the teams prepare presentations to the Quality Council.

These guides were responsible for much of the success of the teams throughout the state. They were enthusiastic supporters of TQM and modeled the true meaning of quality improvement. Meeting regularly in their regions across the state, the PIGs received special training and became familiar with the learning resources that were available to help teams. They worked in this role in addition to the performance of their regular responsibilities, and became experts on quality improvement.

TEAM ANALYSIS

One of the ways to improve teams is to take two or three associates who do not work directly with the process and ask them to evaluate the team. Their purpose is to help the team improve the way the team works together. The two or three selected associates visit the team meetings, and interview the team members as a team and individually. The two or three associates make suggestions on how the team might improve the way they work with each other and improve their processes. Implement team analysis as follows:

1. Invite teams for analysis.

2. Select two or three outsiders to do a thorough analysis of the team.

3. Have the outside reviewing team present the criteria that will be used in evaluating the team.

4. Review criteria with the team.

5. Conduct the team analysis.

6. Interview the team as a whole.

7. Interview individual team members.

8. Provide feedback, both written and oral.

8

LEADING TOTAL QUALITY MANAGEMENT

"Your life is your message. Leadership by example is not only the most pervasive, but also the most enduring form of leadership."
—Gandi

There are perhaps very few jobs more difficult or more challenging than leading the Total Quality Management initiative. Leading TQM means being out in front. It means taking a position. It means being an articulate advocate. Leading TQM may also mean ridicule. It means that people may laugh at TQM advocacy. It means that people may listen politely to a position, but totally ignore it. They may claim that TQM is too ambitious, too expensive, too complicated, too radical, will take too long, just a fad, and that the status quo works fine.

HOW TOUGH ARE YOU?

Organizational change seems to work best in America when the organization is forced to change because customers reject their products. For example, one of the most significant turnarounds in the history of organizations was done by Chrysler in the 1980s. Here was a company ready to go out of business. In fact, if it wasn't for a loan from the federal government, it probably would be out of business. Chrysler understood that it needed to change the way it did business. Even with executives, managers at all levels, and employees knowing that Chrysler must change, it was not easy. However, faced with the reality of either building a quality car or going out of business, it made change a bit easier.

This is not true for government. Most people in government realize that the system is sick, but believe that they personally can outlast the system. In other words, they will retire long before they will ever be forced to change. It is

131

common among government workers to believe that they can withstand any attempts to change them. It is common for government workers to pay lip service to new leaders in government. Sometimes government people even receive new ideas with enthusiasm, but will not take the initiative or the risk of implementing change.

It seems as though government workers would rather spend their working time griping about how poorly government is managed than to take the initiative to fix it. Perhaps the most shocking reality in government is the amount of errors made in practically every process. Perhaps even more disturbing is that government management systems tolerate the errors. For example, one study in the area of disability determinations revealed an average error rate of 56 percent in initial determination for Social Security disability benefits. A process improvement team lowered the error rate to 10 percent! They continue to work on improvements to drive down the error rate, with their goal less than .001 percent. This team showed what could happen if front-liners work on process improvement. Now that they have set a benchmark for the entire country, it would seem likely that the rest of the federal government and state governments would all develop teams and begin working to drive down the error rate. At government's current rate of change, it will probably take years for the rest of the government to change. In the meantime, customer dissatisfaction continues.

Most government workers don't think government is like Chrysler. They believe there is not a crisis. Therefore, to lead a change initiative in government is extremely difficult. When addressing associates on TQM, one might be astounded at their lack of receptivity. TQM advocacy is a speaking challenge. It's like pulling teeth. Government workers generally believe the myth that they are among the best in the country in delivering government services. They will have no facts to document this, and if they do provide data, it's often very selective data. It takes little analysis to show that the data is incorrect.

A common phrase in leadership is "you get what you tolerate." That's exactly what occurs in government. Leaders tolerate poor quality work because it is too difficult to change the system so that it delivers error-free work. Consequently, government is filled with managers, not leaders, who have grown accustomed to tolerating inexcusable quality, and they adopt an interesting management strategy which allows them to claim they are good, blame others for their mistakes, and constantly complain that they could do better if they had more people and more resources. It's been going on for years, and is still growing even in lean budget years. When budget cuts are made in programs, managers usually survive by cutting services rather than positions. There is a slight change in direction at the federal level under President Clinton and Vice-President Gore. Positions, including those in management, are now being eliminated.

People who believe that government can improve and have the desire to improve the way government does business must be willing to take their "hits." Leaders can expect to be sabotaged at all levels, expect to have people lie, expect people to provide phony flowcharts and data, and expect that many people will ignore TQM. Therefore, to lead a TQM initiative in government, one has to be tough.

DON'T GO IT ALONE—GET NEEDED SUPPORT

Soon after one of the authors joined the Department of Labor and Employment Security in Florida, he conducted three seminars for top management on Total Quality Management. It wasn't long when one of the administrative assistants in the office came to him with tears in her eyes. She said to him, "I respect you and believe in what you are saying. I know you're trying to help this department get better, but I can't stand it any more, hearing what people are saying about you. They think your ideas are pie-in-the-sky and are just academic notions. Some believe that they might work in industry, but they won't work in government. They believe you are just wasting their time and that you are a jerk. You are too condescending and insensitive. Further, when you make fun of people who are late to meetings, you are just doing that for your own enjoyment. You say you are trying to get the organization members to value time, but you just like to embarrass people. A lot of people don't like your personality."

After getting her to settle down, after getting her to control her emotions, we talked about the comments and their meaning. She was told, "Don't worry about attacks on an individual's personality, but rather focus on the process. Listen to only those comments that will help us improve the process of changing the culture to the desired state and ignore attacks on individuals." To be tough, one must ignore personal attacks. It is not that government needs to improve the personalities of their workforce. One can't change people's personalities, but one can change the processes of the way business is done. Therefore, focus on any comments that pertain to the way work gets done. This is not always an easy task.

To be successful, TQM leaders need to develop a support team that assists them in the change initiative. For example, the administrative assistant who came to one of the authors with a true intent to help them was recruited for the first support team. We called such workers "internal consultants." These were associates in the organization who gravitated towards the TQM initiative. These were the people who showed the most interest and took it upon themselves to put forth extra energy to improve the organization. This internal support team was people composed of various backgrounds, various ages, and a wide degree of employment in government. For example, one internal consultant was 70 years old, a former senior vice president for a top American corporation, who got bored in retirement and came back to work in the front-lines in Purchasing. Another was a person who had 33 years of government experience and was just plain tired of the way government worked. Still another was a statistician, an economist, who stepped forward because she was tired of inaccurate data.

The internal consultant group had eleven people. We met every Monday morning to chart our progress, discuss our strategy or change strategy and, more important, to give support to each other that we were moving in the right direction. People who want to lead a change initiative can't do it alone. Leaders advocating TQM need to be tough and need people to help deal with the negative personal comments and negative attitudes toward a TQM initiative.

TQM LEADERS ARE BELIEVERS

TQM leaders accept the basic principles of quality management. They never lose sight of the customer and strongly believe that the organizational systems should be designed to meet and/or exceed expectations of their customers. They believe in empowering people to improve their processes. They are willing to work towards the development of a system that allows workers to do the right thing the first time. They believe the best approach to improving processes is for people to work in teams. They believe in themselves, in continued improvement of both themselves and the organization and their mission: the development of a total quality organization.

Trusting one's beliefs in TQM is a difficult challenge. The more leaders believe, the more they realize that they must spend every waking hour at work moving the organization towards TQM. In industry, if a customer rejects products or services, it is not easy to lose the proper focus. On the other hand, in government where the customer is sometimes thought of as an inconvenience who "better adjust" to government systems, it is easy to lose focus. It is easy to be distracted by actions taken by legislators, by directives from the Executive Branch, or perhaps the most common diversion, meetings by bureaucrats who want to control people and resources.

It is amazing in government how much money is allotted for travel to organization meetings that have very little impact. In fact, most government meetings are repeats of meetings that have occurred for the past 50 years. They are discussions about what should be done to change the system. About every year, bureaucrats on the federal and state levels figure out that they need to do something to control government. Therefore, they will be advocating some new system that supposedly is going to reinvent the way we work. These are almost always top-down initiatives that are attempts to gain control of a poorly managed system.

Not long ago, we heard a bureaucrat from Washington stand up and say that the speech he was about to give was the same one he gave in 1978. He went on to advocate that government could be fixed if we only had more auditors. His speech would make any believer in TQM sick, for TQM believers understand that if government had quality systems, there would be no need for auditors. The people doing the work would build in their own "check points." Therefore, TQM leaders maintain a passion for excellence to the point where they are not distracted. In some cases, they don't even attend the typical government meetings. Their time and travel money is spent on TQM initiatives.

TQM leaders do not delegate quality; they lead the quality initiative. It's okay, however, to delegate trivial government meetings that are required to maintain resources to others. Rather than looking to the top leadership of government bureaucracies for answers to problems, look to associates who are working on improving processes. The TQM leaders don't look up for the answers, but look to the data collected and analyzed by front-line associates to determine where to go and what to do.

TQM LEADERS ARE CHANGE AGENTS

The goal of a TQM leader is to transform traditional methods of doing government business to Total Quality Management. The culture should move from one that is presently focused on management by objectives to a culture that focuses on exceeding customer expectations; from only numerical objectives to fixing the system that allows associates to do the right thing the first time; from a system where management does the planning, the organizing, the directing, and controlling to a system of process improvement and team work; from a system where training was mostly for management to a system where associates at all levels are trained; from a system that mainly tries to track individual performance, where individuals are rank ordered to a system where all associates are expected to exceed; from a system that rewards and punishes individuals to a system of performance appreciation; from a system that's organized around functions to a system that is organized around processes; and finally, from a system where management is expected to know best, where management manipulates people to get done what they think needs to get done, and where leaders are only allowed to fulfill a leadership role if they are appointed, to a system where leaders can emerge and empower others.

Total Quality Management leaders have a vision of a quality culture, share their vision, and point the organization in the right direction. They have a sense of where the organization is going and must go.

To be a successful change agent, understand the present state of the organization and have an accurate vision as to where the organization must go, and be willing, committed, and highly motivated to inspire others to help create the desired organizational culture.

WHAT IS TQM LEADERSHIP?

We define leadership as "influencing behavior in the desired direction because you have a vision about where followers should go."

Simply stated, leadership is influencing the behavior of others towards a desired state. Since one doesn't often know what the desired state of a situation might be, one should give away leadership to others. A TQM leader discusses the desired state of an organization over time. There is an important difference between a situational leader and a TQM leader. A TQM leader understands the desired state of the organization and therefore is constantly leading this initiative. However, TQM leaders may participate in teams and in situations where they do not know what is best. Therefore, they allow others to emerge in leadership roles. With this more flexible approach to leadership, it becomes clear why it is difficult for traditional managers in organizations to embrace TQM leadership. Traditional organization leaders are supposed to know what is best. After all, that's why they were selected. They knew what was good for every situation. Traditional leaders are expected to know what to do and act accordingly. After all, they are responsible.

On the other hand, TQM leaders understand that processes are customer driven and therefore they must empower those responsible for meeting and exceeding customer expectations to select the best course of action. The TQM leader is responsible for creating a culture that allows people to use their brains to improve the process. The TQM leaders realize that each situation is different and decision-making should go to those who are the most knowledgeable about the situation. Consequently, leadership in the organization emerges from collective wisdom and not from autocratic control of people. In fact, TQM leaders look to others for leadership. They look to their associates for proposing new ideas, new procedures, new methods, and solutions to problems. They give away leadership to those who are actively interested in improving organizational processes, to those who are willing to express judgments about situations, to those who are willing to collect data and deal with facts, and to those who are willing to put their own self interests as secondary to the improvement of the overall process.

A TQM leader does not have a goal of controlling people, but rather a goal of gaining control of the processes they own. A TQM leader is defined as an individual who influences the behavior of others towards embracing and accepting the *principles* of Total Quality Management. The goal of a TQM leader is to develop a TQM culture. This is a culture which is customer driven, where the focus is on improving the processes by working together in teams, collecting and measuring data, practicing organization values so that the system allows every worker to do the right thing the first time.

TOTAL QUALITY MANAGEMENT LEADERSHIP TRAITS

Traits are identifiable characteristics used to predict success. Every day leaders must respond to stimuli. The way they respond to stimuli depends upon numerous factors. In this section, we will identify those characteristics we deem necessary for total quality leadership. As advocates for change, specific traits are required. TQM leaders will find the road to success relatively easy if they possess the following traits:

1. Energy

TQM leaders must have personal energy in order to motivate others. Leading a TQM initiative requires working harder than anyone else. Leaders can't be the last ones to arrive in the morning and the first ones to go home in the afternoon. They must be willing to commit energy to enabling and supporting associates. People respect others who are not afraid of work. In a TQM organization, all of the associates will expect, at a minimum, that leaders have work-oriented motivation. People need to understand that failure at a specific endeavor does not imply lack of a valiant effort or energy. It's important that associates perceive leaders as action-oriented and eager to make a positive contribution.

2. Tolerance for Uncertainty

For people who must know how everything is going to turn out before they make a decision, TQM leadership is not for them. Frequently, activities are planned and carried out with enthusiasm only to find that a plan has many flaws. There are times when something is done without knowing the consequences. It just seemed to be the right thing to do at the time. Furthermore, it's almost impossible to predict how people are going to respond to initiatives. There will be many successes, as well as many failures. There will be disappointment in people who supposedly supported the TQM initiative but who were actually working against it. There will be unpredictable responses from some people. For example, we asked all of the divisions to flowchart all of their key processes as one of our initial initiatives. Some of the division directors went out and hired consultants to come in and do the flowcharting. Division directors thought that they would handle this request as another administrative bureaucratic directive (if the boss wants flowcharts, give him flowcharts). When we observed the division directors going to outside support for flowcharting, we just let it take its course.

Most managers believe they are doing an effective job when they control people. Do their subordinates get to work on time? Do their subordinates do what they are told to do? Do their subordinates turn their work in on time, etc.? Consequently, it is very difficult for managers to practice the trait of tolerating uncertain situations. However, leaders in American industry have long understood the need to move forward with uncertainty. Perhaps the most distinguishing characteristic for successful leaders in the past two decades has been their ability to tolerate uncertainty.

Since government has had a long tradition of selecting, recognizing and rewarding managers who do an effective job of controlling people, it is sometimes difficult to find leaders in government who can tolerate uncertainty. The best managers in government have often preached that the best way to keep one's job is to "go with the flow." Most managers in government will say, "Just leave us alone." They want to sit back and keep things the way they are. They will report how complex and difficult it is to manage their assigned functions. Many find it very difficult to change. TQM leaders will have to deal with these managers every day. Some days are not much fun. Leaders just have to learn to tolerate the unexpected and move along.

3. Persistence

Successful TQM leaders must put a lot of activities into motion. Since they know where they are going, and many activities they put into motion fail, they need to keep on trying. Generally the first attempt to even get the managers to think about TQM fails. Managers will take the attitude that "This too will pass."

In all probability, the first attempts to start TQM will be largely ignored. Once managers appear to take TQM seriously, they will spend much of their energy figuring out a way not to implement it. But how can they keep TQM concepts away from the people they manage? Managers will begin to huddle and talk about ways to stop the TQM initiative. They will provide every reason why it won't work in their function. They attempt to make implementation so difficult that they hope for failure and a return to the status quo.

Further, they realize that critical appointments come and go quickly. Therefore, all they have to do is wait.

Total Quality Management leaders persist. They accept the behavior of managers, but they don't quit with their initiative. They find another way to bring about change. Practically every week they are thinking of another way to bring about change.

As the TQM initiative progresses, managers become more insecure. Some of them even become frightened. These nervous managers may start to believe that a leader is serious and has found out that they have not been cooperating. At first, the nervousness starts at the top of the organization, and then it flows quickly to the bottom managers. They gradually come to realize that a TQM leader is serious and extremely persistent.

4. TQM Leaders Are Dependable

When leaders tell people that they are willing to work hard and that they will support them in their efforts, they will at first have doubts. The associates who believe in the TQM message and want to practice TQM will need 100 percent of the leader's support. People who share enthusiasm for TQM will come from all levels. Therefore, they should be encouraged to move forward. The first managers who begin to share the excitement will be taking certain risks. Some will want to form teams when the manager above them doesn't buy into the notions of TQM. The managers who are risk takers need to know that they can depend on the leader if everything does not always go well.

The leader's image in the organization should be one of dependability. To achieve that image, one must be dependable. The leader should "do what he says he's going to do." People must know a leader is committed to TQM and will be there when they need you. Leaders can't show up late for meetings, can't fail to return their phone calls as soon as possible, and can't ignore people. Leaders have to be there to help and support associates. Associates must know that they can count on leaders.

5. Positive Self-Esteem

To be an effective TQM leader, leaders must believe in TQM and themselves. Leaders should perceive themselves as individuals worthy of leadership, as people of integrity, having intelligence, and who are genuinely concerned about others in the organization. Leaders with a high self-esteem are not afraid of failure. In fact, effective leaders seldom ever see failure, but rather see failure as something they have tried, didn't work, but it was something that needed to be done in order to achieve success. They only see themselves as successful.

Furthermore, the more they do, the better their self-image becomes. They gain their self-image from clear, measurable evidence of achievement and performance. They think of themselves as winners and believe ultimately that they will succeed in anything where they are willing to put forth energy and to which they are committed. Many people with a high self-esteem also believe that they are "lucky" and in the end, everything will turn out positively. They have a "can-do" attitude. Also, they have a habit of doing things that make them feel good about themselves.

Leaders of a TQM initiative need a positive self-image. At first, people will try to destroy the concepts and, failing to do so, they will attack leaders personally. If leaders don't have positive self-image, they will be worn down by over time and may even begin to believe they're true. Leaders is lacking a positive self-image may want to try some initiative other than TQM. On the other hand, leaders with positive self-esteem will thoroughly enjoy leading an organization towards implementing TQM.

6. Desire To Influence Others

The final identifiable characteristic that predicts success as a TQM leader is a desire to influence others. Some people have very little desire to influence the thinking and behavior of others. The latter would not be conducive to TQM leadership. On the contrary, TQM leaders want to strongly influence others. Total Quality Management leaders believe that their concepts are valuable and worthwhile. Therefore, they want to share their concepts and beliefs with everyone. They usually find an argument enjoyable, discussions valuable, and they rejoice at the opportunity to convince another person that their concepts are logical.

Having a specific trait does not necessarily mean that one will be good at practicing it. For example, one might be a very effective communicator, but have very little desire to influence others. On the other hand, one might be very poor at persuasion and yet have a deep desire to convince others that certain concepts make sense. Having a trait does not necessarily automatically ensure success, but not having a trait makes it practically impossible. One must, at a minimum, want to influence others to be successful as a TQM leader.

TQM LEADERSHIP SKILLS

A skill is an ability to perform a sequence of behaviors that relate to a specific outcome. For example, some people have the ability to convince others that they are correct, i.e., skills at persuasion. Such people can sequence their behavior to attain a performance goal. In other words, they can convince another person that it is in their best interest to follow certain directions.

In this section, we will identify what skills we believe are necessary for TQM success in government. These skills are as follows:

1. Communication

Communication is the process of sending a message which stimulates the receiver to think and/or behave as intended by the sender. Success in implementing TQM requires constantly sending messages with the intent that people receive them as they are intended. For example, the vision of how the organization will function when TQM beliefs and principles are applied must be understood by all. Considerable time will be spent in team meetings, working with groups at all levels, coaching associates, counseling associates, and, in some cases, resolving conflicts.

All of these activities require effective communication skills. Effective TQM leaders are good listeners, good team members, and effective public speakers.

2. Team Building

Team building is the art of bringing people together to want to work toward achieving specific goals. At the start of the TQM initiative, this skill will be needed every day since leaders are expected to recruit people who share the TQM philosophy. Success requires a team that supports these ideals. Effective teams can become powerful by using all of the skills of each team member. With the support of a team, people with below average skills can make sudden, positive contributions to the TQM initiative.

Furthermore, several opinions on what to do can more often than not produce the right course of action. Being able to bring people together, keep them together, and get results is a skill required of a TQM leader in government.

3. Measurement

Measurement is a process of collecting data and determining its meaning. TQM is often referred to as "management by fact" because measurement plays such an important role. A TQM leader is constantly asking questions about data, demonstrating knowledge about quality indicators for all of the key processes, and finally, letting the data guide leadership behavior. Total Quality Management leaders are constantly demonstrating to their associates their knowledge of key result areas and their ability to collect and analyze data.

Leaders use their measurement skill to set priorities and to evaluate process effectiveness. Obtaining meaningful and accurate data along with statistical competence, is a skill that will help leaders to not overly react to incidents, but rather to respond in a controlled, strategic manner. For years, top management in government has delegated measurement skills to others. Now it is imperative that all top managers demonstrate measurement skills daily.

4. Facilitation

Traditionally, the managers delegated facilitation skills to others, e.g., managers who were going to have a difficult meeting might retain a outside facilitator to maintain communication and reduce conflicts. A TQM leader cannot delegate this skill. It is now the leader's responsibility. Consequently, TQM leaders will want to put themselves in situations that require facilitation such as team meetings, customer focus groups, customer-organization members meetings, strategic planning sessions, etc.

For example, the head of the Department of Labor and Employment Security went throughout the state meeting with managers and facilitated sessions which were warmly received by all associates in attendance. For years, managers would go out and tell the troops what needed to be done even though, in most cases, the top leader didn't know what to do. People would listen patiently and tell the top leader how good he or she was doing their job, and at the same time think to themselves how ineffective the leadership was in their organization.

Facilitation skills not only help deal with conflict and build more effective teams, but also help build trust. Generally, people who can facilitate a win-win situation in the organization are leaders who earn the respect of others. Effective facilitators demonstrate sensitivity and are highly aware of the feelings of others. Consequently, the leader can help organization members handle many personal and emotional problems, as well as adjusting to organizational problems.

5. Teaching

Traditionally, leaders delegated this skill to others in the organization. For example, hundreds of consulting companies have made millions of dollars teaching skills in organizations. The organization would do a study and find that most associates thought the company was poor in communication, decision-making, low morale, poor planning, etc. The response by the top executive team in government was to hire outside consultants to come in and solve their problem. They might, for example, retain a leading decision-making consulting firm to come in and teach them a prescribed decision-making approach.

These teaching skills should not be delegated. It's the TQM leader who must teach skills, such as team dynamics, effective presentations, TQM tools, leadership, etc. Furthermore, TQM leaders should never miss an opportunity to teach. Since TQM leaders are often walking processes, attending team meetings, attending quality council, they are often put into situations where they should seize upon the opportunity to teach those in attendance another concept or another way to learn and appreciate Total Quality Management.

6. Decision-Making

There are many leadership books which claim that leaders should be tough minded and not afraid to make a decision. We believe that in Total Quality Management one does not have to be tough minded, but rather well informed. In a TQM organization decision-making is enjoyable and not too difficult a task. Since measurement indicators, graphs and charts abound in TQM organizations, it's rather easy to make a decision when well armed with data.

Perhaps it will be difficult for some to make what they might refer to as tough decisions, that is to remove or transfer a manager because of his inability or unwillingness to participate in TQM. It is certainly not tough to find those who are effectively implementing TQM. It doesn't take too long to determine whether an individual is on the team or not. Some people's personalities may prevent them from facing up to the situation because they are afraid of conflict* but if the customer is the first priority, it will not be a tough decision.

Leaders are constantly making decisions such as what do they do next, where should they be in the organization, how can they facilitate change, how can they learn more about a particular process, etc. Intuition, data and common sense are the guides. What is important is that leaders constantly use decision-making skills. Decisions must be timely and correct. Furthermore, leaders participate on a number of teams and will want to attack problems in a scientific way rather than verbalizing a lot of different reactions. Leaders identify problems, recognize symptoms, causes, and alternative solutions. They make timely decisions and correct decisions even under conditions of risk and uncertainty.

7. Strategic Planning

This skill requires vision. In our study, every Monday morning we would meet with our internal consultants, whom we referred to as our strategic change team. We spent most of our time in TQM strategic planning. In our early meetings, we spent most of our time constructing our vision as to what we wanted to happen. A vision is a clear mental picture of the desired state of the organization. The internal consultants were a coalition of people who were committed to the vision.

As a team, our job was to promote TQM. Therefore our strategic planning sessions always included answers to the following questions: What are we doing well? What are our strengths? What are we doing poorly? What are our weaknesses? What are the barriers preventing us from achieving our vision? What are our threats? What opportunities do we have for improvement? What action should we take?

Strategic planning, like all other skills, is a discipline that requires a sequence of behaviors. Traditional managers have attacked strategic planning by setting aside three or four days a year for top management to get together and form the strategic plan. In a TQM organization, strategic planning is, at a minimum, a weekly skill that should be deployed by all TQM leaders. What is so pleasing about TQM leadership is the great opportunity it gives leaders. Great leaders, for example, do not emerge because they are great, but rather because they are given the opportunity to lead. General Colin Powell and General Schwartzkopf would not be considered great leaders today if it hadn't been for the Middle East crisis. They are now known as great generals and will go down in history as extraordinary leaders. They will long be remembered for their strategic planning skills.

Total Quality Management is an initiative that will allow great leaders to emerge because it provides an extraordinary opportunity. To take advantage of this opportunity, TQM leaders must be skillful in strategic planning.

8. Self-Management

The skill required of TQM leadership is self-management. This is the art. This skill requires people to know themselves, to understand their strengths and their weaknesses, and to be able to discipline themselves so that they receive a maximum return on the effort they put forth. In an earlier section, we discuss the need for energy. However, energy that is misdirected will not result in worthwhile activities. Therefore, leaders need to control their sequence of behaviors in organizations.

Total Quality Management leaders are continually plotting ways to improve their effectiveness. What we've found to be most effective is that the TQM leader serves as a role model in practicing the values of the organization. To be effective, they need to identify behaviors that can be associated with organization values. For example, if time is a core value to the organization, then the leader should always be on time for meetings and in meetings on time. He or she should be a role model in time management.

An effective way to improve self-management skills is to have subordinates regularly evaluate performance. We found the following questions to be very helpful in improving self-management.

PERFORMANCE QUESTIONNAIRE FOR LEADERS

1. Do you feel your leader is doing a quality job overall? Does he or she try to "get the big picture" and understand the whole organization, or is he/she just interested in his/her pet projects?

2. Is he or she accessible? Can you bring bad news as well as the good without fear?

3. Have you been able to receive satisfactory answers to your requests in a timely manner? If not, why?

4. Is correspondence to you readable and easily understood?

5. Does he or she show respect to you and those around you? Will he or she listen to your ideas? Do you feel he/she has your best interest at heart?

6. Do you believe his or her management style encourages enthusiasm and happiness or apathy and bitterness? Do *you* welcome the sight of him or her coming down the hall, or does *your* stomach go into a knot whenever *you* are near him or her?

7. Do you have any suggestions for improvement in any of the above areas of performance? Please list.

8. What questions should have been included on this questionnaire, or what questions would you like to have included for the next evaluation?

Since TQM leaders spend 90 percent of their time working for the people below them—meeting their needs and giving them support—everyone must exercise self-discipline in dealing with their TQM leaders. Frequently, people must fulfill obligations directed by superiors. We have found that it is the best to react immediately to superior directives and handle on-going obligations required from the top with immediacy. Since leaders are anxious to pursue leading the TQM initiative everyday, it's best to take care of the organizational requirements prior to TQM initiatives.

Therefore, we advocate that leaders get to work early and dispense with these obligations. Many bureaucratic managers will spend the entire day working only on superior directives. They believe it's the only thing they have to do. Frequently, they treat these directives as a nuisance and are constantly telling people how hard they are working. The fact of the matter is that many managers want to sit in their office and control people. Therefore, they give the appearance that they are loaded down with lots of work and only have time to deal with personality conflicts that emerge during the day—reactive management.

Total Quality Management leaders are not managed. They manage themselves. They are skillful in planning their day and finding shortcuts and better ways to do the daily requirements so that they can get on with the "real" work of the day. They are skillful in using the energy required for successful leadership.

Total Quality Management leaders handle details. They process or generate information without either overlooking important items or getting enmeshed in technicalities.

9. Empowerment

The final skill a TQM leader must learn is the skill of empowerment. This is the art of granting the authority to others to act. Traditional leaders have frequently delegated some of their power to subordinates in order to get the job done. This power is only given to a particular person and, in most cases, it comes with prescribed directions. In other words, the subordinate can take action, but only if he acts according to instructions. We refer to this skill as delegation.

Empowerment is much more than delegation. Empowerment allows associates to make decisions without being told how to act. Rather, associates are allowed to make decisions that they believe are in the best interest of improving the process and meeting customer needs. It is much more than delegating people to act on behalf of management. Rather, it is the power to make decisions and take action that improves the process without management telling them what to do and how to do it.

Consequently, empowerment is a new skill required of leaders in today's organizations. We believe that the most effective sequence of behaviors for empowering people are as follows:

A. Have associates demonstrate that they know their assigned processes.

B. Make sure associates understand the expectations of their customers.

C. Have associates work in teams.

D. Have the team measure supplier input, process activities, outputs, and customer outcomes.

E. Have associates continually involved in improving the process by using TQM tools.

Traditional delegation was a skill that required effective downward communication so that the associate could follow orders precisely. Empowerment is just the opposite. This skill requires communication both downward and upward; but even more important, it requires communication with other members working to improve the process.

Total Quality Management leaders don't tell associates who are working on the process what to do. It is just the opposite. Associates, closest to the work and given responsibility for the process, tell management what to do. Empowerment is a new skill for leaders, and it will require lots of practice. It will require TQM leaders to exemplify all of the traits discussed in the previous section.

TQM LEADERSHIP BEHAVIOR: WHAT DO TQM LEADERS DO?

In this section, we will cover what TQM leaders do everyday to lead their quality initiative. Traditional approaches to behavioral perspectives of leadership have focused on two dimensions: tasks, sometimes referred to as concern for production, and a second dimension, consideration, sometimes referred to as concern for people. The behavioral approach describes the basic person-to-person relationship in which one person's behavior affects another. There is considerable speculation as to how leaders should behave regarding these two dimensions of leadership.

Some authors advocate a leadership style based on "Follower Readiness." Most authors suggesting the behavioral approach believe that the most effective leaders is to have a high degree of concern for people as well as for the task that needs to be accomplished. Some might suggest that if the situation warrants it, leaders should select one of the dimensions over another. We advocate that leaders' behavior should always take into account both of these dimensions. We, however, cannot see a situation in a Total Quality Management organization that should force one to have a greater concern for one dimension over the other.

In a TQM organization, the task is always to improve the process. The focus, however, is on people closest to the work improving the process. Therefore, it is a given that a TQM leader emphasizes both task and people. However, TQM leadership requires more than an understanding and an application of these two dimensions. TQM requires specific behaviors. Since a leader no longer just makes decisions and has others carry them out, it is not enough for a TQM leader to just show a concern for production and a concern for people.

The behaviors of TQM leaders should focus on assisting teams and organization members to improve organizational processes. We believe that there is a different set of behaviors required for managers who elect management by objectives approach, for those who advocate re-inventing government, and for those who advocate management by participation. Leading a TQM initiative requires numerous behaviors as follows:

1. Develop effective personal relationships with associates. Leaders will want to affect associates so that they will strive to implement TQM. Leaders' behavior, however, will not produce the desired results if behavior is directed towards personal relationships. Rather, leadership behavior should mostly be focused on process improvement. More effective working relationships are established with people if there is no attempt to control them and if the focus is on process control.

2. Be able to effectively work in teams. Many managers often prefer the "Lone Ranger" style and believe that the best way to get things done is to do them personally or direct others. This is not acceptable behavior for a TQM leader. These leaders have a need for participating in teams, a need for team achievement, and will experience happiness while being a team member.

3. Use Total Quality Management language. With TQM comes a new vocabulary which requires leaders to know and understand the meanings of words used in the quality initiative. If a leader doesn't understand the terms or misuses them, the team will know immediately that the leader does not fully comprehend the TQM philosophy.

4. Teach TQM courses and seize every opportunity to provide further understanding of TQM. Total Quality Management leaders constantly elaborate on TQM beliefs and principles.

   Total Quality Management leaders are involved in all levels of the organization. Not only do they walk the talk, but they are readily available and visible to all associates. They know people by name and take an active interest in each process and each process team. Effective TQM leaders are constantly invited by teams to attend their team meetings or to come into their area and see their latest results. Going to where the work gets done is not only an educational and rewarding personal experience for the leader, but is also a recognition and rewarding experience to those associates who invited you. Associates like managers who are interested enough to visit with them in their workplace. It goes beyond "good PR" for it says that associates are important.

5. Ask questions—challenge the process. This behavior is practiced daily. One constantly learns by asking questions. In the traditional management systems, a question was often thought of as micro management, whereas in TQM a question is a positive behavior. Teams are now prepared for questions and are often disappointed if they aren't asked difficult questions about their processes and how they managed to improve processes. Leaders constantly

challenge the system because they never accept "business as usual" as the answer.

6. Demonstrate measurement behavior. Associates will expect leaders to be genuinely interested in data, and, consequently, leaders' daily behavior will require demonstrating knowledge of process baseline data and benchmarks, and leaders will be expected to use the tools of Total Quality Management.

7. Demonstrate facilitation behavior. The associates will expect leaders to be able to assist the team improve its process. Therefore, TQM leadership behavior requires using the magic marker and flip chart to assist the team in working through a situation. Teams will frequently look to top management for an answer out of respect, but mostly out of fear and tradition. To offset their expectations, the TQM leader reverses the process and begins to facilitate the meeting in a manner that has the team looking for answers.

8. Public speaking is frequently required and often required on a short notice. We distinguish between public speaking and teaching behaviors. Teachers use a variety of teaching methods: lecture, teams, simulations, videos, etc. On the other hand, public speaking is generally a short speech which is designed to inspire associates.

9. Demonstrate reward and recognition behaviors. Leaders will be expected to recognize and reward those who support the TQM initiative daily. This will require making short presentations, giving certificates and plaques, and saying kind and thoughtful remarks about the quality of work in front of peers, friends and leaders.

10. Structure the organization. One way leaders can insert power into the organization is to restructure the organization. Rotating managers is very helpful; but reducing the layers of management will remove many obstacles that prevent the TQM initiative from being successful. When a structure is dominated by five to ten levels of management, it is likely that the organization will find it very difficult to respond to customer needs.

Restructuring the organization too soon in a TQM initiative may cause more resistance than it's worth. The goal is to reduce the levels of management, but it should be accomplished slowly.

In a nutshell, TQM requires true leadership behavior. It requires the leader to be out in front, involved, participating, and highly visible. It requires a leader who is supportive, friendly, and encouraging. It requires a leader who believes in education and training, and who is skilled at counseling and listening to others. TQM leaders are not afraid to admit their mistakes openly and communicate to their associates directly and honestly. They make decisions in a timely manner and are not afraid to test suggestions of others and ideas of their own. TQM leaders are constant, consistent, and reinforce TQM principles.

These leaders also provide proper recognition to associates who prove daily they are committed to continual improvement. They don't run away from problems; they appreciate them. TQM leaders see problems as opportunities. It gives them an opportunity to be innovative and resourceful. TQM requires a leader to be passionate, relentless, and dedicated to people and process improvement. Leaders are expected to be creative and select behaviors that stimulate others to work together, measure their processes, and improve the way they do business. The Leadership Criteria developed by the Quality Council in our study summarizes these expectations.

LEADERSHIP AWARD CRITERIA

- *Role modeling the agency's values*—Demonstrates the Department of Labor and Employment Security's values in word and deed.

- *Process management*—Focuses on the way work gets done, on the organization of people, procedures, equipment, and energy into work activities for the purpose of process optimization. Identifies core processes, recruits teams, leads team analysis and flowcharts processes, detects and removes causes of variation, and measures the effects on customers.

- *Quality tools and data*—Uses quality tools and data in managing the day-to-day operation of the organization.

- *Linkages to other processes*—Demonstrates knowledge of customers impact on organization's process. Understands and explains the relationships between his/her process and other affected processes/customers.

- *Customer focus*—Recognizes both external customers, who use and benefit from services offered, and internal customers, those fellow associates whose work depends on the work that precedes them.

- *Empowerment*—Empowers others to improve processes.

- *Recognition*—Recognizes and reinforces efforts in Total Quality Management.

- *Communication*—Facilitates information with the intent to assist quality improvement teams. Solicits information from customers and associates about improvements achieved.

- *Training*—Demonstrates knowledge of TQM concepts. Attends TQM training classes.

- *Risk taking*—Takes chances of losing one's sense of status by stepping out of one's zone of comfort or familiarity to face skepticism, negativity, or adversity.

HOW DO TQM LEADERS EFFECTIVELY USE POWER?

In a TQM organization, there is empowerment and there is power. Empowerment is that authority given to others to make changes to improve processes. On the other hand, power is the authority given or granted to an individual so that they can control people and outcomes. Managers require power. Leaders require the ability to influence others.

For years, traditional management leaders have been required to read Machiavelli. He suggests that effective leaders are power-wielders, individuals who employ manipulation, and exploitation, and who are devious in achieving their goals. Total Quality Management power is just the opposite. It's open, it's honest, and, hopefully, fair. The TQM leader uses power when all other avenues are exhausted.

Effective TQM initiatives require leaders who are desirous of and effective at influencing others, but, at the same time, have the power and ability to control situations. In the early phases of a TQM initiative, many associates will resist attempts to influence their behavior. Leaders may will resent them and at first will want to strike back. People may fall asleep in TQM seminars, even though a leader is investing 100 percent. People might listen attentively then totally ignore TQM concepts. Leaders may be tempted to retaliate. However, leaders should ignore such behavior because it takes time for people to adjust to TQM concepts.

In government, leaders should be far more patient than they might in business because options are not as clear regarding use of power. Therefore, in the early phases of a TQM initiative, the only option is to re-enforce those who support the TQM initiative and ignore the others. The use of power, referred to as transactional leadership and based on the premise of reward for followers and punishment for those who don't comply, is not the best available option.

Regarding power, we believe there are three specific power dimensions that need to be used by TQM leaders.

1. Reward power: The ability to reward those who cooperate with the leader.

2. Relational power: The leader is perceived as being credible, and associates will join the TQM initiative because they personally respect, admire, and have a high regard for the leader. They personally identify with the leader.

3. Expert power: Associates will follow because they believe a leader is competent. Followers will defer to the leader's judgment because he/she is knowledgeable about TQM.

All of the above forms of power can be injected or withdrawn. For example, leaders can withdraw reinforcement of people who no longer meet expectations. Leaders can withdraw from a relationship with an individual to the point where they no longer desire to please, nor does the leader have a desire to please them. Leaders can also withdraw expertise by isolating people so that they do not benefit from particular wisdom.

These are all options available to a TQM leader. What makes transactional leadership interesting in a TQM initiative is one's personal control of power. Leaders know when they are reinforcing and when they are withdrawing support. Traditional managers, on the other hand, generally go to the easiest form of power when they do not receive compliance from individuals. Total Quality Management leaders do just the opposite. They do everything possible to influence associates in positive ways; and, if they are not successful, they at first ignore them.

As more and more associates become committed to TQM, leaders will be expected to use coercive power. Associates may come to leaders to report managers who are sabotaging TQM efforts. They will become angry if leaders do not immediately use coercive power to remove barriers to their success. When these situations occur, they become difficult moments for TQM leaders. There are very few opportunities to remove a leader for not practicing TQM in the early phases of the initiative. And even in the second year, leaders often find they don't have the power to remove government managers.

Associates may become very disappointed when leaders point out that they cannot or will not remove a manager and that they will have to work around their manager. Further into the initiative, leaders will find creative ways to change the organization. For example, one leader rotated all of her managers in her region. This proved to be an exceptionally good strategy, since it allowed her effective TQM leaders to go into other offices and set up TQM teams. Over a period of time, every associate in her region was exposed to quality management. And when another manager was rotated into their office after a good TQM manager left, the teams, the subordinates, trained the "not so willing" manager.

Business executives reading this might be totally confused about how we dealt with the situation. Why don't we remove the managers who don't comply? There are two reasons: first, removing managers in government is not an easy task; and second, training managers from a subordinate perspective, since they are truly the customers of the manager, is an effective method. We believe in going the extra mile in government.

If, however, government systems begin to break down to the point that both taxpayer and government associates believe we're in a crisis, then TQM leaders' ability to remove managers will happen much faster. Business organizations were not known to take timely action regarding personnel during the days when business was good; but when business became bad, they weren't afraid to release poor managers.

Leaders need to use caution in exercising coercive power in government and must be creative in dealing with people who resist TQM. Total Quality Management leaders do not rely on coercive power. They focus on processes rather than on individuals. They stimulate a new way of thinking and not just trying to figure out new ways to force people to keep doing the same old thing. Total Quality Management leaders do not need coercive power since they do not have complete control of the decision-making, nor do they need complete control of people since they are not out to compare one individual against another.

If TQM leaders believe it's in their best interest to lead from a transactional power perspective, then they should use three dimensions of power: reward power, relational power, and expert power. Leaders can build a power base by rewarding those who exemplify desired TQM behaviors and can develop relationships based upon personal respect and admiration along with credibility with people who cooperate, who support the TQM initiative. And, finally, by continuously demonstrating competence and expert knowledge, leaders will find that associates will defer to their judgment and believe that by following leaders' examples, they will make better decisions.

Remember, the aim of TQM leadership is not to control people, but to gain control of processes.

HOW CAN PEOPLE AND SYSTEMS CHANGE? TRANSFORMATIONAL LEADERSHIP

Total Quality Management leadership calls for a leadership style and approach that goes well beyond the thinking of traditional government managers. It requires the ability to transform the present culture of an organization to a desired state. Although every individual who studies a particular organization will have a different view of the present state and a different vision of what the organization ought to be, those who subscribe to TQM are likely to reach consensus on the desired state of the organization.

Transformational leaders have the ability to cause others to engage in extraordinary efforts. They cause people to put the interest of the mission— organization—above their own self-interest. Transformational leaders are change agents. They perceive the need for a change and are confident that they know what the future state of the organization should be. They see their role in the organization as being the leader of change, to move the organization to its desirable state. They are catalysts to precipitate change by acknowledging dissatisfaction with the status quo. They have a way of bringing people together, convincing them that change is necessary, and showing them how changing processes can improve the organization.

Transformational leaders believe in people and are sensitive to their needs. They are aware and sensitive to individual and team needs. They are sensitive to the fact that it is difficult for some people to understand the need for change and that even if they understand the need, they often will not accept it. Such people don't believe change is necessary and are unwilling to help facilitate the change. Some may understand the need for the change, but because of their own personal insecurity, they resist the change. Leaders need to realize that people do build up anxiety, sometimes become paranoid, and often feel that they are losing organization power. Transformational leaders are understanding and work hard to help people alleviate their resistance. Transformational leaders work to drive out fear in the workplace. Associates should be comfortable about making changes and feel that they can effectively work together.

Transformational leaders know where they want the organization to be in the future. Knowing, however, is not sufficient. They must be capable of sharing vision with others and influencing them to accept the vision. The vision sets the direction, and it is the role of the transformational leader to get everyone in the organization going in that direction. Leaders must have the ability to translate vision into action. Therefore, leaders hold numerous meetings, conduct numerous seminars, and at every opportunity share the vision with all associates.

Communicating the mission of the organization is just not a one time effort where three or four people write the mission and then it is distributed throughout the organization. The mission should be everywhere. People should constantly be provided with the mission and discussion of the mission should be a part of every significant management meeting. It's the reason why the organization exists, and no associate should lose sight of the organization's purpose.

Included in the mission should be a reference to continual improvement. As Deming suggests, "Create constancy of purpose towards improvement of product and service."

Focus on quality, not numerical goals. Many organizations are ineffective because they only judge their success by an increase in numerical goals. Government, like the American automobile industry, has an outstanding production record. It's difficult to read an annual report prepared by a government agency that doesn't highlight its increase in productivity. Over the years productivity indicators perhaps change, but generally speaking, if one can believe government reports, government productivity has increased immeasurably.

There is no doubt that government is far more productive than it has ever been. It helps more people, collects more money, and provides services at a record pace. The problem that almost any government worker will admit is that although production goals are met, it is difficult to meet and exceed customers' expectations. The amount of errors in government and the amount of re-work is astonishing. It seems as though government operates like many industrial organizations formerly did. Every time there was a flaw in their product, American industry would just hire more quality inspectors and improve their re-work department. Now, in an effective business organization, there is hardly ever an inspector or re-work area. Quality is built in up front and not something performed at the end.

The same should apply to government. The focus must be on quality. Consequently, management by objectives should be replaced with management by fact and improvement. Management should move away from individual work standards and numerical and allow process improvement teams to deal with numerical quotas.

Quotas will probably be a part of government until time knows when without the change to quality improvement. It's hard to visualize top government managers eliminating quotas. If they eliminated quotas, many of the top managers would believe that they no longer control their agency. The practical approach is to allow teams to deal with the quota problem inherent within government management practices.

Transformational leaders are visible. They role model the behaviors they desire. They don't expect others to do what they don't do. Many managers in government are selected because they have effectively used the "kiss-up factor," and when they take a management position, they think that they have arrived and that they no longer have to do what they ask other people to do. They believe they can delegate quality. The problem in today's organization is that government leaders can't hide. Their office is no longer a sanctuary.

One of the perks for moving up in government organizations is a parking place or a large office. These are signs of success. A transformational leader will need neither. They don't need an office to impress, nor do they need a parking place. Transformational leaders are the first people in in the morning, and they don't need a monument as an office. They understand that associates are impressed more by what they do than their overall power appearance. They are out in front and use their energy to work with people, not to dictate.

Transformational leaders believe in people. They have confidence that people want to work hard, give more than they take, and when trusted, prove to be worthy of trust. Transformational leaders spend much of their time building the self-esteem of associates. A great teacher once said, "At the end of the course, it is not important that they have increased their image of me as a teacher, but rather have they increased their self-image."

This doesn't mean that after every interaction associates should increase their self-image. There will be times when a transformational leader is sending a message that hopefully has the reverse effect. A letter of warning, a letter asking for the government administrator to take corrective action is sometimes necessary. Sending a negative message may have a positive effect. We have found that there is a better than fifty percent chance of saving a government administrator by sending them a negative message.

Leaders need to be concerned with their long-term effect on people. After working with associates for six to nine months, transformational leaders should have caused the self-image of all of the associates close to them to dramatically increase. Transformational leaders have extremely high self-images. They have learned from past experience that they can rely on their own judgment.

Some leaders have what they will often describe as a history of being "lucky." More often than not, successful transformational leaders will attribute their success to being lucky. They know that if they don't do anything, they can't be either lucky or unlucky. They are not afraid to take a risk. In fact, their self-image is often so positive that many of them do not even see failure, they only see opportunities. In fact, they look for challenging opportunities. Without opportunity, they don't have a challenge. People around them gravitate towards them because they are sometimes awestruck by the risk transformational leaders take and the positive outcomes they achieve. It seems as though every time the transformational leader makes a decision, it's the right one. Consequently, the leader is perceived as having extraordinary skills. And if they combine these skills with also being perceived as a person of character and knowledge, associates will go the extra mile to help the leader succeed. The transformational leader projects enthusiasm and self-confidence.

Transformational leaders have high expectations of people they lead. Since transformational leaders articulate ideological targets, what they want the organization to be, they find it difficult to encourage others who have lower expectations. Therefore, transformational leaders communicate to their followers high performance expectations. They have confidence in their followers and do what's necessary to increase their competence in getting the job done. Consequently, they also increase their follower's self-esteem. They are not afraid to give their followers challenging tasks, support them, and help them succeed.

Transformational leaders strongly believe in the development of people. They sponsor strong educational programs and are willing to invest in associates at all levels. They provide training, whether it be in the classroom or on the job training, for all workers. Every time they get the opportunity, whether it be in the classroom or on the job, associates should expect to learn.

The first challenge to leaders will be to get the associates to want to learn TQM tools. And as they get more and more interested in improving their work processes, they will make numerous demands for more education and training. The transformational leader is prepared to deliver what the associates want and need.

To change the organization to a desired state, transformational behaviors are required daily. By putting forth energy, having a sincere desire to lead, believing in oneself, having a passion for quality, and trusting oneself that the chosen direction is in the best interest of the organization, a leader will be able to inspire others, inspire change, inspire a continued improvement, and revitalize the organization.

Leading a TQM initiative requires the behaviors discussed in the earlier section of this chapter. Transforming the organization into a TQM culture requires transformational leadership behavior. Most government organizations have entrenched production cultures where attitudes, values, and beliefs have been passed on over time. Even though many government workers are highly critical of government systems, they will still find it very difficult to change. Attitudes towards government work, beliefs about management systems, and a clinging desire to maintain the status quo in government will require leaders to go beyond the skills of a TQM leader and embrace transformational leadership concepts. It will require the transformational leader to accept the responsibilities for the overall success or failure of the organization. He or she will have to elevate the values of the organization to a higher level.

Since transformational leaders can't order or command that TQM in its purest sense be implemented in the organization, they will have to learn to trust their intuition, trust their decisions, and trust in the goodness of other people. The ultimate objective is to create a culture where processes meet or exceed customers expectations, where each process is error-free, where measurement of processes is a daily and pleasant experience, where teams can achieve success, where every worker contributes, where associates publicly state that they are proud of their government agency, proud of their processes, proud of themselves, and respect leadership.

TQM leadership is a difficult challenge in government. It requires intelligence, sensitivity, and perseverance. TQM leadership in government is a process of energizing resources (inputs) to intentionally influence and cause TQM actions (activities) that produce quality results which meet or exceed customer expectations (outputs) that ultimately benefit the public served (outcomes).

9

COMMUNICATION, TRAINING AND RECOGNITION

James "Ernie" Riddle, Vice President of Marketing and Business Operations for Xerox Corporation's U.S. Marketing Group stated, "But the most shocking thing we discovered is that the Japanese could sell a copier for a price it cost us to manufacture one." Therefore in 1983, senior management at Xerox developed an agenda for change called "the quality policy." Riddle states, "We wanted quality to be the center of all strategic efforts and to involve all employees." The effort included three major planks— "Adopt the best ways of doing business, get the power of all the company's 100,000 world-wide employees behind the effort, and focus on the customer." Riddle went on to say, "I'm a real disciple of quality. I believe it saved our company."

Like all organizations that want to change to a quality culture, Xerox understood one of its most effective tools for change is communication. And if any government organization desires to implement Total Quality Management, it needs to understand it has to make a major investment in communicating quality.

WHAT IS MEANT BY "COMMUNICATING QUALITY"?

Let's begin first by defining communication. It is a process of sending symbols, messages, which stimulate an intended thought in the mind of a person(s). Communication is said to be effective when the intended receiver comprehends the message as intended by the sender and/or elects to behave or take action desired by the sender.

To establish a successful quality organization, associates at all levels should be continuously bombarded with quality messages. Messages need to be sent that stimulate all associates to think about what they can do to improve their processes so that they are able to do their work right the first time. Even though there are thousands of different messages and hundreds of different methods, all

159

communication should be directed at leaving the following residual messages in the minds of all associates. In other words, when all is said and done, what is the message that is left, and will it stimulate the desired behavior?

TQM RESIDUAL MESSAGES

A. Quality work: To do it right the first time.

B. Quality goal: To meet or exceed customer expectations.

C. Quality philosophy: To provide taxpayers a significant return on their investment.

D. Quality beliefs: To improve organizational processes by granting authority and responsibility for improvement to associates closest to the process.

E. Quality values: To role model the department's desired behaviors of all associates.

F. Quality principles: To accept and practice the fundamental axioms of Total Quality Management as the most effective approach to managing the organization and achieving desired outputs and outcomes.

G. Quality planning: To involve all associates at all levels in the organization in designing, structuring, and implementing procedures that improve organizational effectiveness.

H. Quality strategy: To focus on continual improvement of our processes, to work in teams, to be customer driven, and to manage by fact.

COMMUNICATION GOAL

With very few exceptions, the target of communications is all associates. On a few rare occasions, only our managers might be targeted. Prior to quality management, organizations were often very selective in defining their targets. For example, an organization might conduct a survey and find that morale is low in one area and institute a motivational program in that area. Or the organization might be falling behind on its profit goals, and therefore communicate to selected associates the start of a cost cutting campaign. The goal in the latter case would be to send messages that stimulate people to concentrate on cutting costs. If costs saving practices begin to work, company officers may regroup and begin to send messages to stimulate their associates to start thinking about ways to improve quality. For years, government organizations have sent mixed signals from the top. For example, in the Department of Labor and Employment Security, the federal government may ask them to start focusing on reducing their error rate. And after some time passes, they may consider the No. 1 priority is to get jobs for people who come in for unemployment benefits. And then some time later, the No. 1 priority is to see how many more employers can be served. In the meantime, the top of the organization is trying to devise ways to help the front-liner do a more effective job. Therefore, a program becomes the No. 1 priority. Today, in the Department of Labor and Employment Security, job profiling is the highest priority. It's no wonder that practically every survey in organizations shows that communication is the No. 1 problem.

In a Total Quality Management organization, the dominant message sent to all associates is quality. The goal is to send messages that stimulate associates to use their brain power and skills to improve their assigned processes. The goal is always the same, whether it be upward, downward, or horizontal communication. Whereas upward communication in the past was primarily positive (letting top management know how well things were going) and downward communication was primarily negative (top management telling lower levels things they needed to do to improve), communication in a TQM organization is far more open and honest. Information is not judged as being either positive or negative, but, rather, facts are communicated and are treated as opportunities for improvement.

Horizontal communication in traditional organizations has frequently proved to be a difficult process. Because of organization silos and a protection of turf, associates find it very difficult to communicate and very frustrating. In a TQM organization however, horizontal communication becomes an everyday practice. It is not difficult and frequently is very rewarding. Therefore, in a TQM culture, communication plays a major role in the success of the organization. Associates are free to make suggestions, are well informed about processes, and since facts speak for themselves, associates don't have to guard their communications.

COMMUNICATION STRATEGY

In developing the communication strategy in our pilot, we took into consideration the 10 common mistakes organizations make in implementing quality as outlined by C. Jack Grayson, Jr., Chairman, American Productivity and Quality Center. In a speech made in Houston, Texas in May 1990, entitled "Communicating Quality: The Communicator's Role in Quality Improvement Process," Grayson suggested that organizations generally make the following mistakes: (1) Take a piecemeal or fragmented approach, (2) Limit the effort to one area, (3) Implement quality while retaining a business-as-usual mentality, (4) Omit structural

Implement quality while retaining a business-as-usual mentality, (4) Omit structural changes—not rewarding people who put high values on teams and quality, (5) Focus on quality *techniques*, (6) Voice rhetoric without substance, (7) Fail to involve customers and suppliers, (8) Do too little training, (9) Set sights too low, and (10) Have poor communication.

We set out to avoid these mistakes and adopted a communication strategy aimed at integrating quality into the whole organization and sent messages that it was not "business-as-usual." Our strategy was "communication by action," and we focused on process. We did not want to see our TQM initiative perceived as a program, for it is a process, a mindset. It's a new way for government to work. We avoided editorials, banners, and slogans as part of our strategy. However, from time to time, teams and overly enthusiastic associates would propose slogans and banners.

Our most effective communication strategy was to report successes as often as possible. Another effective strategy was to allow the newsletter in our department and the newsletters within the division to take a natural course of action. We did not instruct the Director of Communications or the department or provide any special instructions to the divisions to include TQM in their newsletter. Although over time, newsletters became dominated by TQM articles and success stories, it was not because of a management directive.

Fortunately in government, senior executives are often slow to respond to new initiatives. Therefore, it's easier to let the natural order of events take place. Where an enthusiastic Communication Director exists, it could present a problem. Such as person could become so imaginative and creative that he or she could get too far ahead of the process, and the associates might begin to believe that it's a PR campaign to make top management look good. Although the Communication Director might believe he or she is winning approval by making top management look good, the Communication Director, in fact, could be hurting the initiative.

Since top management frequently has the least effect on improving organizational processes, top management should receive the least recognition. The challenge is to make TQM a way of life within the organization. Consequently, even though messages often have a persuasive intent and early on, messages are designed to persuade associates to give TQM a try, the most effective communication strategy is "Let it happen."

As the organization becomes more and more successful at implementing TQM, significant interest in communication will emerge, and in all probability, a quality communication team will evolve. The purpose of this team will be to help the organization change to a customer-oriented, process improvement thinking organization. They can help break down the barriers to quality, help all associates, as well as management, concentrate on meeting and exceeding customer's expectations, and that all associates participate on process improvement teams.

Furthermore, they can be very creative in designing recognition programs. The quality communication team emerge should naturally, and a team should not be appointed immediately. If the communication team begins too soon, it will probably do more damage than good.

QUALITY AWARENESS

In the Department of Revenue in the State of Florida, we started our total quality initiative by meeting for a couple of days where the senior author presented Total Quality Management beliefs, assumptions, and principles. Soon after our meeting, we established a Quality Council. The purpose of the Quality Council was to guide the TQM initiative. We met every two weeks for two hours, discussing what actions the department could take to initiate TQM.

The senior author had acquired most of his TQM knowledge from working as a full-time TQM consultant in industry and had observed very successful quality councils. However, for this particular agency, even though it was composed of the top management, a few middle managers, and some front-liners, it had a very difficult time fulfilling its mission. Many of the council members wanted to be active and take the lead, but the organization was very slow to respond. After the initial two-day seminar on TQM, the senior author, serving as an external consultant, directed top management to begin identifying and flow charting its core processes. And shortly after this directive, the Quality Council was formed.

The senior author miscalculated the time it would take to identify and flowchart the core processes. Whereas business organizations frequently find the identification of core processes in flowcharting a somewhat difficult task, it gets done in a relatively short period of time. However, even though the Director of the Florida Department of Revenue was a strong supporter of TQM, it became clear that division directors were slow to get on board and that the top management was so far removed from their processes that they didn't have a good understanding of how work flowed in the divisions they managed. Furthermore, the Department of Revenue was a perfect example of organization silos. Each division was managed from the top down, and there was an obvious protection of turf, even though their No. 1 core process, collecting sales tax, flowed through each division.

The senior author quickly realized that he made a mistake in establishing the Quality Council too early. It took months to finally identify and flowchart the core processes. In the meantime, the Quality Council attempted to justify time spent at the meeting by debating what actions they could take. They made all of the mistakes a Quality Council can make. They even violated one of Deming's principles by creating a slogan, "Rev up for quality." They did do some good, however, for they developed a very effective quality training program.

When the senior author instituted quality awareness in the Department of Labor and Employment Security, he waited until the core processes were identified and flowcharted. While he waited, knowing that it would be a slow process, he conducted over 50 seminars on Total Quality Management beliefs and principles. Over 1,000 associates attended these seminars. It took approximately seven months to initially understand the core processes within the Department.

Although there are numerous different ways one can implement TQM, the most effective method is to first obtain an understanding of the core processes in every organization. Even though it would be preferable that the processes be identified and flowcharted by the people closest to the process, many division directors do not trust front-line associates to do this task. Therefore, they will generally assign two or three of their best managers for the task. One division director, in fact, even hired a consultant to identify and flow chart the core processes in his division. As an aside, when the process was finished, the consultant came to the senior author with the proposal that the director be fired and the consultant hired as the director, since the consultant knew the processes better than the director.

When a quality initiative begins, two messages are communicated. First, the organization must identify and flowchart their key processes; then, all associates should be exposed to TQM beliefs and principles.

SELECTING A TEXT AND CREATING A BOOKLET

When the senior author began the TQM initiative in the Florida Department of Revenue, each member of top management, members of the quality council, and selected managers were given a book, *Kaizen: The Key to Japan's Competitive Success* by Masaaki Imai, published by McGraw-Hill, 1986. Although this is an exceptionally well-written book which thoroughly describes TQM, many people in senior management positions rejected the book because of its Japanese title and constant use of Japanese examples. Many executives told me they liked the book, but it wasn't accepted by their associates because of their attitude towards Japan.

Therefore, when the senior author began the TQM initiative in the Department of Labor and Employment Security, he selected another book, *The Deming Management Method* by Mary Walton, published by Perigee in 1986. This book was well-received and served as a foundation for our TQM initiative.

We also provided our own TQM booklet aimed at helping departments take the initial step towards TQM. If an organization elects to do a booklet, and we believe that it's a good idea, at a minimum it should include: (1) a letter from the top administrator, (2) a discussion of assumptions and beliefs, (3) the TQM principles that will guide the organization, (4) philosophy of training, (5) a section on TQM tools, (6) a section on the steps of improvement, (7) a section on how teams can facilitate process improvement, and (8) a description of the recognition program for those who improve their processes.

THE USE OF INTERNAL FOCUS GROUPS AND SURVEYS

The purpose of internal focus groups is to gain an understanding of associates' attitudes towards TQM. The goal is to determine the progress the organization is making in implementing TQM. We have found success in gathering associates into a room and employing the SWOT System, where the associates are asked to identify the strengths, weaknesses, opportunities and threats relative to our Total Quality Management initiative.

Traditionally, organizations have used surveys to determine the climate of the organization. Information obtained from these surveys often provide data on job satisfaction, job commitment, etc. Based on data obtained, management might elect to change their strategy regarding motivation, communication, organization structure, etc. In most cases, however, other than instituting a quick-fix program, the information is largely ignored. Two problems are common to survey research. First, it's often difficult to define the exact meaning of the results. Second, in a TQM organization, it is often too late to tackle the problems the survey uncovers because of the lag between the time the survey is administered and the time the data is reported.

We are strong believers in surveys; however, the most useful surveys are very specific, relatively short with data that is easily collected and analyzed. The best type of surveys is developed by teams who are improving a process. The large overall organization survey which is commonly sponsored by the communication division can provide some interesting information, but is not very useful. The most effective method for collecting information that is useful to the communication division is sent to them by front-line teams.

THE NEWSLETTER

The newsletter is a vital medium for getting messages across. A frequent mistake that some organizations make when they initiate TQM is to have a TQM newsletter. If TQM is to become a natural part of the way daily business, then the existing newsletter should be allowed to slowly change as TQM continues. When one of the authors was in the Department of Revenue, as an internal consultant, he quickly realized that the newsletter was getting ahead of reality. The director of the Florida Department of Revenue was a very well-respected and well-liked individual. People around him wanted him to succeed. Consequently, even though TQM wasn't really occurring, the newsletter was reflecting that it was going along smoothly.

In the Department of Labor and Employment Security, the Office of Communications was responsible for the primary newsletter, which was not dominated with stories about TQM. This was good because we did not want their office printing stories that would "please" the Deputy Secretary and might not be totally accurate.

The Department's newsletter usually consisted of a letter from the Secretary, a major article, and generally an award one of the associates might have won. In addition, there were many articles about top management, some special articles like recycling done in the department, latest information on what the telephone system can now do and its cost, maybe a special article on taxes, and a report from each of the divisions about what was occurring with them. One of the more interesting articles was written by the employee advocate, where she generally covered a topic of interest and then answered questions that she received during the last month. There was also a section on moving up which dealt with promotions and retirement, and a section called the "Best Foot Forward" where people were honored for receiving commendation for exemplifying the quality service that the department strives to offer.

A year later, the same newsletter had a headline, "Another Year of Celebrating Quality," with pictures and names of all of the teams that appeared that month before the Quality Council. What was rewarding was that any mention of quality in the newsletter was because it really happened and not because we had a communication office that wanted to "kiss-up" to the Deputy Secretary. The newsletter served as a very effective medium to stimulate associates to get on the TQM bandwagon. What's important to remember, however, is that the newsletter should not be used as a vehicle to draw undue or exaggerated attention to TQM.

THE QUALITY COUNCIL

After each division had flowcharted their key processes, we started the quality council. The council was composed of the Secretary, Deputy Secretary, division directors, one member from each division representing middle management, and one person from each division who was a front-line associate. The

Division Directors selected their own council representatives who showed some interest in TQM and whom they thought would be effective advocates.

The council, meeting twice monthly, encouraged participation in continual improvement activities by providing the resources needed (training, TQM materials, etc.), tracking improvement processes, assessing effectiveness, rewarding teams' improvement actions, and leading by example. Examples of assistance provided by the council included the development of training programs that helped prepare facilitators, reading materials and videotapes that were circulated throughout the divisions, specific techniques to analyze and identify causes of problems (with the assistance of associates in the data center), systems to collect and analyze data for team members, and evaluation of improved processes.

During the first year of existence, the department Quality Council members developed criteria for membership on the Quality Council. The criteria became necessary since a number of team members who presented to the Quality Council thought it was hypocritical that they were judged by some members of the council. They suggested that some members of the council were not "fit" to judge their work since the members of the council were not on teams and were not taking an active role in TQM. Therefore, we developed the following criteria.

- LES Quality Council Members demonstrate both tangible support and enthusiasm for our goal of achieving Total Quality Management throughout the Department of Labor and Employment Security.

- Members must demonstrate their commitment by having attended the core courses offered by the department on TQM or by timely scheduling and completing such courses after becoming a member of the council.

- In addition, members should demonstrate their support of our goals by working on teams, knowing and understanding the processes in their work units, promoting the measurement of the processes, measuring customer satisfaction, insuring meaningful data is maintained, documenting continual improvements in their work units, and assisting fellow associates in learning the principles of TQM.

DEPARTMENTAL VALUES

Soon after we initiated Total Quality Management in the Department of Labor and Employment Security, we asked the division leaders and the bureau chiefs to come up with a set of values. We would discuss them at meetings and some would even write them up. In fact, some managers complained that we spent a lot of time talking about values, but we never got them published.

We did not push to have the values published and distributed to the organization for two specific reasons. First, even though values are discussed by senior managers, it doesn't mean that they accept them. Second, it is hypocritical to publish values that are not practiced by top management. Consequently, top management needs time to begin practicing the values before they are published. In fact, if we had our choice, we wouldn't publish the values at all. If top management practices the values, it won't take long for others in the organization to follow.

Implementing TQM may require certain events to occur sooner than what might be ideal. We asked each of our process improvement teams to come up with a set of values for their team. Therefore, when we formed the Quality Council, our first act was to define our mission and values. The mission was:

> "To empower all associates to improve
> processes throughout the department."

After defining our mission, we spent several hours discussing the development of a set of values that would guide us. The values we developed were as follows:

Florida Department of Labor and Employment Security Values

* **Quality**—Quality is meeting customer requirements the first time and every time. Our internal and external customers include individuals, teams, and organizations who receive and use the output of our work process.

* **Responsiveness**—Responsiveness is the willingness and ability to provide information, reply to requests, answer questions, and complete tasks promptly. In order to create and maintain an atmosphere of "total quality," it is necessary to have the ability to respond in a positive and timely manner. With regard to providing quality customer service, it is absolutely essential to meet or exceed the expectations of all customers in terms of responsiveness.

* **Flexibility**—Flexibility is the ready capability for modification or change, and the adaptability to new situations. Flexibility in the workplace allows for acceptance of change in processes, procedures and requirements to support the accomplishment of the agency's mission, goals, and objectives in light of an ever-changing environment, and the demands of shifting priorities. Continual improvement requires flexibility, and positive changes are constantly sought.

- **Respect**—Respect is the quality of accepting and holding in high esteem all persons' rights to their beliefs, values, autonomy, and differences while treating them with dignity, worth, courtesy, civility, and politeness. Respect is the ability to actively listen to others without interruption, prejudice, judgment, or reservation, and is the acknowledgment of the worth of others' time.

- **Sense of Total Commitment**—Commitment is carrying out the pledge to do something. Total commitment is awareness of the responsibility to be continuously involved in the activities intended to achieve quality work. Continual improvement is an integral part of our daily operations.

- **Honest Communication**—Open and honest communication is an expression of a professional work environment which facilitates the exchange of information, ideas, and divergent opinions between all levels of an organization in an atmosphere of respect and genuine concern for the best interests of the organization, its associates, and customers.

- **Humor**—A characteristic disposition or state of mind that allows oneself and others a perception of amusement. Inoffensive humor provides a link between individuals and creates unity out of diversity. A shared bit of humor encourages the development of "common ground." It serves to motivate workers to carry on in their jobs despite occasional unpleasantness.

- **Empowerment**—Empowerment is the freedom and power to act, command, or decide upon a course of action. Teams are empowered with authority related to the work and processes for which they are responsible, in order to achieve gains in quality and productivity.

- **Teamwork**—Teamwork is the ability of a group of individuals to work together toward a common vision by each doing a part to achieve the efficiency of the whole. It is the capacity to direct individual accomplishment toward organization objectives. It is the fuel that allows common people to attain uncommon results.

- **People**—We believe that people are intelligent, creative, knowledgeable, loyal, desirous of freedom for job enhancement, and can develop systems that will improve job outcome and customer satisfaction, if given the opportunity.

- **Customers**—Our goal is to meet or exceed customer expectations. We are continually measuring and evaluating internal and external perceptions of our performance. We use customer feedback to improve our processes and services. We will meet customer needs at all levels and seek their input and direction on how we can better serve them.

- **Diversity in the Workplace**—We can realize the full potential of our workforce if we celebrate both our unity of purpose as an organization and uniqueness as individuals. Through the recognition and affirmation of diversity within our workplace, we foster associates' personal growth, strengthen our ability to respond to challenges, and improve service to our customers.

VALUE-SIGNING DAY

On March 22, 1994, nearly 7,000 associates in the Florida Department of Labor and Employment Security signed an agreement with Secretary Shirley Gooding reaffirming the values of the agency. We made available to all of our departmental offices a beautifully printed document that included our values and a description of each of them. On the bottom part of the document we left room for those associates to voluntarily sign their name, which meant that they agreed to uphold the department's values.

The Office of Communications first came up with this idea and presented it to the Quality Council who approved it. At first, the senior author resisted the idea since he was of the opinion that a value signing day could have a negative effect rather than a positive one. He was wrong. People eagerly volunteered to sign the document. Only one letter of dissatisfaction was received by the Secretary, and this associate criticized the expense of printing the document which was signed and then placed in a visible barrier for each office. The newspaper coverage was very positive, and associates thought of it as a good idea and welcomed the attention. Some newspapers even carried pictures of our associates signing the document.

QUALITY IMPROVEMENT TRAINING

Perhaps the most significant departure for a TQM initiative from the traditional organization is the shift from learning for the special few to everyone in the organization. In the traditional organization, education was primarily designed for management, primarily because management did the thinking and the employees did the work. If employees received training, it was generally to improve their skills for their specific assignment. The management objective was to keep management informed by allowing managers to attend seminars and to participate in strategic planning sessions and organization retreats. Workers were motivated to get promoted into positions where they could use their brain power and have an opportunity to attend various educational sessions and to participate in executive meetings and retreats.

On the surface, this rational model of upward mobility makes a lot of sense. Practically everyone enters their first organization in an entry level position. Because of their motivation, their talent, and overall competence, they get promoted to higher positions. It only seems right that those who prove themselves and move up the organization ladder should get the most perks, including the best education. On the other hand, those who aren't motivated, those without talent and competence should remain at the bottom of the organization. This appears to be a very rational model and has merit if all one expects from employees is that they "do as they're told."

The rationality of this approach dissolved upon realizing how much brain power you is lost if by not tapping the minds of workers. In an organization with, say, 10,000 employees, of which 1,500 are managers who believe that they do the thinking and that employees do the work, the loss of brain power becomes very obvious. On the other hand, visualize an organization where 10,000 people are treated with respect and have a management system that allows each associate to use brain power daily for the purpose of improving the organizational processes. The latter is a Total Quality Management organization. It is a management system designed to tap the brains of all of its personnel. Therefore, no individuals working in a TQM organization are excluded from learning no matter what their job or position in the hierarchy. Personnel are not only given the opportunity to learn, but over time are expected to know, understand, and practice competencies required of all personnel working in a TQM organization.

The most significant difference between personnel training in a traditional management-by-objectives organization and a TQM organization is in the breadth of competencies that are required. When individuals in a traditional organization are given a job, they are told what to do and how to do it. Therefore, their training was only in the development of skills for a specific job, whereas in a TQM organization, all personnel are expected to develop competencies which not only are job specific, but competencies that allow them to improve any process they're assigned. All personnel in a TQM organization are expected to develop the following core competencies: (1) assessing customer expectations and satisfaction, (2) using TQM tools for diagnostic use and decision-making, (3) using process improvement methodologies, (4) working efficiently and effectively in teams, and (5) communicating effectively in interpersonal, small group, and large group settings.

Our training strategy began with an orientation for all associates prior to forming TQM process improvement teams. In the orientation session, we exposed our associates to the beliefs and principles. We were very explicit about what competencies were required to practice TQM principles. The primary goal of our orientation program was to introduce associates to the fundamentals of TQM. After the orientation, we allowed process improvement teams to form. It wasn't long after we formed a few teams that we heard the cries for TQM training.

Our associates were demanding that they have a better understanding of TQM competencies and specifically how they will relate to process improvement. Our challenge was to have the training immediately available. After the teams who requested the training went through the training, they would usually complain that they wish that they had gone through the training first. We believe that this is a positive complaint rather than a negative one. Associates who go through the courses without an immediate use for TQM competencies will not understand and appreciate the value of their training and will not know how to directly apply these competencies to continual process improvement success.

Self-assessment is an extremely vital step in learning and that self-assessment can be the most effective when the associate is not only learning the competencies, but practicing them daily. In training sessions, instruments and tests can provide feedback on specific competencies. If these efforts are combined with on-the-job application, a very effective training and development program will be in place. Furthermore, competencies development can improve significantly with experimentation. By attempting to use the competency at higher levels of effectiveness, the associate can experience significant personal growth.

W. Edwards Deming stated that only by improving the processes, systems, and tasks can an organization excel at meeting customer needs with quality products. To improve processes, systems, and tasks, each associate must be capable and motivated to improve processes, systems, and tasks. The associates can only contribute if they are fully trained in the competencies required for effective Total Quality Management.

EFFECTIVE TRAINING LEADS TO PERSONAL DEVELOPMENT

One of the significant outcomes from TQM training is the personal development of individuals. The basic TQM courses are just the beginning. When combined with the opportunity to make process improvements on a daily basis in an organization, effective training begins to develop the whole person. No longer are associates trained just to do "a job." In a TQM organization, they are trained to learn, to learn about their customers, their processes, their tasks, and the entire organizational system. Organizations that have implemented TQM are often referred to as "learning organizations." No matter what their job, in a learning organization, the associate must accept the responsibility for personal development. Learning opportunities occur every day at both unconscious and conscious levels. In the workplace TQM provides a system that allows many learning opportunities every day. In fact, learning from experience in a TQM organization is a more conscious and deliberate process. People can learn from successes as well as mistakes and can articulate what has been learned and communicate it to others.

Frequently in traditional organizations, meetings were called to motivate, to give directions, or to maintain control. Sometimes management would let people participate in making recommendations to management. In other words, in management by participation, the team participates and management makes the decisions. These meetings have always presented an opportunity to learn; however, continual process improvement teams require participation, and the team is empowered to improve the process.

INVESTING IN HUMAN CAPITAL

Without question, the biggest investment for government is in people. Government is people driven. It is not driven by the best product, international competition, etc. Government is only as good as the people working in government; whereas in industry an innovative method of doing x-rays can be worth more than the sum of the people working in the organization. However, government is people. Industry is the combination of competition, market, product, and production. Yet, in the last few decades industry has come to realize that the vital factor is its workforce. They understand that human capital has become the prime source of wealth and power. Consequently, the best industries invest significantly in human capital. Government has fallen behind industry. Government has invested mostly in management training. Since government takes the attitude that front-line employees should do what they are told, then government will only invest in training programs that tell the front-line employees how to behave. Government doesn't realize losses are resulting from a poorly trained workforce. Government must come to the conclusion that they must make a significant investment in every individual who works in government. While some corporations are spending as much as 20 percent of their time in training and development, government front-liners are fortunate to get an hour a month in training, and the kind of training they receive will be essentially how to do their task more effectively.

Government needs to invest in human capital since it is the most effective way to get a return on their investment. It must decide that the people in the front-lines, those working the process, are in the best position to improve the process, and therefore front-liners need to be fully trained, not just to do a task, but to participate in a total quality improvement initiative.

MOVING AWAY FROM THE WIN-LOSE MENTALITY

Since our culture is so competitive, people tend to believe that the most effective route to success is to become the "rugged individualist." They believe that there will always be winners and losers and that the winner is the person who stands out above all of the rest. Therefore, working on a team does not always appeal to everyone, particularly those who have a personal agenda and are looking for ways to move up the organization ladder at the expense of others. Many people with personal agendas are reluctant to use data and measuring points because it becomes a risk to them. It might show their own inadequacies. Furthermore, many people would rather rely on their "kiss-up" skills as a means to advancement, as opposed to scientific methods.

When there is a win-lose mentality in an organization, winners will identify the best path to success. If it requires training in specific areas, such as the functions of management, they will seek training. When others ask them about the training that they will receive, they will make light of it since they don't really want others to have the same exposure that they have received. It even becomes more obvious as to who has a personal agenda when they are confronted after an important management meeting by their subordinates with the question "What happened?" And the response is, "Nothing." When people are unwilling to share, that means that they have a personal agenda. Having information to them is power, and their approach to sharing it is only when it's to their advantage.

TQM training should produce win-win situations. First, all associates should be encouraged to volunteer for training when TQM training starts in the organization. Try to put everyone on an equal plane. Make sure that everyone has the opportunity for the same education. Without training all of associates, government organizations will continue to run with a win-lose mentality. Society readily demonstrates the results of using a win-lose approach to life. Some people claim that more money will be spent on losers than on winners eventually. For example, everyone in the United States can receive 12 free grades of schooling. When an individual falls out or quits before they graduate from high school, they often become a loser. Many people may not care whether that person finished high school or not since it's one less person that's going to get in their way and it increases their chances of being a winner.

Organizations cannot adopt the same mentality. Everyone in the organization must be a winner. Everyone in the organization must be able to read, write, and do mathematics at a high school level. Each associate in the organization must understand TQM tools and be able to use them. Each associate must be able to participate in a team and articulately express themselves. Everyone must be a winner.

HOW DOES EVERYONE BECOME A WINNER?

When we first started implementing TQM is state government, our obvious strategy was to only develop winners. We did not focus on people who did not want to participate in TQM. We spent our energy on helping those who wanted to change the way they do business. As we progressed, however, in our TQM initiative, we began to link all of our processes, and associates were encouraged to attend TQM training. Associates who were relying on another process for their supplies would complain about the poor quality of their suppliers. Furthermore, many processes were so poorly managed that our results became public and were a focus in political debates. Our associates who had pride in reducing the error rate were angry at the other associates who didn't seem to care. Therefore, peer group pressure became a very powerful force to get everyone in the training. Although our goal was to have every associate get into TQM training, we never made that statement formally. We were afraid that most top managers would use a management-by-objectives approach to TQM training. They would force all of their associates to attend training, then they would say that they are successful as managers. The result would be that we would achieve our goal, but would have many associates who resented TQM. Therefore, we let training become a very natural part of Total Quality Management.

TQM AS A PROFESSION

Although TQM is not considered a profession, we adopted an attitude that TQM is a profession. Therefore, all associates should be treated as professional when they have embraced TQM concepts and skills. Like all professionals, whether it be medical doctors, teachers, lawyers, etc., the people who work in those professions require exceptional knowledge and do not stay in the profession without continuing education. An effective TQM initiative considers all members of the organization as having the potential of becoming professional. As a TQM initiative becomes more and more successful, everyone will want to be trained and join the professional workforce. Over time, it will become required.

EMPOWERMENT AND TEAMWORK PRODUCE SELF-MOTIVATED AND SELF-DIRECTED LEARNERS

Perhaps the most gratifying result of our TQM initiative was that motivation and interest in TQM actually increased in an election year. A 30-year veteran of the Department of Labor and Employment Security remarked: "This is the first time since I started working here that the associates didn't slow down before the election." He was amazed how many associates ignored the daily developments of campaign rhetoric and focused on their work.

Why is TQM the reason that they didn't slow down? Since customers and data drive the organization, associates realized that it didn't make too much of a difference who got elected, but what was important was our error rate, our time cycles, our output, and customer outcomes. They knew that no matter who was elected or who became their new boss, they would be asking the same questions: "How good are we? What do the quality indicators show? Are our customers satisfied?" Quality individuals and members of quality teams knew that they were focusing on what was needed and what management wants. Therefore, it wouldn't make too much difference who was the next political appointee running the agency.

What TQM does for individuals in the organization is that it replaces the need for leaders to motivate people; rather, people rely on the system for their personal motivation. When people are empowered to improve a process, they are more likely to take the initiative to learn and to find new ways to make improvements. Associates are far more self-directed than management-directed. They realize that they need to learn and appreciate the opportunity to improve their skills and themselves. Associates first look to the organization for training; then as they begin to use the results of their training, they are motivated to become more professionally developed. They realize that they need development in such areas as planning, leadership, communication, problem analysis, decision-making, quantitative areas, personal organization, group skills, etc.

Rather than the organization telling associates what they need, associates realize that if they are going to play a significant role in continuing improvement, they need training and will direct the organization to assist them in fulfilling their needs.

TRAINERS

At the beginning of a TQM initiative, there will be very little demand for training. Our approach of not requiring training has both positive effects and serious limitations. It's the old chicken and egg discussion, which comes first, process improvements teams or training? However, about ten months into our initiative, the demand for training mushroomed. We had anticipated this demand by recruiting associates who took the lead in their respective divisions in implementing TQM. For example, a bureau chief in one of our divisions became one of our most effective teachers on TQM tools and trained hundreds of associates throughout the state. His overheads are now being used by other trainers who were trained by him.

At the beginning of our TQM initiative only a few of the professional trainers in the department bought into TQM. They wanted to continue to teach traditional training and development programs. Therefore, we encouraged associates from all divisions who had any inclination or interest to teach TQM. It was amazing how much interest people had in teaching and how much teaching talent we had within our department. The demand for training drove the training department. Whereas in the past, trainers have always developed courses to be taught based upon survey "needs," the trainers were now reacting to the "demands." In other words, associates knew what they wanted and needed from training. Trainers now were able to see their associates as customers, and the trainer's job was to meet or exceed customer expectations.

TRAINING AND EDUCATION: PERCEIVING ASSOCIATES AS CUSTOMERS

We did not go out and purchase any outside courses or trainers. We developed all of our courses based upon the needs of our customers. Many organizations make the mistake of buying TQM courses from outside vendors in the beginning of their TQM initiative. We believe that the best method is to develop your own department courses and publish training booklets in-house. The development of TQM courses is extremely important. Designing what is needed based upon customer demand, developing the content and using skills to implement TQM are important phases in the TQM initiative. The associates preparing the courses take pride in authorship and become extremely knowledgeable about the beliefs and principles of TQM. If outside programs are purchased or outside vendors are used to teach TQM, the opportunity for associates to use their brain power in the development of TQM courses will be lost. Furthermore, and perhaps even more important, you lose an opportunity to recruit highly committed associates will also be lost.

TQM TRAINERS: CHANGE AGENTS

The trainer plays a vital role in changing the organization. How the trainers respond to the criticisms in their courses determines how associates will react to TQM. Since TQM requires, at a minimum, development in the four areas of customer service, process improvement, total quality tools, and teams, there is ample opportunity to help associates comprehend TQM and change to process improvement methods. Trainers must be extremely enthusiastic, believe in TQM, and be willing to take ownership of the department's TQM initiative.

Effective TQM Trainers

1. Perceive themselves as change agents. They see their job as a facilitator of change.

2. Perceive their students/associates as customers who need TQM knowledge and skills, and their job is to sell TQM. Whereas in most traditional training programs the objective is purely education, in a TQM initiative, especially in the beginning, the trainer's role is to persuade as well as teach.

3. Represent themselves as the organization. When TQM trainers teach, they are the spokespersons for the organization. They are committed to the organization's beliefs, values, and principles and communicate that message to their associates. They enthusiastically endorse top management and find it troubling when their associates viciously attack top management.

Total Quality Management trainers are there to facilitate change, but that doesn't mean that they take the easy way out when confronted with criticism of the administration in the classroom. In fact, they are staunch defenders of TQM and those who advocate TQM in the organization. Too often in organizations, the trainer takes the easy route and agrees with the students that the organization is ineffective in communication, incompetent in decision-making, has serious deficiencies, and would be much better without the present top management. Most trainers let their students ventilate and then agree with them. Not so with a TQM trainer. They believe in their organization and in their top management. Total Quality Management trainers are not afraid to take a stand. If a trainer is not willing to make a commitment and share their commitment with others, they will not be very useful in a TQM initiative.

QUALITY IMPROVEMENT RECOGNITION

Our Quality Council developed the criteria for team awards. We followed a similar process in how we set values. We first identified the criteria and then members of the council volunteered to write a description of the criteria. We believe that each Quality Council should develop its own criteria from scratch. It helps the council to better understand TQM and to have a thorough understanding of the criteria. The criteria our council agreed to is as follows:

Criteria For Team Awards

Impact of change (15)

Describe the actual impact of the change. How are customers better served as a result of this change? Examples might include improved productivity (i.e., shorter waiting lines for our customers), lower costs, happier customers, better quality jobs for our customers (both external and internal), increased status of our programs in the community, "thank you" letters from our customers, etc. Provide actual data, including charts whenever feasible.

Process supports mission, goals, and values (15)

Describe how the change supports the goal, mission and values of the department. The process improved should relate directly to one of these with a description that clearly demonstrates this connection. For example, one component of the department's mission is to help return to work those individuals who have experienced injuries while working and almost any improvement in the workers' compensation program could be related directly back to this part of the mission.

Team participation (15)

Describe how team members were selected and how roles and responsibilities of each member were decided. Did the team clearly understand its purpose and was it empowered to create change? Provide evidence. How was consensus reached on assignments of work to be done? Provide evidence of cohesiveness, trust, open communication, mutual support, and empowerment.

Customer feedback (10)

Describe how the team determined who were their customers and what were their needs. Were customer surveys well designed so that customers had little difficulty expressing their concerns? Include a brief description of methods, and measurement scales used, including frequency of customer contact.

Ongoing improvements (future plans) (10)

Describe how the team may continue to address future improvements in the process. No process is static and improvements are always possible. For example, a future improvement may be in a sub-component of the previous process identified. Once the suggested improvement is implemented, the team may find additional refinements or changes in policy that will improve the process even more. These future plans should be presented.

Identified/documented process (10)

Describe how the team defined the problem and identified the process to study. How was the process charted and studied? Did team members complete a flowchart working together and was there agreement by all? Include a copy of the process flowchart and any other documentation tools used.

Quality data (10)

Describe how and why data were selected and collected. Include discussion of any special collection efforts related to customer satisfaction (i.e., mail surveys, telephone calls, visits to individual customers, focus groups, complaint letters, etc.). Also, include any reports or special studies (government, etc.) that were used by the team. Were any of the data used developed within the department or were any purchased outside? Were team members assigned responsibility for collecting any data? How were samples selected? How did the team try to ensure that the data were reliable?

Use of quality tools (5)

Describe how the team used the quality improvement tools (flowcharts, cause and effect diagrams, histograms, Pareto charts, scatterplots, run charts, control charts, etc.). How did the team decide which tools were most appropriate? Attach copies of graphs and charts used by the team.

Linked process to other processes (5)

Describe how the team considered how the process improved is linked to other processes that will be impacted by the improvements made. For example, an improvement may be made in a process without direct impact on customer satisfaction, and yet through linkage have a profound impact on another process that does. How does the improved process fit into the global picture (linked to other processes)?

Level of risk involved (5)

Describe the level of risk assumed by the team in its study and improvement of the selected process. For example, a process improvement that identifies top management as a prime cause of a bottleneck in a grant review may be perceived as more risky than identifying a problem in the mail room. Although this is not true in an organization committed to customer satisfaction, there is still the perception that suggestions involving executive problems are more risky. Another risky improvement may call for a personnel or legislative action that may not please everyone.

The Quality Improvement Recognition Form

Since we were evaluating teams in our first year of TQM for a possible monetary reward, it required that we have a systematic process. Therefore we assigned points to each of the criteria. After each team made their presentation, members of the Quality Council would complete the following form.

Criteria for Team Awards

Impact of change _____points (15)

Process supports goal, mission, and values _____points (15)

Team participation _____points (15)

Customer feedback _____points (10)

Ongoing improvements (future plans) _____ points (10)

Identified/documented process _____points (10)

Quality data _____points (10)

Use of quality tools _____ points (5)

Linked process to other processes _____points (5)

Level of risk involved _____ points (5)

Total points _____ Recommended Award _____

Team Presentations for the Quality Council

We also gave the team members a little help on how to make a presentation. First, we suggested how to prepare their text, and second, how to make a presentation. Below is a copy of the document that we gave them:

Team Name Here

Process that was identified/documented: (Flowcharts are encouraged to facilitate understanding)

Quality Tools Used: (Provide a listing of the quality tools used, e.g., flowcharts, cause and effect diagrams, histograms, Pareto charts, run charts, etc.)

Quality Data: (Briefly describe data collected and used by the team to measure the impact of changes implemented to bring about quality improvements.)

Impact of Change: (Briefly describe the actual impact of the change(s), contrasting benchmark information with conditions after process improvements were implemented. Provide actual data, including charts when possible.)

Ongoing Improvements/Future Plans: (Briefly tell how the team may continue to address future improvements in the process.)

Process Supports Mission, Goals, and Values: (Briefly tell how the process improvements support the mission, goals and values of the agency.)

Team's Awareness of Linkages with Other Processes: (Briefly describe how the team considered how the process improved is linked to other processes that will be impacted by the improvements made.)

Team Participation: (Briefly describe how team members were selected and how roles/responsibilities were decided.)

Team Nominations

To appear before the Quality Council, each team had to be nominated by their Division. Therefore before any team had appeared before the department's Quality Council, they have already been reviewed by their division and had the division's sponsorship. Each team was required to fill out the following nomination form:

Process Improvement Team Registration Form

Team Name_____   **Date Formed**_____

Team Leader_____   **Telephone #** _____

Members

Definition of Process to be Improved

Who are Your Customers?

What are Your Quality Indicators?

Team Meeting (One hour per week): Day   Time____

Please attach copies of your values, mission statement and flowchart.

Team Booklet

Each team provided a written document which generally followed the criteria that was used to evaluate the team. In our first year, the team booklets were overwhelming. Teams were so interested in making a good impression that they probably spent too much time preparing the booklets.

In our second year, we sent out the message that teams do not have to develop elaborate written documents. We thought that since the financial incentives were withdrawn that the written documents would be more condensed and strictly data oriented. However, we found that the teams were extremely proud of their work and wanted to present their results so that they properly reflected the quality of their work.

LEADERSHIP AWARD

Well into our first year of our TQM initiative, we begin to recognize that there were a lot of people who stepped forward, took some risk, and were responsible for making TQM a reality within the department. Therefore, we developed a leadership award which resulted in a plaque for the individual selected. Our process for selecting TQM leaders was first to develop a set of criteria in the same way we developed criteria for other awards. First, we identified and agreed to criteria and then Quality Council members volunteered to write a description for a specific criteria. We then published the criteria and asked divisions to nominate individuals for the leadership award.

When the division concluded that an individual warranted the TQM leadership award, the division sponsored the selected individual and he or she appeared before the Quality Council. Generally, the director of the division described why this person deserved the award and then the leader being nominated made a brief presentation. Immediately thereafter, this individual was given a plaque. The department Quality Council's policy was to automatically present the TQM leadership award to the individual sponsored by the division.

From time to time, we would critique the leadership award process and division nominees. This of course was never done in front of a TQM leader selected for the award. These critiques served to be useful because council members were allowed to comment about the quality of leaders selected by each division. The criteria used for the leadership award were provided in the Leadership chapter.

TQM DIVISION AWARD

The Quality Council felt that if one division was exemplary, they should be eligible for a division award. Therefore the Quality Council developed criteria which would be used to assess a division's progress in implementing TQM. Below is the criteria we developed to assess division TQM effectiveness.

CRITERIA FOR DIVISION AWARDS

1. Customer Expectations

The focus of all quality process improvement should be to exceed customer expectations and delight the customer. A number of questions follow which may help determine the importance placed by the division on customer service and how well they have done. Each of these questions could be followed by other questions such as how, how do we know, how much, how often, etc. Have customers been identified? How do we know what customers want and what their expectations are? How do customers feel about service? Do customers feel that service has improved? How do we measure customer perceptions and how often? Does the division have customer focus groups for customer listening and feedback? Does the division include customers and suppliers on process improvement teams? Do managers and supervisors all work with associates on the line and provide direct customer service for some period of time during the year? Does the division use customer complaints to identify problems and make improvements? How? Does the division recognize associates and process improvement teams for great customer service?

2. Leadership

Describe how the division's leadership (directors, administrators, managers and supervisors) demonstrated their commitment to quality. What is the evidence of the division's commitment to change? Cite examples of this commitment (i.e., the division director's personal commitment—time, resources, etc.). Provide copies of the division's vision statement, and goals and describe how these were developed. How were barriers to successful implementation removed? How did the leadership walk the talk?

3. Process Improvements

Describe how the division implemented process improvements. How were new procedures established? Have the new procedures been published? Are there evaluation measurements established for the new changes in processes? Have the flowcharts been changed to reflect the new processes? What feedback instruments have been provided? How were teams encouraged to define problems? Cite evidence of team empowerment to identify the processes to study. How were processes charted and studied? Did team members complete flowcharts working together? Include copies of flowcharts and any other documentation tools used. Describe the actual impact of the process improvements. How were customers better served as a result of the changes?

4. Meaningful Data

Describe how and why data were selected and collected by the division. Include discussion of any special collection efforts related to customer satisfaction (i.e., mail surveys, telephone calls, visits to individual customers, focus groups, complaint letters, etc.). Also include any reports or special studies (government, etc.) that were used by the division. Was any of the data used developed within the department or was any purchased outside? Were team members assigned responsibility for collecting any data? How were samples selected? How did the division try to ensure that the data were reliable?

5. Teamwork

Describe how team members were selected and how roles and responsibilities of each member were decided. Did the team clearly understand its purpose and empowerment to create change? Provide evidence. How was consensus reached on assignments of work to be done? Provide evidence of cohesiveness, trust, open communication, mutual support, and empowerment.

6. Training

Describe how the division provided training to meet the needs of team members. How were team members empowered to request training at any time, regardless of work load?

7. Process Linkage

Describe how the division linked each process to the mission, goals, values, and principles. Were all process improvements valued and rewarded by the division regardless of immediate impact on external customers? For example, an improvement may be made in a process without direct impact on customer satisfaction, and yet, through linkage, have a profound impact on another process that does.

8. Associate Performance and Recognition

How are associates recognized for quality performance? Does the division foster a work environment in which positive morale can flourish? Did the division establish a nonmonetary award system?

This was a good exercise because it helped the division leaders understand what was needed to be a successful TQM organization, and it helped the leaders visualize what a TQM organization would look like.

We never used this criteria to evaluate any division, however. We decided that one division, the Division of Unemployment Compensation, was superior to the other divisions in implementing TQM. Therefore, we encouraged the Division of Unemployment Compensation to apply for the Florida Sterling Quality Award. The division accepted the challenge and made application.

Applying for the Sterling Award is no easy task. It takes considerable work just to make the application. However, we found the exercise of applying for the Sterling Award to be very beneficial. The team that prepared the document learned a lot about their own organization as they used the Sterling Award criteria to evaluate their own organization.

After the Division of Unemployment Compensation completed their Sterling Award application, the team that compiled the data for the application and wrote the document made presentations throughout the Department about this experience.

The Sterling Award review team was thorough in their evaluation of the division. Listed below are just a few of the many questions they asked:

- How are customer survey results mapped into the process improvement process?

- Who maintains your customer complaint log?

- How do you know if you are meeting customer expectations?

- How did customer needs drive the design of the process system?

- What is the percent of customers surveyed?

- What is the percentage of responses received on the customer survey?

- Who are your customers?

- Were customers involved in the development of the process?

- How is feedback from your client used to improve the service standards?

- What is your biggest TQM accomplishment?

- Did your reported results include any customer feedback, why, how, when, etc.?

DIVISION QUALITY COUNCILS

Each division within the department had its own quality council. These councils were put together in a similar manner to the department's Quality Council described above. The divisions developed a number of unique awards.

BEST OF THE BEST

At the end of our first year, we selected the top eight quality improvement teams that appeared before the Quality Council. Teams were selected based on the points they received when they appeared before the Quality Council. The eight teams who scored the most points as rated by the department's Quality Council were considered to be the "Best of the Best." They were honored during the end of the year quality forum. We extended invitations to the Governor, Lt. Governor, members of the Commission on Government Accountability, Tax Watch, legislative and Governor's Office staff, the federal U. S. Department of Labor, and members of the press.

ARTICLES WRITTEN BY ASSOCIATES

One of the most effective ways to communicate to associates is to encourage articles that are written by associates and published in the newsletter. These articles are extremely powerful and have a positive effect on change. Below is an example:

Quality Incentive Program vs. Total Quality Management by L. Gammons-Thurman

Under the old pilot, the incentive was to produce quality through numbers. You exceeded a certain level with minimum errors, and you were monetarily rewarded. Well, that was great and easy. We proved to ourselves that we could work faster. But did we prove that we could work smarter? No. We didn't have to. The criteria was to produce more, not to work smarter. The standards were set, and the goal was to meet or exceed those standards. This experience, however, did help some to realize their potential, generated competition, recognized individual successes, and, most importantly, enhanced the record-keeping skills for supervisors. It was like being in the car alone going down an open road with no speed limit. The faster we drove, the more exhilarating it was. Speed meant everything, until we came upon that stop sign called "Total Quality Management."

What does this mean? Well, it means you must proceed cautiously. You are no longer traveling alone. The car is now filled with car-poolers called "team members." Quality is achieved through the collective efforts of everyone. Results are achieved by involving everyone in the improvement process. Internal and external customer feedback is important. Improvement is a continuous effort. Flow-charts must identify key processes. Data must be collected and documented. Meetings must be held regularly. A mission statement must be developed. Diversity and creativity are key tools. Commitment is a must. Now, with all these things being of value to each team member, the ride is bound to be a smooth one, and the goal of results through Total Quality Management achieved.

GRAPHICALLY DISPLAYING DATA

An effective TQM organization has data readily available for team use and accessible not only to team members but other associates interested in their processes. Bulletin boards frequently contain graphs and charts. By graphically displaying their data, all team members as well as other interested associates can observe how well the process is working. Traditionally data was not available to all associates and if data was available, it was not presented in a meaningful way. In a TQM organization, quality indicators for all processes are tracked and openly displayed.

CELEBRATIONS WITH THE TQM BAND

TQM band members were available for all major celebrations, as well as for special training seminars. The band members were also TQM advocates and had a special interest in not only playing as a band member, but helping to ignite some enthusiasm in our seminars and celebration ceremonies. The appearance of a "band" during a state sponsored seminar was unusual to say the least, and helped confirm that TQM advocates and those in training were special people.

THERE'S NO CEILING ON RECOGNITION

To emphasize the importance of recognition, the senior author would tell his division directors that more than half of their time should be spent in recognizing people and their contribution towards improving the organization. Of course, most ignored this advice and went about their routines. Because most managers believe that they must control people, they often say that, "If I could only get my people to do what I want them to do, this organization would run effectively." Consequently, their recognition system consists of recognizing those people they can control with positive messages and using negative messages with their personnel who do not cooperate.

Traditionally in organizations, we have given both informal and formal recognition to those who role model the desired behavior of the top executives. Only in areas where results could be measured objectively were people recognized who might not always model the behavior that management wants. Consequently, many people with achievement personalities got into jobs where objective measures were applied, and therefore, they could exhibit their own desired behaviors, provided they were delivering on their goals.

When objective measures are clear, effective managers will often say that they helped the individual set their performance goals, got out of the way, and developed recognition programs to keep the individual moving.

When Total Quality Management is implemented in the organization, leadership should take the same approach. Help the teams define their mission, empower them, get out of the way, and recognize their improvements. Leaders respond to facts. They respond to data and use data to help them control the process, and therefore, do not have to concern themselves with controlling people.

Verbal communication is extremely critical in TQM organizations. Associates can accent the positive since their focus is on continual improvement. Negative information is a constant in the environment. Data that becomes available should not be perceived as being negative, even though associates will frequently think that the data they display are negative. However, all data should be perceived by leaders and associates as an opportunity to improve.

Every time teams make an improvement or when a team is moving in the right direction, recognition should occur. Leaders in the TQM organization are very close to the work, know the process, and are able to draw meaningful conclusions from the data teams present. Therefore, leaders in a TQM organization have significantly more opportunities to reward and recognize continual improvement. Recognition is a daily role for all TQM leaders.

10 PERFORMANCE MANAGEMENT

*"It's vital for every employee to share
a sense of urgency about quality performance."
—John C. Marous
Chairman and CEO,
Westinghouse*

Perhaps the most difficult concept to work into the TQM organization is the performance appraisal. In fact, W. Edwards Deming suggested removing performance appraisal systems from the organization, and the organization would be more effective. For traditional managers in organizations, the removal of the performance appraisal has to be one of the stupidest ideas of the century. How dare you remove the traditional managers' biggest gun in controlling people? What better legal way to control people is there than the performance appraisal? It is the ultimate weapon for organizations. People who don't get in line, and do what they are told, are often threatened by the dreaded performance appraisal.

It can be used as a positive instrument for "giving" a person a salary increase, a promotion, and a pat on the back. On the other hand, the performance appraisal can be used to terminate workers, demote them, build a case against them for possible termination, and can irritate them by making negative statements about their behavior that become a permanent record.

Top down, authoritarian, "know-it-all" managers in government have relied heavily on the performance appraisal to control people. If their most significant threat is removed, authoritarian managers would be at a loss on how to control subordinate behavior. It is easy to understand why middle managers often resent moving to a customer service, data driven process managed with teams as the central focus. Most middle managers feel as though they are losing control, and the fact is, they are.

Even though top management reluctantly accepts the principles of Total Quality Management, they ultimately are not as threatened by a TQM organization

191

because they do not believe that they are going to lose control of people. Most top managers know that in the end they will "get their way," whereas middle management is not quite sure how to respond. Therefore, the performance appraisal is far more important to the middle and lower managers in controlling people. In fact, top management in government organizations seldom rely on the performance appraisal as their annual way to "get" someone. Our experience in government has shown that the higher one is in management, the less likely he/she will conduct a performance appraisal on a subordinate. Most top managers in government will complete a performance appraisal on a subordinate only if required by law. Top management in government relies on other forms of communication to send messages that stimulate positive reinforcement or negative criticism. Top management realizes that they have a number of avenues to control people. The higher up one is in the organization also makes one realize that controlling subordinate behavior does not necessarily help achieve personal objectives. In fact, effective top managers understand that one of the most effective methods for managing people is to give them a job and let them make something out of it. Effective managers realize it's the day-to-day communication that's important, and waiting for an annual event to appraise an individual's performance is illogical. Feedback to subordinates, whether it be positive, negative, or neutral, is a daily, weekly interaction. The best appraisals are open, honest, and should be given at the most appropriate time rather than waiting for a specific time identified by the organization.

ANNUAL PERFORMANCE EVALUATIONS

In a Total Quality Management organization, the annual performance appraisal is logically perceived as an organization relic. It has little merit. It should be replaced by day-to-day communication. Both verbal and written communication are used to keep individuals informed on their progress. To document performance, from time-to-time, customers, suppliers, fellow associates, and managers may write letters that are placed in a worker's file. In a TQM organization, everyone who works in the organization is striving to succeed. It is not a contest as to who is better than whom, but a culture that allows every individual to exceed. Quality managers have long known in the traditional organization that a good manager designs a system where all subordinates exceed or excel on the job. They are good at getting people to work together and tap the strengths of their subordinates. Therefore, if a top government official comes into an organization and wants to rank order people, the quality manager resists. The senior author once observed a large organization that was experiencing significant profit losses. The chief executive officer of this organization held a number of beliefs that were inconsistent with TQM principles, but perhaps the most ridiculous belief was that managers needed to control their people through competition. Therefore, he instituted a practice where every manager must rank order the people who worked for them. Then he instructed the managers each year to get rid of the bottom 20 percent. Therefore, if there were 10 subordinates working for a manager, he had to remove two of them. His belief was that if the worst performers in the organization were fired, the organization will be successful. People often say in government, "If I could only get rid of my worst performers, my organization would be effective."

It's very difficult for traditional managers to accept the fact that 90 percent of their problems in the organization are caused by systems failures rather than by an incompetent workforce. Government is not ineffective because of government's inability to hire qualified people, nor is it ineffective because individuals don't do what they're told to do. Government is ineffective in many cases because the management system is poorly designed, developed, and implemented. People failures are mostly the result of a system failure. Yet, traditional managers rely heavily on rating and ranking the performance of subordinates as a meaningful and useful tool.

PERSONAL AGENDAS

In a TQM culture, people learn to trust or not to trust, to respect or disrespect, to be open or to be closed with associates, team members, and management. Some associates will put their personal agendas ahead of organization agendas. That is, it's more important to them to control others, to develop conflicts, to promote counter-organizations, to build barriers, etc., than to contribute towards improving the organization everyday. Associates, whether they be peers, superiors, or subordinates, often easily recognize the personal agenda types when they work with them in teams. It is not as easy to recognize people with personal agendas where management assigns work, holds the individual accountable, and compares them to others in the organization. In these situations, it is very easy for subordinates to fake out management by pretending to please and support management. Since practically everyone understands the "halo" effect where it is believed that if the person doing the performance appraisal likes an employee, then he or she is very likely to rate that employee exceptionally well. Most people realize that one of the best methods in government for getting a high performance rating is to fake support of supervisors. They believe that they can manipulate managers by telling them what they want to hear.

WORKING IN TEAMS

On the other hand, when people work in teams, the work itself determines success. People no longer work just for the manager, but work for the process, and peers evaluate each other on how much they contribute to improving the process. Teams expect other members to practice the values of the organization, and they also expect that an individual team member will contribute. If any team members are unwilling to contribute, some members will first go to management and ask that dissenters be removed, and if management won't remove them, then the team may reassess their situation and might decide to give individuals another chance or to exclude them altogether.

We have found in implementing TQM that letting teams handle their own problems is the most effective strategy. Since we used volunteers to form teams, it was not as difficult for a team to remove one of its peers. Once the person was removed from the team, then it became management's job to figure out what the person can do and can't do. The manager at that point in time could decide if the person was worth keeping working individually or to begin building a case against them that would ultimately lead to the subordinate's termination. The reality is that teams provide instant feedback about performance, and, therefore, if an individual can effectively work in a team, management should not interfere.

Furthermore, if a team functions effectively, why should managers intervene by rating and ranking the performance of the individual team member? It would be far more effective if the manager's evaluation of the team member's work was a statement that the person exceeds at his or her performance since they are part of a team that is producing exceptional outputs and outcomes. In fact, the manager can say that about all of the team members. In a traditional organization the problem the manager experiences is that if he or she develops an effective process improvement system, the effective manager will be seen as ineffective by superiors and peers because he or she does not control their people by the traditional ways and, second, will be considered weak because he or she gives praise to all the people who work for him or her.

We recommend a natural process of selection and appraisal. The role of the leader is to assist the organization in identifying and defining processes and then develop a team-based culture which allows associates to systematically improve the processes. Performance appraisal is a daily interaction among team members, subordinates, peers, customers, and suppliers. If the system is designed well, associates working in the system should receive a performance appraisal that indicates that they are exceptional. The entire team can and often should receive a performance appraisal that indicates that they exceed in their job. They don't need to be measured against each other, ranked, or rated. Exceptional performance becomes the standard. The performance goal of the organization should be that everyone receives a performance appraisal that indicates that they exceed.

BACK TO REALITY

It's practically inconceivable that organizations will ever have a policy of no performance appraisals. For sure, government organizations are not going to replace the performance appraisal in the conceivable future. We must accept the need for annual formal performance appraisals. Therefore, we decided to devote considerable time to finding a method for measuring and evaluating associate achievements during a specified time period (normally one year) that did not interfere with the practice of TQM. We are aware that a few TQM organizations have either made or are in the process of making significant changes in their performance reviews. These organizations have tried to link individuals to team performance, link individual performance to the person's ability to function as an effective team member, link individual performance to customer satisfaction, link individual performance to process improvement, etc.

Furthermore, business organizations have also found ways to link pay for performance, or link TQM behaviors to bonuses, promotions, stock options, etc. There are many advocates of TQM who are concerned about trying to link individual performance directly to TQM activities and rewarding individual efforts with salary increases bonuses, stock options, etc. They think that these rewards will destroy teamwork and promote individual competition among team members. Consequently, many TQM experts advocate team rewards as opposed to individual rewards.

At the present time we believe that the most effective path for organizations is to continue with the formal annual performance appraisal for two reasons. First, our legal system requires it, and, second, a formal annual discussion with each associate that provides feedback on their personal performance can be beneficial. Rewards, such as salary and bonuses, however, should be directly related to team performance. For years many of the top corporations in America realized that the best bonus system was a fixed percentage going to each of the members of the top executive team if the organization exceeded their goals. When individual pay-off is tied to team performance, the team is more likely to foster a climate that is conducive to effective working relationships.

STANDARD PERFORMANCE APPRAISALS

For years, business and government organizations have spent millions of dollars on trying to find ways to develop more effective performance appraisals, and they will continue to do so. It seems that there are few organizations satisfied with the formal annual performance appraisal process, criteria, and outcomes. They are dissatisfied for many reasons, but the most often stated reasons are that the job criteria doesn't fit the job and, second, most bosses do a very poor job of providing feedback to associates. In other words, the boss takes the performance appraisal lightly. In fact, in one government organization, over 30 percent of the people being appraised received their achievement rating by default. In other words, the supervisor didn't even bother to complete a performance appraisal. The most likely reason a supervisor uses for not completing a performance appraisal in government is that the appraisal doesn't make any difference, because in their opinion there would not have been any raises that particular year. Their subordinates are likely to say that their supervisor is not effective in communication skills and often does not like to be up-front or direct with people. They report that their supervisor uses "other" means of control. Furthermore, subordinates will frequently claim that the supervisor would not conduct a performance appraisal because no one bothered to update the standards for the subordinate's position. In other words, the subordinate was performing differently from his or her written standards.

With all of the faults of the present performance appraisal systems in both business and government, Total Quality Management perhaps only adds to the problems of performance reviews rather than simplifies the process, especially in government. Government workers frequently receive what are called job standards. Shown below is an actual copy of Performance Standards and Expectations for an associate working as an Employment Security Representative I:

Performance Standards and Expectations

Employment Security Representative I

Standards:

JOB ORDERS RECEIVED FROM LOCAL OFFICE MARKETING—Ensures that Jobs and Benefits is promoted to the Employer Community and guarantees a minimum of 2010 job orders received of which 10% are from NEW (non fast food) employers visited no more than one time in a 6-month period. Satisfaction of the aforementioned = PASS.

JOB BANK—80% of all job orders, excluding Mass Recruitments, must be received through the Job Bank to PASS.

RECRUITING AGREEMENTS—Promote the use of recruiting agreements and obtain 1-2 formal agreements per year to PASS.

Expectations:

VETERANS AND MIGRANT SEASONAL FARM WORKERS (MSFW)—Adheres to all Federal guidelines assuring that appropriate services and goals are met or exceeded.

WORKSHOP/EMPLOYABILITY SKILLS PROGRAM—Actively promote Employability Skills Workshops, and other Jobs and Benefits workshops, i.e., Profiling, Job Clubs, Demonstration Project, and Eligibility Review Program to employers and to applicant groups.

TQM PHILOSOPHY—Participate in process improvement teams. Act as Process Improvement Guide. Document, measure, and chart data regarding continual process improvement. Assist in helping at least one team in office to go before the Region VIII Quality Review Board every 6 months.

PROFESSIONAL PLACEMENT NETWORK—Actively participate in the recruitment of participants in the PPN Program. Advertise, promote, and demonstrate a commitment to this program's success.

MARKETING—Develop and maintain up-to-date marketing plans, and actively market the agency's ideas, objectives, and activities.

REPORTS—Must respond timely to all reports (including Officevision).

JOB SERVICE EMPLOYER COUNCIL—Actively maintain, participate, and promote JSEC. Increase JSEC membership, involve JSEC in creative, supportive and enhancing activities that will promote Jobs and Benefits.

PRIVATE INDUSTRY COUNCIL—Work cooperatively with PIC and its agencies regarding partnerships and relationships with Jobs and Benefits.

PROJECT INDEPENDENCE—Work cooperatively with projects and processes that can better serve Jobs & Benefits and PI customers.

INNOVATIONS—Continually strive to improve the Jobs and Benefits image by suggesting new ideas.

The problem with standards in any organization, and particularly in a TQM organization, is that they are generally too narrow and become outdated shortly after they are written. We suggest that government agencies implementing TQM move away from employee standards, which we define as a stated measure of the level of performance the employee is expected to achieve or the objectives the employee is expected to accomplish. Performance standards should become performance expectations, which we defined as job-related goals set at the beginning of the performance planning period. The primary difference between the two definitions is that a stated performance standard is a stated measure, whereas performance expectations are job-related goals. A standard, for example, for an employment interviewer might read that the person is expected to see a new customer every 15 minutes; whereas, a performance expectation might read that the employment interviewer is expected to fulfill a number of functions in the organization without specific measurements. In a TQM organization, there is more concern for process measurements than individual measurements. Therefore, associates should be evaluated on job expectations, not on individual standards.

Government organizations have been sent messages by its customers and the taxpayers that they are tired of an ineffective and an inefficient government. Government mistakes appear daily in every newspaper. But even more important than customers and taxpayers, people who work in government are frustrated by how government works. For years, government has tried to put a square peg in a round hole when it comes to performance measurement. The assumption has been that if management writes the standards correctly and the employee is held to that standard, then government will work effectively. When it doesn't work, government management uses excuses that the standards have been changed, new standards need to be developed, employees aren't held accountable for the standards, and that when employees are held accountable for the standards, nothing can be done about it when they don't meet their standards. These excuses fill top management meetings. What top management should just do, however, is come to a conclusion that even if the standards were correct and if all government workers did what they were told to do, government would still be ineffective. In other words, the sum of the parts does not make a whole.

TQM PERFORMANCE EXPECTATIONS

When we developed a method for tracking and evaluating associates in a TQM culture, we established two objectives. First, our goal was to help our associates succeed. Therefore, our appraisal process focused on the success factors which produce superior performance. Second, our goal was not to develop a system which forced associates to be ranked or compared to other associates. Our system should not force managers to distribute evaluations that forces comparisons. Therefore, we developed behaviorally based measures of job performance that focused on detailed evaluation of specific acts or behaviors.

This process is fairly straightforward an organization that establishes a TQM culture because a complete list of behaviors that apply to all jobs in the organization can be created. The following behaviorally based measures apply to all associates in a TQM organization: (1) the associate is expected to know, understand, and explain the process(es) to which they're assigned, (2) the associate is expected to contribute as a team member of a process improvement team, (3) the associate is expected as a team member to embrace and implement organization values daily, (4) the associate is expected to contribute as a team member to documenting their assigned process(es), (5) the associate is expected as a team member to measure the output of their assigned process(es) supplier(s), (6) the associate is expected as a team member to measure the output of their assigned process(es), (7) the associate is expected to work as a team member in measuring the outcomes of their assigned process(es) on customers, and (8) the associate is expected to work as a team member by graphically displaying data generated that indicates process effectiveness.

Not all associates volunteer to work on a team. In the initial phase of implementing TQM, those who do not volunteer are generally ignored (processes are not ignored). They should not, however, be ignored as TQM progresses. Most associates will eventually join a team. However, there are some who will hold out and will want to work by themselves. In business organizations, hold outs do not last very long. With career service protection, many associates, both the front-liners and managers, will insist upon their right and challenge management initiatives. A time will come when they should not be ignored. Therefore, we recommend that the following behavioral expectations be included in their position descriptions: (1) the associate is expected to practice departmental values, (2) the associate is expected to contribute to process improvement, (3) the associate is expected to embrace and implement organization values daily, (4) the associate is expected to contribute to documenting their assigned process(es), (5) the associate is expected to measure the output of their assigned process(es) supplier(s), (6) the associate is expected to measure the output of their assigned process(es), (7) the associate is expected to measure the outcomes of their assigned process(es) on customers, and (8) the associate is expected to work to graphically display data generated that indicates process effectiveness.

The following behaviors are expected of all leaders in the organization. Leaders are: (1) expected to know, understand, and document their assigned process(es), (2) expected to measure and chart data that factually describe their assigned process(es), (3) expected to measure the effects of process(es) on customers, (4) expected to empower and facilitate associate(s) participation in working as members of process improvement teams, (5) expected to work as a member of continual process improvement teams, (6) expected to role-model departmental values, (7) expected to recognize continual process improvements, and (8) expected to document continual improvements.

Performance appraisals may include Total Quality Management support if quality measures are spelled out in the position description. The following is suggested wording to be used on all position descriptions for managers/supervisors:

"Managers/supervisors are held accountable for the achievement of the department goal of Total Quality Management. In order to demonstrate support of the department's goal of TQM, the associate in this position must: (1) know and understand their processes, (2) measure their processes, (3) measure customer satisfaction, (4) have meaningful data, (5) work in teams, and (6) document continual improvements."

It's recommended that the above be listed on the addendum to the position description for supervisors and managers and that it be listed on the reverse side of the position description under knowledge, skills, and abilities.

These behavioral expectations should be included in each position description where applicable. Begin with managers-leaders and then follow-up with their associates. Each manager-leader should meet with associates and provide them a copy of their position description and discuss their TQM performance expectations. Also, at this time, the associate and manager-leader should sign and date the review and performance planning form described below indicating that the position description and performance expectations have been discussed.

Review and Performance Planning

Name:_____ SSN:_____ Position # :_____

Class Title: _____ Class Code:_____

Division/Bureau/Unit:_____

Beginning of the Review Period

Planning for Period beginning:____/____/_____ ending: ___/____/___

    This is to acknowledge that in planning for my initial or subsequent performance review(s), my supervisor and I have discussed my official position description and work standards/expectations and any documented changes in work standards/expectations for the next review period, as applicable.

Employee's Signature:_____ Date:_____

Supervisor's Signature:_____ Date:_____

End of the Review Period

(If different) Period beginning: ____/____/___ ending: ___/____/___

    This is to acknowledge that I have discussed my work performance during this period with my supervisor.

Employee's Signature:_____ Date:_____

Comments:

Supervisor's Signature:_____ Date:_____

Comments:

Reviewing Authority's Signature:_____ Date:_____

Comments:

PERFORMANCE ASSESSMENT (BEHAVIORAL OBSERVATIONS)

In that the practice of TQM clearly defines required behavior, it is relatively easy to observe TQM behavior. Furthermore, there are many occasions to observe associates and their team performance. In addition, performance assessment is more likely to be performance appreciation rather than performance criticism. Since poor performance is more likely a result of system failure rather than associate failure, the focus should be on fixing processes rather than "fixing people." However, occasionally there are individuals who, in most cases "self-select" out of the system, but who are unable to find another position in their agency. In government, these are the most difficult associates. Their attitude and work performance actually create a barrier to continual improvement. They don't want to work on a team, they don't like measuring their work, and they spend most of their time criticizing the TQM initiative. Eventually such associates will need to be reprimanded and, in some cases, terminated.

TQM allows leaders to gather significant data from a number of sources regarding team and individual performance. For a manager-leader, data about his or her performance can be gathered from his or her superior, peers, subordinates, customers, suppliers, and from the individual (self-assessment).

An associate can be evaluated by his or her leader, peer assessment (team members), assigned process customers, assigned process suppliers and also through self-assessment. We believe the most effective method for gathering data about an associate is to work with associates and their teams to develop criteria that can be used by customers, suppliers, peers, and leaders to evaluate the associate and teams.

Self-assessment is an effective method for understanding and evaluating an individual in a TQM organization. We found the following method of self-assessment to be very effective. Each leader was sent a letter that asked them to reflect on their past year's performance using the following criteria: (1) departmental values, (2) process management, (3) quality tools and quality data, (4) linkages, (5) customer focus, (6) empowerment, (7) recognition, (8) communication, (9) training, and (10) risk-taking.

We asked each leader to assess themselves regarding each of the criteria. This proved to be an excellent tool for understanding and evaluating the leader and at the same time proved to be an excellent development tool. It made the leader stop and take a "time-out" during the year to check his or her own progress to understand deficiencies in areas that needed improvement. Just as important, after they completed the document, they began to realize how much they did achieve during the past year and, therefore, they were able to engage in "self-appreciation."

The leader should make the performance appraisal activity a positive one. Associates should be pleased with their own personal performance and, of course, be appreciated by his or her leader and peers. The aim should be to build the person's self-image. According to Barbara Ilardi of the University of Rochester, New York, "People who view their job performances through rose-colored glasses are happier at work than their more realistic colleagues. People who look at themselves just a little bit better than they really are have better mental and physical health than people who underrate themselves." She concluded in her study that "What the worker believes about himself or herself in terms of motivation, competency, and opportunities provided by the workplace is a better predictor of overall job satisfaction than what the supervisor believes."

Leaders should be more interested in developing a positive self-image within their subordinates than trying to build their image in the eyes of the subordinates.

Information from various sources can provide valid and reliable information because peers, subordinates, customers, and suppliers are often in a good position to observe and evaluate performance on several dimensions. Observations from these sources provide insight on how well leaders and associates are meeting the expected behaviors. For leaders, subordinates provide valuable information. Leaders who are not facilitating teams, gathering measurable data, improving processes, etc., are easily detected when looking at subordinate performance appraisals. On the other hand, the leader who is doing an outstanding job receives accolades and is appreciated even beyond the leader's expectations.

The value of other sources, such as subordinates, is more of a prevention as opposed to detection methodology. When leaders know they are going to be evaluated from numerous sources regarding their fulfillment of job expectations, they realize that playing games with multiple sources of information is very dangerous. Consequently, leaders are more likely to walk the talk, get involved in TQM, provide accurate data, and exceed customer expectations.

If an associate is not measuring up to job expectations, then a performance improvement plan should be completed by the leader. This plan should clearly outline what needs to be done for the associate to attain successful performance. The leader should clearly identify the performance deficiency of the associate and then identify what the associate can do to improve their performance, what corrective action should be taken. A date should be set for timely conferences to review associate's performance. Below is the performance improvement plan worksheet used in Florida state government that we found to be effective in implementing TQM.

Performance Improvement Plan

Name:_____ SSN:_____ Position # :_____

Class Title: _____ Class Code:_____

Division/Bureau/Unit:_____**Review Period: From:__/ /__To:__/ /__**

This is to provide you with a formal Performance Improvement Plan in order to correct performance deficiencies. To attain successful performance, you must improve in the specific areas noted below and continue successful performance in your other areas of responsibility.

Performance Deficiencies
Specific work deficiencies:

Performance Improvements
Corrective action to be taken and dates for conferences (attach additional sheets as needed):

This is to acknowledge that I have, on the date indicated below, discussed my performance deficiencies and corrective action to be taken as indicated by my supervisor. I have also been notified that if my performance is not successful within the next 60 calendar day period, action will be taken to remove me from the class.* My supervisor and I agree to work together to enable me to improve my performance to a successful level.

Employee's Signature:_____ Date:_____
Comments:

Supervisor's Signature:_____ Date:_____
Comments:

Reviewing Authority's Signature:_____ Date:_____
Comments:

* Employees without career service status may be terminated at any time during a 60-day extension if performance does not meet work standards/expectations.

PERFORMANCE DEVELOPMENT

If the organization is going to continually improve, so must the workers. TQM requires personal development. Therefore, it is in the best interest of both the organization and individuals to continually improve their performance. The most effective way to achieve individual growth in a TQM organization is to focus on planned personal change. The planned personal change process requires a vision, goals, a plan, action, and reinforcement. Every associate should link to someone higher in the hierarchy of the organization that can serve as their mentor or coach. This person does not have to be the associate's immediate supervisor; however, all leaders in the organization should spend considerable time mentoring and coaching associates.

Personal planned change begins with a vision, a brief statement expressing the ideal future state of the associate in his or her organization. Questions that need to be asked are: What will the organization look like in a year, two years, etc.? What will be the primary focus of most workers? What skills are needed? What opportunities will become available?

Because the organization will inevitably change, associates must question how they are going to change with the organization, and second, how such a change would enhance their career.

Process planned change also requires a vision. Coaches and mentors can help associates visualize what the process is capable of doing if time and resources were unlimited. Many government workers have worked so long in a job that it is extremely difficult for them to "think outside of the box" and to use their creative thinking skills.

For years, organization leaders have paid lip-service to the development of personnel. Only a few selected individuals were singled out for personal and professional development. Although many organizations invested significant amounts of money in training, the training was still designed to control personnel rather than to enlighten them. Personnel were developed in such courses as communication, listening, conflict management, stress reduction, motivation, etc. The assumption was that if people communicated more effectively, if they listened better, were more motivated, etc., then the organization would improve. Most organizations wasted their money.

Government organizations spent most of their training money on sending upper echelon government managers to workshops. Training money for middle level and front-line personnel was spent on telling personnel how they could do their job better if they would follow the directions of the training course and their boss. Training for front-line and middle management personnel largely became a substitute for what poor managers couldn't deliver in the first place. With evolution of training, one can understand why it is so difficult to implement TQM in organizations, and especially government. Middle managers and front-liners have been manipulated most of their career and feel that TQM is just one more instance of being manipulated. Generally, they can beat back attempts to manipulate them with just a little resistance. For example, they may complain to the top manager when he or she comes around and try to slow down or even stop the "new" program. They become increasingly upset during TQM implementation because their normal resistant behavior doesn't slow down the process. Many associates have to take other extreme measures like filing a grievance, refusing to work in teams, writing nasty anonymous letters, constantly criticizing management, etc.

It is the TQM leader's responsibility to work with these individuals so that they can begin to have a positive vision of the organization in the future and how they function within the organization. Our experience has shown that the first step towards helping an associate plan professional change is to help them visualize how their assigned *process* might be or could be in the future. The leader needs to help them visualize how they might participate on a team to improve the process.

Whether a leader is trying to help a person in career planning, process improvement, or in overcoming an unsatisfactory performance assessment, coaching begins with a vision of the desired state. For example, in coaching a subordinate who has received an unsatisfactory performance assessment, the following questions might be asked:

- Does the subordinate know performance is unsatisfactory?

- Does subordinate know what is supposed to be done and when?

- Are there obstacles beyond subordinate's control?

- Does subordinate know how to do it?

- Can the subordinate do it if he or she wanted to?

The subordinate's behavior should be redirected through coaching, and it begins by the subordinate visualizing a satisfactory performance. Once satisfactory performance is visualized, the associate can then begin setting goals.

PERFORMANCE GOAL SETTING

Performance goal setting is a process aimed at developing a statement or statements which identifies an achievement that an associate proposes to attain in a specific time period. During initial TQM implementation, associates are in search of mentors and coaches. They are looking for direction. An associate may see that the organization is offering training courses in TQM orientation, TQM tools, TQM teams, etc. The associate is confused because the courses aren't mandatory and the alert associate needs direction. Since there are very few managers in the organization that support TQM in the early stages, the alert associate is confused. He or she is getting mixed signals. The organization offers the courses because obviously they think they are important. On the other hand, people around him or her and even their managers criticize the courses and offer no support.

Associates who have the desire for learning or who naturally want to understand more about Total Quality Management take the risk and begin enrolling. What is mind boggling is that so few government workers are willing to take the risk of learning. After interviewing numerous front-line workers, supervisors, and middle managers, the authors were struck by the fact that so few had any personal goals, let alone performance goals. The vast majority of associates had one objective, and that was to survive another administration.

TQM leaders must, at a minimum, assist all associates in identifying goals that will assure them they are going in the right direction. Organizations can no longer afford to have workers who are not interested in bettering themselves and the organization. Organizations make a significant investment in people when they move to a TQM culture. To achieve a return on that investment, the organization has a right to expect that each of its members is committed to self-improvement and to organizational improvement. Total Quality Management organizations don't have jobs that allow an individual to be "brain dead." All associates must be goal oriented and have an action plan.

ACTION PLANNING

Action planning is a specified course of action designed to attain a stated objective. It outlines a step-by-step process the individual is going to take in order to make improvements. Planning itself is a simple process. However, completing a plan is a complex process. It should answer the question: What is the best path to take in order to achieve the identified goals?

A plan may include reading specific books, completing TQM courses, completing a college degree, completing courses at a university, attending seminars, meeting with a mentor once a week, cross-training to learn other jobs, visiting other organizations, viewing other teams, etc. Furthermore, a plan may include personal behaviors that need to be improved, such as attending meetings on time, showing interest and having enthusiasm at meetings, not being afraid to assert oneself when around top management, speaking to other associates, smiling, volunteering for assignments, taking on more responsibility, etc.

Total Quality Management organizations provide a great opportunity for people at all levels who desire to improve themselves and their organization. We believe that with the help of a mentor or coach, people at all levels are able and willing to set forth a plan and take action.

ACTION

Some people are capable of setting goals and developing a plan, but are rather poor at taking action. This phenomena occurs at the beginning of every new year. Many people have a New Year's resolution, their goals are clear, they have a plan, and within a few weeks the objectives and plans fall by the wayside because of a lack of action. We believe that people fail to take action because they are either uncommitted to measurement or they don't understand the importance of measurement as a motivational tool. People excel at sports, that is put forth energy and try to live up to their full potential, primarily because of the measurements of success provided by the sport. For example, it's fun to take a basketball and just shoot it at the hoop even though there is no competition, just to succeed for personal satisfaction.

Without measurement, we would not have sports. There must be a way to track degrees of performance. These measurements are extremely motivating. For some people, competing within themselves (internalizers) is sufficient motivation. They can play a round of golf by themselves and end up the game as motivated or even more motivated than when they started. On the other hand, there are those who require outside stimulus to motivate them (externalizers). They require competition or external sources of motivation such as bonuses. The important point here is that whether one is an internalizer or an externalizer, measurement is required. It's necessary to record progress. Therefore, we advise that associates their plan carefully, but during the action phase they track their activities by measuring the critical points in their plan. If individuals are going to achieve their objectives, they've got to know more than just feeling they're going in the right direction, they need to know the facts. We recommend the use of quality tools for personal performance development.

REINFORCEMENT

Even though the results of collective data are motivating, each individual needs reinforcement. Reinforcement comes from the mentor or coach sending messages that stimulate the associate to continue with their actions. Just a comment in the hall a couple of times a week can be exhilarating for some people. Leaders should go out of their way to recognize associates who are making continual improvements in the organization and in themselves. Leaders should find numerous ways to identify and recognize positive actions taken by their associates. Leaders must understand that many people in the organization at all levels will want to break out of the pack and take the opportunity for personal improvement offered by a TQM organization.

However, it's not as easy as just saying, "If you want to, do it." People around the ones who want to break out of the pack will intentionally, and often unintentionally, discourage their behavior. There are many people in government jobs who are not necessarily happy, but content to get a paycheck and spend most of their time as an organization critic. These critics enjoy holding others back. Therefore, particularly in government organizations, TQM leaders have got to put forth extra energy to assist associates in performance development. They need a coach who is on their side, sincerely respects them, appreciates them for what they are, and is willing to make a significant effort towards helping them improve. The leader reinforces positive actions at practically every observation.

SELECTION PROCESS

The purpose of the selection process is to identify and recruit personnel who have a commitment to Total Quality Management and the skills that enable them to participate on teams and contribute to process improvement. Our legal staff advised top management in Florida's Department of Labor and Employment Security that TQM questions during the employment interview can be asked and expected to be answered if the position description reveals the criteria discussed above under the heading of "Performance Expectations." In addition, the Legal Department recommended that the job announcement include a statement, "Requiring knowledge of TQM," or "Requiring experience in TQM." Legal also provided examples of questions which they thought could be asked in the selection process as follows: (1) How would you define quality? (2) Do you have any experience working with teams? If so, please explain. (3) Do you have any experience flowcharting a process? (4) Do you have any experience with customer's surveys? If so, explain. (5) Do you know now to document a continual improvement in a process? (6) Do you know how to analyze data?

In summary, the focus of this chapter was on performance management, and the very difficult need to intertwine into the TQM environment the performance management requirements that most government agencies must use. We said that in a genuine TQM organization the need to complete a performance appraisal not only violates one of Dr. Deming's principles, but 90 percent of the problems in any setting are caused by system failures, not people. Nevertheless, because of the legal requirements mandating performance reviews and because periodic feedback on personal performance is beneficial, we suggest that appraisals focus on the success factors which produce superior performance and that associates not be ranked or compared to their peers. We defined behavioral expectations for all positions that are to be included in writing on the actual position description. The value of self assessment cannot be overstated, for individuals need time to reflect upon their progress, both in terms of deficiencies and achievements. Through a structured strategy of performance goals, action plans, and reinforcement, as well as a selection process that recruits good future team players, it is possible to have a true TQM environment within required personnel rules and regulations.

11 IMPLEMENTING TOTAL QUALITY MANAGEMENT

"The customer, in spirit and in flesh, must pervade the organization—every system in every department, every procedure, every measure, every meeting, every decision."
—Peters, Thriving on Chaos

And this crap about TQM...let's get real, do you really think that we are all so simple minded to think that calling us associates and even more stupid—your customers—makes us 'feel' good? Please stop looking so stupid...nobody pays customers...we're employees. The taxpaying public is the customer along with the constituents we serve. So please tell your top management that calling us customers makes you look really stupid.

Do you really want us to be happy...then stop this nonsense and do your jobs.

Get off the processes and get on the product. We are supposed to be providing services or producing goods, are we not? Then, for God's sake, let's take a look at the end product. While you're sitting around with these feel-good Fridays on process, who is finding out if the services are even relevant? Shouldn't (sic) the review be based on the goal of what we do, not just a review of process for process sake and 'sharing'?

—Anonymous letter

I hope this is the last meeting that people's opinions are referred to as TQM. I mean that's just another disguise for the 27 other consulting firms teaching that other stuff. Before they called it all these other things, now it just happens to be TQM. It's all just a way to make themselves some money. To me it doesn't mean much.

211

Everybody has got to work TQM into their conversation so they feel like, well, we sure got that in there you know.
　　　　　　　　　—State Senator at the 1993 Productivity
　　　　　　　　　Advisory Group meeting

TQM was real successful in post-war Japan. The three stooges could probably have made progress in that environment. This country, state government, and you (letter to the Governor) and I have not gotten to where we are because TQM is the only way to manage. In fact, Japan is now struggling in the world economy. Let's face it, common sense, good judgment, and giving a damn has carried us much further than the latest management craze.
　　　　　　　　　Anonymous Letter

We could provide many quotes from anonymous letters we have received since implementing TQM. It is doubtful that any one organizational intervention has had so many critics. We recommend that anyone who wants to be loved, consistently strives to avoid criticism or lacks the courage to always do the right thing not take the leadership role in implementing Total Quality Management. Implementing TQM in industry is an extremely difficult challenge. We believe it's twice as hard in government. In industry organizations, personnel will give the appearance that they are "buying in" to TQM. In government, personnel are more authentic and will overtly reject TQM, and in many cases personnel will openly try to sabotage the effort.

HOW TO MAINTAIN SANITY

Given all the critics both within the organization and outside, and with the amount of rejection TQM receives, the personality of an individual trying to implement TQM will be tested. We recommend, therefore, that two important rules be adopted:

1. Remember that TQM has many critics, but there are no rivals.

2. Respond only to attacks on the process and not to attacks personality.

The U. S. Government management system has been under attack for many years. More recently, taxpayers are revolting against higher taxes and desire less government. Further, government workers have long been the target of criticism. Public remarks about government workers being lazy and only interested in receiving their checks are numerous. We believe that taxpayers will continue to revolt; however, pay little attention to the criticism that government workers are lazy. We have concluded, however, that government needs to become more effective, more customer oriented, less wasteful, and focus on providing quality service.

Few advocate that government should continue in its present management system, operating from a top-down perspective; that is, the people at the top know best. Recently, we received this memorandum from the Department of Labor and Employment Security—

> "Government management systems have long assumed that top management is in charge of the organization and therefore should direct the organization from the top. Rather than building their organization to meet the needs of front-line associates, government organizations are designed so that the associates at the bottom of the organization can meet the needs of those above them."

For example, on November 25th, 1994, the U. S. Department of Labor Employment and Training Administration in Atlanta, Georgia, issued a memorandum regarding employment service revitalization work plan. They state that the employment service mission and goals become the "[N]ation's leader in providing services to its customers and serving as a universal gateway to work force development resources by professional, empowered staff." To help them with their efforts, they awarded a million dollars to states to gather data regarding some notions of the plan. First, they wanted the State of Iowa to determine staff training needs that may be available from current reports and develop from them a core training curriculum for adaptation by each state to meet the front-line staff training needs. Iowa received $340,000 to do this job.

The above shows how far the top of the organization is removed from what is happening in the front-lines. Government might as well have taken this money and thrown it away. It would have been far better had they given the total sum to a front-line worker as a bonus. Any TQM organization knows the training needs of front-liners. What is sad about giving away this money is that top government bureaucrats frequently go on television and talk a good game regarding quality and listening to front-line workers. It's obviously a case of leadership at the top doing a good job of talking the talk, but not walking the talk.

In this same memorandum on the employment service revitalization work plan, the government gave Texas $100,000 to provide an opportunity to extend the best practices of successful local office managers to other local offices. They gave Maryland $504,000 to collect and review information on resource center concepts and activities throughout the nation, develop requirements, define options, and review prototype models. Once they've developed these models, they will disseminate them to the rest of the states. Rhode Island was granted $400,000 to analyze existing customer needs documentation from national studies and the work of leading states, and collect additional information required through employer surveys and front-line staff. And, finally, Ohio was given $447,000 to provide comprehensive information on present job matching approaches and methods. They were to identify and document the best practice methods, research the use of job matching data, labor market analysis, and curriculum development, and disseminate the results through a national conference.

This shows how wasteful government can be when it assumes that the people at the top "know best." It appears as though the Department of Labor's Employment and Training Administration has money every year for grants, and they have got to find some way to spend it. Their approach is rather obvious: use today's language to construct research grants, but yesterday's management approach. While traditional organizations are looking for the answer at the top, Total Quality Management organizations know that if there are any answers they will be developed by the people who work on the processes.

Front-line workers know what the customer needs and wants. The question for government is, are they going to empower front-liners to meet or exceed expectations of those customers? Is government going to change and put their resources where they belong, closest to where the work gets done? Further, will government bureaucratic leaders switch from just trying to survive by kissing up and meeting only the needs of the people above them to meeting the needs of the people that work for them?

It shows that the Department of Labor had over a million dollars to give to states for modeling specific programs. The people at the top continue to look for model programs, when the answer to effective government lies with the people who provide the service. Therefore, even though Total Quality Management has its critics, no one is advancing a more effective approach to managing government. There are those who believe that government is such a failure that they don't want to improve management systems, but rather reinvent them.

Our approach is one of continual improvement. Reinventing government is necessary in some systems; however, reinvention is not always the answer. It is selective and only deals with parts of the system, whereas TQM is concerned with the total system.

Critics of TQM abound. They attack people who advocate TQM, constantly looking for TQM advocates to make a mistake. Workers frequently say that "If they would just let us alone, we'll get the job done." It is a very difficult transition to go from a management by objectives approach to a Total Quality Management approach. Most government workers, however, don't even realize they might be using MBO. Therefore, what TQM really replaces is a reactive management system in government. When many of the personnel become frightened by this change, they will counter-attack with an assault on a leader's personality. Critics are hoping that with these continuous assaults, the leader will not be able to survive, or at a minimum become a walking-wounded leader.

Another way to attack TQM is to find situations where TQM did not work and then spread the word among associates that the "truth" is that TQM doesn't work in other places and therefore won't work here. For example, even though *Business Week* has published numerous articles describing the TQM successes, on August 8th, 1994, they published one of the most ridiculous articles on TQM. In the article, they claimed that TQM didn't work because one company, named Varian, lost business when they implemented it. Even though their on-time deliveries went from 42 percent to 92 percent and they cut their time significantly for designing semi-conductors, TQM was judged a failure because of lost market shares and posted losses. Critics were soon copying this article and sending it to all associates. It was obvious to anyone who read the article that the author knew very little about TQM and that all along Varian was attempting to use TQM disguised as MBO. For example, the writer states: "Obsessed with meeting production schedules, the staff in the vacuum-equipment unit didn't return customer phone calls, and the operation ended up losing market share."

The article goes on to say that "Radiation-repair people were so rushed to meet deadlines that they left before explaining their work to customers." Any writer who would try to associate the two above sentences with quality obviously doesn't understand the first principle of TQM, which is to meet or exceed customer expectations.

Implementing TQM is a constant struggle, and one cannot be distracted by attacks on the concept or on the personality attacks of people implementing the change. However, information on how processes are working or not working effectively is very important. Anonymous letters, hearsay evidence, gossip, etc., are all valuable sources of information that should not be ignored. It is easy to document the accuracy of most information. Focus on the processes that need improvement. The data derived from those working to improve the process is the ultimate judge of process effectiveness.

The purpose of this chapter is to describe the steps we used in implementing TQM in the Department of Labor and Employment Security. Our first step was to develop a vision of where we wanted the organization to be in two years.

TQM VISION

A vision is a view of the ideal future state of the organization. The vision describes what everyone wants the organization to become. We envisioned an organization where the focus was on the customer, on continual process improvements, and associates working in teams to improve the processes. We saw an organization that had adopted, accepted, and practiced Total Quality Management beliefs and principles.

OUR GOAL

Our goal was to transform Florida's Department of Labor and Employment Security from its traditional way of doing business to the TQM culture we had envisioned. Our aim was to move the present culture from being top-down—or management "knows best"—to a culture where those closest to the work would be empowered to manage processes. This bottom-up approach argues that the associates know best.

Our aim was to move the traditional culture away from being results only, from only focusing on numerical objectives set by management, to focusing on doing the right thing the first time so that customer expectations would be met or exceeded. We wanted to move away from a culture that focused on detection of errors (according to Al Gore, one out of three government people are watching the work of others, Inspector Generals, auditors, etc.).

In the past, when an error was found, the goal was to find someone to blame rather than helping them diagnose the cause of the error and help them fix it. We wanted to move away from the set of old management principles—plan, organize, direct, and control—to a set of TQM principles that focused on customer satisfaction, process improvement, process measurement, and team work.

We wanted to move away from a culture where loyalty was the primary value to a culture where values are shared, where respect and open communication are encouraged, and where data guides behavior. It is a culture that does not focus on playing up to management, but on rather quality data.

Our aim was to dramatically change training policies which focused mostly on training middle and top management and how they can plan, motivate, communicate, and control others to a culture where all associates receive training that helps them improve the quality of their work.

Our aim was to move the organization away from a performance appraisal which rank ordered individuals, promoted competition among each other, and penalized associates for failures to a culture where all personnel can exceed, where personnel are appreciated, and encouraged to learn from process failures and not penalized. Our desire was to move away from recognition of only individuals to recognition of teams and individuals.

Our aim was to move away from organizing around departmental functions where we would divide and cluster work to a culture where we organized around the core processes of the department.

Finally, our aim was to develop TQM leaders, to move the present leadership style of taking and giving orders, setting goals for subordinates, solving job problems, defining rules and penalties, tolerating marginal performers, and manipulating values to get what management wants to a culture where leaders emerge because they are willing to empower others, role model organization values, assist teams in making continual improvements, facilitate communication, and provide recognition.

With our vision in mind and our goals clear, we implemented the following change strategy.

CHANGE STRATEGY

Our change strategy was a simple one. First, we would begin by creating a readiness for change. We wanted our associates to see a "need for a change," creating dissatisfaction with the present state. Many people working in government may be critical of the way government does business, but not willing to accept the idea that dramatic change in the way that government does business is necessary. Even though change did not come easy at Chrysler, it helped Chrysler personnel understand a need for a change when their very existence was being threatened. People in government have survived many hollow threats made by taxpayers and legislators and therefore are somewhat immune to change attempts. However, our initial attempts to change the department to a TQM culture was to generate dissatisfaction with the present system by revealing discrepancies between the current way it did business and the desired way we wanted it to do business.

Second, our strategy focused on overcoming resistance to changing to a TQM culture. We understood from the beginning that many of our associates would endure considerable anxiety and would find it difficult to let go of the known (what they're presently doing) and move to an uncertain culture. They knew the consequences of the present way they did business (no one was likely to lose their job; it's doubtful that the taxpayers will ever do anything about government ineffectiveness other than talk about it; and what we do now at least keeps our boss happy and it's good enough for government work). We understood that any attempts to change our associates would be met with significant resistance. Therefore, our strategy included empathy and support for those having difficulty accepting the advocated changes. We adopted continual improvement as our change barometer and took pleasure with the smallest of incremental steps that moved this in the direction we desired. TQM implementation requires suspending judgment, being patient, and being willing to take a few arrows.

We did not take the approach some business organizations have taken and that is to proclaim TQM as the new management system, assign it to management to implement, and if any employees did not like it, they could find something else to do. By decreeing TQM as the management approach from the top, the organization will adopt the new beliefs and concepts quickly; however, it will take considerable time for personnel to accept them.

In government, overcoming the resistance to change is much more difficult. Government managers and subordinates will unite to resist change attempts. Therefore, any change effort in government requires significant participation and involvement. We needed to get all employees involved, first to understand the need for change and second, to help us to design, develop, and implement the desired TQM culture.

PHASES IN IMPLEMENTING TQM—PART I

Phase 1: Indoctrinating Top Management

To be successful in Total Quality Management, the organization must be changed from top-down to team driven. Focus on delighting the customer, meeting or exceeding their expectations. Train all associates in the basic TQM tools. And, finally, reward, recognize, and promote continual process improvement by teams.

We started at the top.

Dreadful Friday Afternoons

Our first attempt at creating a need for a change began one Friday afternoon where the senior author gave a two-hour TQM lecture to division directors and bureau chiefs. This lecture outlined TQM beliefs and principles. Subsequent Friday afternoons focused on measurement and plans for implementation. For the measurement section, we used the head of the Statistics Department at Florida State University who had a layman's approach to measurement, and the implementation plan was directed by a TQM scholar who had a very disarming approach to implementing TQM.

Like any change effort in government, very few jump aboard. Even though the audience was the top leaders in the department, they behaved more like middle managers who are frightened by the prospect of change. Most of the directors and bureau chiefs leaned towards the idea that government must change, but changing to TQM may not be possible, nor is it a good idea. Therefore, unlike lower and middle managers, the top managers were good at acting. They would compliment us on the seminar and tell us how much they appreciated it, then take the road of most leaders who focus on surviving, and that is "do nothing." At the end of our seminars we felt exhilaration, but it didn't take long to realize that the top leaders in the department rejected TQM, with one exception.

This was not totally unexpected by the senior author since he had experienced a similar reaction when he first exposed the Florida Department of Revenue top management to TQM. Division heads are often very political, will say what they think they should, but then will take the safest route. Many government managers are survivors, not leaders. Being out front on any initiative is not a risk many will take.

Further, even when the head of the organization is willing to take the risk, government managers are unwilling to share in the risk since they are not sure how long the risk taker at the top will want to stay in his or her job, get fired, or be willing to accept the heat or criticism of the planned change. Managers don't want to go down with a political appointee. Contrary to popular belief, political appointments don't just come and go after elections. Therefore, even though the division directors and bureau chiefs were political appointments and can be given two-week notice without cause, most people occupying these positions try to position themselves to survive no matter who gets elected. Therefore, it's easy to understand why so many administrations get elected to reduce government and manage it more effectively, and yet, at the end of their tenure, more people are working in government and government is still perceived as ineffective.

What we found out in our first attempt to change government was that there are few managers who are willing to stand for a cause. The vast majority of government managers are more concerned about their own survival.

After we completed the dreadful Friday afternoon series, we waited for division directors to take the lead. Not much happened. Therefore, we implemented the following steps.

Phase 2: Labelling Employees "Associates"

Shortly after being appointed Deputy Secretary, the senior author was having a meeting where he referred to employees as associates. The bureau chief in charge of personnel liked the label and requested that we use it throughout the agency. The secretary of the department heard the term used and liked it so much that she began to refer to everyone as associates. Then she issued a memorandum indicating that the department would use "associate" as opposed to "employee" in its literature. The senior author anticipated a significant backlash. He was under the opinion that people would naturally use the term if they liked it, and then if it became a norm, the department could officially accept it. He was wrong. The Secretary's announcement had a positive effect. Of course, most people who heard the concept for the first time probably thought it was rather ridiculous and got a good laugh. However, over time most personnel within the Department grew to appreciate the term and expected to be called an associate.

There is a very good reason for referring to all employees as associates. First, it helps move the organization away from the idea that there are people who know, the managers, and the people who do, the employees. Second, it helps people in the bottom of the organization hierarchy acquire new level of professionalism. It helps them to improve their self-image regarding their self-worth and helps them to think of themselves as professional people who are empowered to improve processes and provide quality service. If they think of themselves only as an employee who does what he/she is told, the associate's full "brain power" is not contributing to the organization.

Everyone in the organization should perceive of their colleagues as professionals and as associates who provide professional services. Organizations must break away from the idea that there are only a select few who make a difference in the organization. For the organization to be total quality, it must involve everyone.

Calling our colleagues associates rather than employees helps them to understand that they are not just minions to be directed, but rather associates to be appreciated because of their value to the organization. Calling people associates will not liberate them, but it helps to serve notice that employees deserve the highest respect. Professional people have never accepted the label "employee"; they refer to their counterparts as colleagues and associates. They do so because it shows respect for the individual. It might be difficult for some people to accept, but even those getting an unemployment check want to be treated professionally. And, one of the most effective methods for teaching an individual how to provide professional service is to sincerely and truly treat the person giving the service as a professional.

Government workers need to become empowered to make suggestions, make changes and collectively work together in order to improve customer service. The level of respect within organizations must improve for TQM to be effective. Government needs to break the mold and rethink the way it does business. Albert Einstein was correct in saying, "The problems that exist in the world cannot be solved by the level of thinking that created them."

Today, "associate" has become a part of most everyone's language in the department. There are still a number of naysayers, but in most cases these people realize that they have a personal agenda and are not coming to work every day to improve the organization, but rather come to work with the attitude that everything should be done for their personal benefit.

Phase 3: Identification of Key Processes

Since each division was a bit slow in getting started, we sent a message that we thought would stimulate activity. We asked each division to identify and flowchart their key processes. This assignment was met with some hostility, not from the division directors or bureau chiefs, but from those people assigned to flowchart the processes. Top management might grumble a bit, but they are accustomed to receiving directives from the top. Since this was a directive that they could understand and easily delegate, it was thought that it would keep the Deputy Secretary (in charge of Total Quality Management) content while the division worked on the flowcharts. Most of the divisions put together three or four people who were in charge of providing the senior author with a document that described the processes within their division.

Even though the divisions did not get into the spirit of what was requested, we wanted them to form teams and flowchart their own processes. We found out, however, that division directors often did not trust people who were working on the processes to flowchart them, and second, were afraid to form a team and let the team flowchart their own processes because this assignment would get in the way of productivity. Division directors understood that when people were asked (people presently working a job) to do extra, workers on the job would complain that they did not have enough time. Therefore, the division director would have to accept lower productivity. It was a dilemma for them, and they elected not to allow the people working in the process to flowchart their work.

Consequently, when we received the flowcharts, they were highly inaccurate. They did not reflect how the work actually got done. Even though we understood how the flowcharts were prepared and how inaccurate they might be, the senior author exhibited all of the flowcharts on his walls in his office. Then he scheduled a meeting with each of the division directors and tried to explain the flowcharts, knowing full-well that he did not understand them. What he also found out while he attempted to explain the flowcharts was that most of the division directors didn't understand them either. The senior author was amazed that the top director, the CEO of the division, did not understand basic processes.

We were somewhat in disbelief that we were directing an initiative in a $2.5 billion agency, and top management, including the Deputy Secretary, didn't know how processes worked. Therefore, we made it our goal to understand each key process and its measurement points.

Phase 4: Measuring Key Processes

When the senior author met with the division directors, he was complimentary and attempted to provide empathy and support. Realizing that one of his perceived shortcomings is empathy for those who are experiencing trouble in accepting change, the co-author of this book, who naturally demonstrates empathy, was assigned the task of helping all the divisions identify the indicators within their processes.

The assignment given to each division director was to identify these measurement points and then each month produce a report on how well the process was functioning. This assignment was also met with some hostility since most of the people who were given the assignment of flowcharting the key processes thought they were finished and now had to identify the measurement points in their key processes.

The teams assigned to do the flowcharting were probably wondering how they were going to complete their task since the flowchart was so inaccurate. They had just come off of a victory in which they thought they snowed the Deputy Secretary; now as a reward, they had to identify the key measuring points and then send a report each month to the Deputy Secretary. This was undoubtedly perceived by the people doing the work as more bureaucratic demands and something else to get done because the boss at the top wanted it. The consultant hired by one of the divisions to do the flow charting was given an extended contract. He became more and more important since he was the only one who understood the flowcharts that were submitted.

For the next few months, each division promptly sent in their reports. Each month the reports got bigger, and each month we would hear through the grapevine that the reports were inaccurate and loaded with fluff just to impress the Deputy Secretary.

When the senior author was directing the TQM initiative in the Florida Department of Revenue, he had similar results. Very few division directors were willing to make the commitment to TQM and consequently tried to delegate quality. It's easy to know when division directors are delegating quality because they will not participate in the flow charting process. Leaders who truly want to know TQM know that they have no option. They must understand how business is conducted in their organization.

In the Department of Revenue the assistant director, who provided the most resistance and was perhaps the biggest critic of TQM even though his director supported the TQM initiative, finally became disturbed by the lack of progress. He decided to flowchart the key process (the sales tax) himself, along with a team of people he recruited. After he completed this task, the assistant director became a staunch advocate of TQM. What made his initiative so successful was that he formed his own team and had a genuine interest in knowing how the processes within the department worked. We would often say that he was the first and only person who truly understood how the Department of Revenue collected taxes.

Even though the initial attempts at flowcharting key processes and the initial attempts at measuring these processes could be considered failures, they were, in fact, just the opposite. These two assignments proved to be very beneficial. First, it was an effective way to intervene within the divisions. Second, many people learned one of the TQM tools, flowcharting. Third, top management began to get a fairly good understanding of at least how work flowed. Fourth, even though many people who worked on the processes found the initial task irritating, they began to understand the merits of the assignment. And, finally, division directors and top management began to realize that the Secretary and Deputy Secretary were extremely serious about TQM and willing to take the risks associated with TQM implementation.

Phase 5: Forming Process Improvement Teams

As division directors, bureau chiefs, and other leaders within the division became interested in learning more about their processes, they realized that if they were going to improve their division they must form continual process improvement teams. Furthermore, as they studied flowcharts they came to realize that there are natural places to put teams, each process having a supplier and a customer.

We made a strategic decision not to assign people to processes, even though it was obvious that they were working in a specific process. Rather, we chose to ask for volunteers to improve processes.

While these teams were forming and getting started, the senior author was conducting two-hour TQM orientation seminars throughout the department. The purpose of these seminars was to provide a background on TQM, communicate TQM beliefs and principles, and hopefully ignite interest in some of the associates. Over 1,800 associates attended the orientation seminar. That is not to say that they all listened. Some slept and others served as nonverbal critics. One associate, in fact, came to the seminar with her coat and folded herself into a chair towards the front of the room and promptly went to sleep. Many people wanted to communicate that they just wanted to be left alone to do their work.

On the other hand, each seminar had some very positive effects. Contrary to popular opinion, many government workers do want to work and improve their system. Many people who attended these seminars volunteered for teams. Those, of course, who didn't volunteer claimed that the others were coerced. We truly admired the ones who took the risk and volunteered for teams. At first, peer group pressure was obviously against such a move.

One of the ways that top management will try to deflect TQM is by acting as though they are going along with the initiative by forming teams. However, the teams that they form are project teams and not process improvement teams. In other words, they continue with their old committee approach and ask teams to explore topics on which they need advice.

When implementing TQM, be very careful of this deception. It is a management-by-participation approach. The team participates in making recommendations to management regarding a problem, and management makes the decision. For example, a division director had to implement new personnel policies required by the State of Florida. To do so, he implemented what he called TQM teams. These teams got together and obviously developed personnel policies that favored the associates of the organization, and if implemented by top management, would cost 20 times what the budget would allow. These teams were obviously trying to make government work to their benefit. When they reported their findings to the Secretary, Deputy Secretary, and division managers, they became upset when their ideas were rejected.

Many of the people who participated on these teams represented their personnel departments which had a very poor record of TQM participation. They now took the position that they participated in TQM, and it was clear what would happen. Management had empowered them, but then when their ideas were proposed, their ideas were rejected. Their conclusion— don't participate in TQM. By his actions the division director just threw up another roadblock for us to go around.

Team members who volunteered to improve specific processes were often eager to start, but lost much of their enthusiasm during team meetings. They were not prepared for the difficulties that confronted them during team meetings. They needed a lot of help and what was amazing is that they received it. Volunteers from throughout the organization crossed division lines to help teams get started. One bureau chief in the Division of Unemployment Compensation became an expert on flowcharting, another leader became an expert on facilitation, another in team dynamics, and one of the trainers in the Training Development area stepped forward as a specialist in customer service. It was truly amazing how much talent there is in an organization when people are given an opportunity to develop their skills. Even though practically every team leader wished that they had training prior to their process improvement meetings, most of them were very effective in achieving their process improvement goals.

At about the same time that the teams were forming, it became rather obvious that the divisions would all be moving at a different pace. One division, Unemployment Compensation, jumped out in front. The division director and the bureau chiefs were strong supporters of TQM. On the other hand, the Division of Labor, Employment, and Training gave no indication that they had any interest at all in TQM. In fact, it appears as though they'd built a fort around their division to make sure that anyone with a positive attitude towards TQM would not be admitted.

Phase 6: Internal Consultants

Although there was activity in Total Quality Management within the Department, the Deputy Secretary was having a problem tracking and understanding all of the activities. Therefore, he brought together a team of associates representing all of the divisions that had already demonstrated their enthusiasm for TQM. These volunteers maintained their regular assigned duties and, at the same time, were willing to help the Deputy Secretary implement TQM.

Meetings were every Monday morning for the purpose of tracking progress and initiating actions to advance the TQM initiative. Each of the consultants was assigned to a division other than the one they worked for. Their job was to meet with the division director to which they were assigned and assist the division director in implementing TQM. This proved to be one of the most effective steps in our implementation plan. Since the Deputy Director had had considerable experience as an external consultant and one year at Honeywell Space Systems as an internal consultant, he understood the difficult task of each of the internal consultants' assignment.

With one exception, the division directors gave the appearance that they truly appreciated the internal consultants. Their support for the internal consultants was a significant hurdle in our advancement. We were able to make significant progress in most of the divisions.

The Monday morning meetings which started promptly at 8:00 and were to be finished by 9:00 became marathon meetings. Each consultant would pose questions or problems that they were experiencing in their division, and the rest of the consultants would give advice on how we should approach these problems. This meeting also served another important purpose. Implementing change requires lots of support. Therefore, our morning sessions usually began with generalizations on how people felt about their progress. In practically every meeting, one of the internal consultants would be discouraged, and other team members had to help boost morale.

Further, it seemed like in every meeting one of the team members would bring to the meeting information about TQM that enhanced our understanding of the subject. Therefore, it also served as an educational program. Finally, we developed our approaches to initiating change at all levels of the organization that proved to be very effective. For example, we set up the training program for the department. Even though we had a Training Department, most of the trainers were very slow to get involved in TQM.

With one exception, the trainers gave the impression that they wanted to continue teaching traditional training programs that dealt with best practices, motivation, communication, stress management, managing difficult employees, managing difficult customers, etc. The internal consultants concluded that either the Training Department got involved with TQM or that each of the divisions will have to do their own training. Practically all of the training for TQM was being conducted by volunteers who had other jobs to do. Once the internal consultants developed the curriculum, however, the Training Department got aboard and proved to be extremely effective in meeting or exceeding the educational needs of their customers.

Phase 7: "Just-in-Time" Training

As the continual process improvement teams began to make progress, they immediately began demanding training. Our approach all along was to only offer training to those who wanted it. Our training focused only on those who wanted to volunteer. We only wanted associates in class who saw the need for their own personal development and wanted skills that would help them achieve success with their teams. We were amazed at how many people came forward. Many of the associates who asked for training did so without the support of their managers.

Since many of the division directors were strongly behind TQM at this point, the managers who worked for them were put in a difficult situation if the manager was working against the TQM initiative. Their subordinates knew this and concluded that their manager was unable to block their activities if they persisted. Many of the managers who were against TQM were hoping that the teams would fail and that then they could go back to controlling people, not processes. We were fortunate that so many front-line associates came forward, probably because the managers in government do not control salary increases (all associates receive the same percentage increase granted by the Legislature), and most managers in government aren't willing to put forth the energy required to terminate an associate.

Our TQM training focused on what our customers demanded. Our goal was to meet or exceed their expectations. We taught them five basic TQM courses. The courses were taught by instructors from the department's human resource bureau, as well as several internal consultants and process improvement guides throughout the state.

Our instructors were given extremely high ratings, and demand for training was so heavy that our Training Department could not meet all of the requests. They had to go back and ask the volunteers who helped us get started in training for their services. Having an effective training program is a must for a successful TQM initiative.

TQM Trainers as Change Agents

As training progressed, it became more and more obvious how important the trainers were for TQM success. Some leaders were becoming impatient with the lack of activity on the part of their associates and began to require their participation. The trainers were instructed to start each session with the question, "Are you all volunteers? If not, raise your hands." In practically every session a number of hands would go up, and the trainer then asked them to leave. The associates would then say that they were forced to be in the session, that they would like to leave but were afraid to. The trainer then would ask the associates the reasons for their feelings, and in most cases associates replied that their manager ordered them to come to the course. The trainer then would even volunteer to call the manager and tell them that it was not supposed to be mandatory. However, the associate would give up and stay in the class.

Then the trainer had an extra difficult challenge. Trainers not only have to teach the people that want to be there, but they have to deal with people who have a negative attitude and who are generally cynical about TQM. Therefore, trainers have to change their approach and work through all of the cynicism that's in the class before they can even begin teaching.

When the Deputy Secretary asked trainers where they had been, they would respond, "Taking arrows for you." The Deputy Secretary, realizing how difficult TQM training was in the department, met from time to time with the trainers. These became valuable sessions. Also, the internal consultants met with the trainers to provide the trainers feedback about their effectiveness and at the same time learn more about the divisions to which they were assigned. The training sessions became a valuable source of communication. Eventually, the director of training was invited to the internal consultant meetings and became a permanent member.

Phase 8: Submarine Attack

In an interview with a front-line worker who strongly endorsed TQM, the interviewee indicated that there was just too much dead wood in her division, and then she said, "If we did everything right the first time, there would be a lot of people out of a job." Her statement accurately describes why so many people in government fear Total Quality Management. Government inefficiency produces a lot of jobs. Another fear is that someone will find out there are too many managers and do something about it. Because of these fears, there are many associates out to derail TQM. These fears, along with the normal fear of the unknown that is a natural response to change, force leaders to take many different approaches to change.

One of our best approaches, which we called the Submarine Approach, starts with the customer. It begins by analyzing customer needs to see how the organization can be structured to meet those needs. For example, for people to get their unemployment checks, they had to first go to one of the offices in the

Division of Unemployment Compensation to sign up for benefits. Then, to prove that they were looking for a job, which is required of most people who ask for unemployment benefits, they had to go to job services, which is part of another division within the Department of Labor and Employment Security. Job Services is usually located in another office and required the customer to complete practically the same form that they completed when they signed up for unemployment benefits.

Prior to implementing TQM, it could take as much as three or four hours to get signed up for unemployment benefits alone (in one of the offices, if one didn't get to the unemployment office by 9:00 A.M. that morning, it was doubtful that the paperwork would be processed that day). Then on to another office the next day to wait in line, and do practically the same task as the previous day. When we put customers first, we developed a system that accommodated their needs, not the department's. Now the customer comes to one site, has one interview, and is free to start looking for a job. What used to take two days and many hours now takes less than 15 minutes in many of the offices and no more than an hour in most of the offices.

For years the department treated the customer as if he was "trapped," and the only way to cope with the trap was to go along with a system that was designed more for workers' convenience than for the customer's convenience. To merge these services and cross-train all front-line associates took a little more than two years. Even though the managers knew that this was one of the Secretary's highest priorities, many failed to do anything to support this change, and it wasn't until the Secretary showed her impatience with how slow the process was going did all of the managers get aboard and make the merged services work.

The Deputy Secretary saw how slow it was going and asked to take over the management of a pilot project known as the Tampa Employment Service Center. His approach was to go directly to the front-line and ask them to make the changes. Even though a Big Six accounting firm had been sent in to show how to merge the services, management still rejected the change.

The managers would block the change by taking their time in cross-training front-line associates. The excuse for not implementing the change was that the associates were never trained. The Deputy Secretary decided to "submarine" the managers and met with the front-line associates. The Deputy Secretary then asked for volunteers to form teams to implement merged services. Out of 32 front-liners, 25 volunteered, and the Deputy Secretary then turned over to the management of the front-line processes to the front-liners. He then met with the managers and instructed them to find something else to do. Only one manager supported this move. He said that he had plenty to do and welcomed the teams by saying that, "If they can find a better way, more power to them."

There were 32 front-liners, and they had 11 managers. It was quite obvious that's why management was so slow in making this change. They were afraid they would lose their jobs. We assured our associates we were not out to terminate people, but rather place people in positions where we could get a better return on investment. We had a significant need in the area of finding and posting jobs and helping people to get into training and/or a job. There was plenty of work to be done if, as an organization, we became more effective at achieving our mission, which was returning people to work.

The submarine approach worked. The front-liners were very successful in shortening the process and reducing errors. We began using this approach throughout the organization, not just with front-liners, but at every level which we were having difficulties getting management to change. Submarining managers will work if one understands their processes and then begins expecting their divisions, bureaus, and offices to provide data on how well their teams are functioning and what improvements they are making.

It was interesting when we first asked the divisions to flowchart their processes and form teams that many of the divisions made up the teams by writing in an associate's name and submitting their team reports to the Deputy Secretary with the names of team members. When the Deputy Secretary would visit these teams, many times he would find out that the teams never even met. Many of these managers were trying to hang on to the past by doing what they had traditionally done over the years, and that is to meet or exceed the expectations of the person to whom they report. In the past, well written bureaucratic reports were all that was needed. Managers did not work for the customers they served, but worked for the people above them.

A lot of anonymous letters to the Governor, might result from the submarine tactic. For example, one person complained to the Governor that front-line associates were told that "Managers and supervisors are useless and not needed. Managers/supervisors are held accountable for the performance of local offices, but do not have the authority to manage/supervise their area of responsibility." Negative feedback should be evaluated carefully. If the negative feedback can help improve the process, use it and appreciate it. However, if the negative attack regards someone's personality, color, gender, or defense of how things used to be, ignore it.

Implementing TQM requires attack at all levels—top, middle, and bottom. We found the submarine approach to be a good one.

Phase 9: Quality Council

A full description of the Quality Council appears in Chapter Nine—Communication, Training, and Recognition. In that description we discuss the "nuts and bolts" of our Quality Council and provide copies of criteria used by the council to assess improvements, forms used by teams, etc.

The importance of the council to our success cannot be overstated. The council played a key role in directing and coordinating the department's continual improvement efforts in every way. The council not only provided structure to the new order, but proved that top management was serious about the changes to be made. We selected as members top administrators and managers (see Chapter Nine), but as importantly, people at every level including a "front-line" associate from each division. The message was clear_ all associates in the department were considered equally responsible for quality. Every council member had one vote, regardless of being a first line worker or the Secretary of the Department.

Not only was the message clear to members of the council that everyone was responsible for quality, but also that everyone's opinion on how the department would implement TQM was important. During the council's meetings, front-line associates, those individuals who served customers directly, also served on the council helping provide direction. Just a few examples of the subjects addressed by the council in their bi-weekly meetings were:

- The Mission of the Quality Council
- Customer Surveys
- Development of Team Feedback
- Training for Team Members
- Leadership Award Criteria
- Managing Baseline Data
- Quality Principles
- Automation of the Team Tracking System

The first meetings of the council were held at headquarters in the state capital because most of the early presentations to the council were made by teams in the central offices. As teams formed throughout the state later, the council held regular meetings in Miami, Orlando, Tampa and Jacksonville. Thus, associates throughout the state had the opportunity to make presentations to the council without the need for extended travel.

As the council held its meetings throughout the state, associates from every region had the opportunity to witness the key role the council played in every component of the Department from personnel and training through budgeting, strategic planning and even the recruitment of new associates. It was obvious that everyone in the department was represented on the council and that they had a voice on its direction. The number of teams continued to grow throughout the state as a direct result of the visibility of the council.

Phase 10: The Quality Council as the Instrument of Change

One of the most effective methods of change was developed by one of our regional managers. She rotated the management of each office in her region. This maybe the fastest method for implementing TQM. In her region, there were only a few managers who practiced the beliefs and principles of TQM. And, therefore, she only had a few offices that were trying to meet or exceed customer expectations. The TQM managers had exemplary offices and were held up as models. But even holding up an office as a model of quality will not stimulate other managers in government to change. Most government managers flippantly disregard change efforts by others with an old phrase, "It won't work here."

For years, government managers have gotten away with poor results and have successfully fought efforts to change process. The assumption behind rotating managers is that if associates at the front-line become exposed to quality management and learn that customer service, data, process improvement, and teams are the driving forces, and then another manager comes in and tries to control them and not the processes, he or she would fail. Although the regional manager was heavily criticized for using the rotating system, and it even stimulated one of the managers to write the Governor, of course anonymously, complaining about "This authoritarian method," the approach proved to be a very effective change strategy, and we would recommend its use.

Below is a letter we received from one of the associates who happened to be in one of the offices where we rotated managers. The results speak for themselves.

Deputy Secretary
Dept. of Labor and Employment Security
303 Hartman Building
2012 Capital Circle, SE
Tallahassee, FL 32399-2161

Dear Deputy Secretary:

I wanted to share a little excitement with you regarding TQM. I attended the PIG training in September, 1994. Thank you, it was great! I returned home full of enthusiasm with new ideas and reported to a PIG Manager. This one is really walking the talk.

Within the week a huge 3-color banner appeared in our office that proclaimed:

"Celebration!!! Let's all Celebrate! Last Month
this Office Assisted 275 Customers Find Jobs."

Not bad for a small rural office with a placement goal of 182–214. Next, a cow bell showed up on the counter, and associates were encouraged to ring it when they had performed a quality service or made a placement.

Prior to his coming to this office, we were a typical state employment office. We had four paper teams that had been created by drawing names out of a hat and working on whatever management told us to. Needless to say, we had accomplished very little.

One of the first actions was to make team membership voluntary. No one left. Then the teams were encouraged to reorganize based on interest and knowledge. The teams were advised of their right to change names and take ownership of the teams. They did.

Consequently, we now have three teams doing what they want to do with whom they want to do it. All three teams are moving at a swift pace and yes, this little piggy is excited. We really do have associates coming to work with smiles on their faces.

The reason I want you to know this is because several weeks ago I had an appointment with a very smart lady who was depressed. During the interview, without being malicious, she stated she had noticed our staff was more depressed than she was. She explained by saying "Look out there on your counter — two need antidepressants and one looks like he was just hired and he's still smiling." I walked out to the front and saw that she was exactly right. Then I got depressed.

Last week another gentleman came into my office for counseling. During the conversation he said "I've been going to another Job Service that is closer to my home. But when I came in here and saw this office bragging about their placements and all of the staff smiling, I knew I was in the right place." Again, I walked out to the front and took a look for myself. Guess what, same three people, only they were now happy and smiling. This office is becoming a quality workplace.

The PIG Manager is Ken Castillo. In less than four weeks he has introduced a new TQM into this office and made it fun and creative. He has empowered the associates, and they have responded with enthusiasm. Could you please find a Recognition Award for Ken? I can't think of anyone more deserving.

Once again, I would like to thank you and Ken for your guidance and assistance. As I look around, I can truthfully say that I am proud to work for the Department of Labor.

Sincerely,
Caroline E. Hanley
Employment and Training Counselor

IMPLEMENTATION OF TQM—PART 2

Changing a traditional management-by-objectives organization to a TQM system is similar to planting the Chinese bamboo tree.

The Chinese bamboo tree grows from a very hard nut. According to an article in *National Geographic*, it takes the Chinese bamboo tree approximately five years until it sprouts and begins to grow. During those five years, the nut requires watering, fertilizing, and nurturing everyday. And if during that five-year period, the nut misses a single day of watering, fertilizing, or nurturing, it dies in the ground. After five years, if the nut has received the necessary watering, fertilizing and nurturing, then within six weeks, the bamboo tree grows to over 90 feet tall.

Implementing Total Quality Management can be thought of as a similar process. Each day the beliefs and principles infuse the culture. Associates are constantly reminded about the basic tenets of TQM. The process begins by disseminating TQM concepts throughout the organization. Associates gradually begin thinking about processes and not about specific tasks. Associates begin thinking about customers and how they may meet and exceed their expectations and not about how they are going to satisfy their superiors. Associates begin thinking about how they can gather meaningful data, data that helps them improve processes and not just data put together for senior management. Associates begin thinking about how they can use Total Quality Management tools to improve their processes, rather than to focus on traditional data processing requirements of the department. Eventually associates understand that if the organization is going to improve its processes, then each associate must grow professionally. Like the Chinese bamboo tree, it takes time to nurture associates, bring them along slowly, and after a time, the associates will grow dramatically and so will quality grow in the organization.

Office of Prevention

After approximately eight months into our TQM initiative, an auditor, seeing the need for prevention rather than detection, volunteered her services to begin focusing on prevention rather than detection. We welcomed her attitude and her creativity. She was assigned to begin preventing problems in the Division of Administrative Services. It wasn't long before we realized how valuable this person was to the organization. She was able to uncover significant problems that eventually would have led to an audit and an audit criticism. Her skills were phenomenal. She was able to show the organization how, if it continued in its direction, it would experience significant losses in the time it took subordinates to do things, significant losses in rework, and potential losses in money. She initiated activity-based costing.

The Department of Labor and Employment Security captures costs in two accounting systems. The first is the State Automated Management Accounting System (SAMAS). This is a statewide general ledger system based on the organization charts. The second system, used by the department, is referred to as the Grant Automated Management Accounting System (GAMAS), which is a combination of the SAMAS Grant Accounting Subsystem and a cost allocation system used by the department. The system's purpose is to assign costs to the department's various funding sources (grants/contracts, etc.). The system includes a time distribution subsystem by which all personal service charges (salaries and benefits) are directly charged to a funding source. The time charges in each organization code become the factor by which all costs which are not direct charged to a funding source are allocated. Neither one of these accounting systems provides process or activity based cost data. In order to provide management with the information about what causes costs within an organization, process analysis must be coupled with activity-based costing.

Activity-based costing is a relatively new accounting technique used to determine the cost associated with processes and/or products. Activity-based costing performed in conjunction with process analysis provides the cause of costs and with this information available, the means to manage these costs. Our department tested the use of activity-based costing in the vendor payment process. We would expect activity-based costing that is performed after a detailed process analysis to provide the following: (1) cost of performing this process, information which is necessary to adequately evaluate the cost effectiveness of alternatives such as privatization; (2) causes of costs, particularly overhead costs, which will supply the support needed for cost reduction; and (3) an ongoing basis by which management can measure performance.

The implementation of activity-based accounting was exactly the right thing to do at the right time. The problem, however, came when another government organization realized that the auditor had talents that went beyond auditing, and she was recruited for a top flight managerial position. Her efforts, however, did not go unnoticed by the Inspector General and the auditing office. When the Inspector General took over the management of the auditors as well as his own Division, he proclaimed that the role of the Inspector General, as well as auditors, is to prevent problems and not just detect problems.

We believe that the Office of the Inspector General and the auditors should become a part of the senior management team and play a significant role in prevention rather than detection. We also believe that activity-based costing has promise in government and needs further development.

Data Measurements, Data Processing and Data Management

We realized that if we were going to change government to adopt a TQM approach, then we had to become involved in changing the present information systems approach. Prior to TQM, the goal was to see how much data could be generated for the main frame computer. The Division of Information Management Systems employed over 250 people to write programs and maintain the mainframe computer. Millions of dollars were spent each year to collect data and to develop an information system, it seemed as though the data collected was generally never accurate, nor was it useful. The data collected, however, seemed to fulfill the objective at the time—to generate reports for the organizations that funded the Department of Labor and Employment Security. The objective seemed to be to collect as much data as possible and then disseminate the data with a rational explanation that met the needs of the intended reader.

Even though the organization had getting jobs as its objective, we were never satisfied that the data was accurate or properly reflected the efforts of our front-line associates. Furthermore, the data, even though it was accepted by many organizations such as the legislative staff, Governor's Office of Budget, and the federal government, etc. was challenged regularly. For example, when the department was a pilot program for the State of Florida, the Department reported data that showed we saved the State of Florida government millions of dollars. However, when we were audited by various agencies, our data was heavily criticized, and our departmental image fell significantly because it was difficult to determine the accuracy of the data and its reliability.

When we initiated TQM, senior management began to become increasingly uneasy. In fact, a few senior managers told me that if we accurately collect our data, it could have a far-reaching negative effect on the department. They offered that since the federal government is satisfied with the data, then why change?

Changing the way data is collected and interpreted may just be one of the single biggest barriers to implementing TQM in government. One top government administrator, for example, said, "If they find out what we're really doing, they won't fund us next year." This is a difficult barrier to overcome. Consequently, TQM requires working past these attitudes, since it relies on data-based decisions rather than gut-level feelings. Total Quality Management systems rely on statistical methods to measure and analyze the degree of process control in order to identify and implement process improvements, and thereby prevent defective goods and poor customer service.

Government has relied on "visible numbers only" and on management by objectives. The system is designed to reward or punish government workers based on how they produce in relationship to other workers. This method fosters an environment of fear and of competition, and often leads to job dissatisfaction and poor quality of work.

In TQM, the data drives decisions, and measurements determine if a process is in control or out of control. Data measurements are necessary to define the process even before changes are attempted. This is a difficult challenge since most associates in government often fear the process of determining what they "really do."

It often takes three or four serious attempts and approaches just to get associates to collect accurate data regarding a process. When a team is first approached about making quality improvements, they will immediately provide solutions. However, teams shouldn't become solution oriented as soon as they start. They first have to collect the data so that baseline data can be developed to evaluate the effects of the improvement. The effects of the change, once implemented, should be measured,. The success of process improvements depends largely on data and measurements.

When we first approached the Information Management Systems division on helping us to change the attitude of our associates and to work closely with us to initiate a TQM environment, we received practically no assistance. It was obvious from the beginning that the programmers and maintainers of the mainframe wanted to be "left alone." They took on the attitude of "If you'll just leave us alone, we will get the work done."

Therefore, we made a change in leadership. We developed a new position entitled Chief Information Officer and hired an individual who understood TQM and how computer specialists could be helpful in the TQM initiative. One of the first actions taken by the new Chief Information Officer was to set up customer councils in each of the divisions. These customer councils determined the priorities and plans for the Information Management Systems Division. He set the tone for a "new way of thinking." Changing the mentality of over 250 computer specialists is like planting a bamboo tree—it's a very slow process. It was an even a slower process since all of the personnel, with only two exceptions, were protected by career service. We are making progress in this area, and over the years this division will be customer-oriented.

Perhaps what was most interesting about making this change in the Information Management Systems was the reluctance on the part of computer specialists to collect meaningful data regarding their work. Although the computer specialists constantly complained that they were overworked and underpaid, they never collected data that would show their claims to be true, even though the senior management of our department probably agreed with them. They had many excuses, and perhaps the one they cited most was that their customers were always changing their priorities, yet the computer specialists never had time to collect the data to prove their claim. Under the direction of the new Chief Information Officer, a system was implemented that began gathering data that allowed us to make improvement in this vital area.

Changing Government—Pushing a Bus That's Stuck

Changing government is like pushing a bus that's stuck. Government, in this case, is the bus, and the people in it are the employees of state government. The drivers are the Legislature and the Executive Branch. Outside of the bus are the taxpayers who have an opportunity every two to four years to change the drivers. Since the taxpayers know that the bus does have a purpose and that the people inside of the bus provide services that are needed, the taxpayers bring the government employees food and gas for the bus in hopes that the bus will get going.

The people who need the services realize that they have to go to the bus to get what they need because the bus will not go to them. The employees in the bus know that they could provide better service; however, they feel like they are abused by their customers and are not paid a decent wage. Furthermore, the people in the bus are complaining that they, themselves are not moving up or going anywhere either. Also, they like to blame the drivers of the bus for being stuck. The drivers of the bus are constantly criticizing them, often running on platforms that they are going to reduce the employee size, and they have little respect for each other. In years past, the drivers have said they were going to do something to help the bus get out of its rut; however, the drivers actually added more people to the bus so the bus got heavier and heavier. The taxpayers bring more food and gas, the customer begs for customer service, the employees continue to complain, the drivers continue to ignore them, and the taxpayers hope that something will change.

The employees are afraid to get out of the bus and push. It may happen that the bus starts to move in a positive direction and that the management systems in government become effective and, consequently, many lose their jobs. The employees know that the elected drivers don't know how to get the bus going. They have been changing gears and pushing on the accelerator for years, and nothing has changed. In fact, the more they change gears and the more they hit the accelerator, the more government becomes larger and ineffective. Therefore, when one of the state employees suggests that change is imminent and it's time that the state employees get off the bus and make some changes for the betterment of government, the employee is heavily criticized.

Government employees often lose sight of the primary purpose of government. Rather than government existing to provide services for the taxpayers, many government workers have the attitude that government exists for their convenience. The purpose of the bus is to haul state employees around; therefore, when one suggests a system of management that is contrary to government employee convenience, the person takes significant risk. It is difficult to get the state employees to want to push the bus. Furthermore, it is just as difficult to get the drivers to understand that if they continue with the way they are presently driving the bus, the bus will not move. Consequently, it would take a major shift in thinking both by the drivers and the employees to move the bus. Both the drivers and the employees need to become process thinkers, process improvers, and customer driven.

Driving Out Fear

W. Edwards Deming points out that for Total Quality Management to be successful we must drive out fear in the workforce. During Japan's rise to becoming a world class competitor, the companies in Japan were able to guarantee lifetime employment to their employees. This helped Japanese corporations enormously since their employees were assured that if they improved the process, they would not be out of a job.

We were fortunate in the Department of Labor and Employment Security in Florida that we could make a statement that we were not going to replace people if they improved a process. However, we did not guarantee people that they would be able to keep the jobs that they have, but rather we would find them a position in the organization. Since the Florida Department of Labor and Employment Security had a need for more employees to help our customers find jobs, we knew that we could place people in job finding positions. However, whatever assurances that we made mostly fell on deaf ears. Many people were afraid to change. Most state workers tend not to trust people above them.

Furthermore, it's just not a matter of front-line associates trusting or distrusting management, but it is management throughout the organization that distrusts the Executive Branch, the Legislative Branch, and government political appointees. Therefore, even though we were able to make a significant statement of guaranteeing people that they would not lose their jobs, we were not successful in driving out fear.

It is interesting that in government where employees have significant rights barring any catastrophic mistakes, such as stealing or intentional misuse of funds, employees are afraid to make improvements because it may result in a loss of their jobs. Rather than putting the customer first, state employees will often put themselves first. Even though we appreciate Deming's eighth point of driving out fear, we are not sure that it is worth all of the effort it takes to drive out fear in government. In fact, from our experience, we believe that fear may be a positive development in implementing TQM.

Instilling Fear

The only way to motivate some people in government to change is to scare them. In fact, it just may be that the best, most effective way to implement TQM in government is to institute a freeze on hiring. This sends a message to all state employees that there is a better way to do business.

The public is fed up with government and is asking government to change. If government doesn't change, the options are raising taxes, hiring freezes, delaying capital projects, cutting back on public service, layoffs, salary cuts or privatizing processes and services. It is unlikely that the public is going to continue with the first option of raising taxes. Therefore, to avoid the other options, which all come at the inconvenience of people who work in government, we believe that Total Quality Management is the most effective response. Therefore, we instituted in some cases "fear in the workplace." We were not sure about the effects of instituting fear, but we know that, for many people, we got their attention.

Appealing to Fairness

Perhaps, our most effective means of persuading government associates to change was our appeal to fairness, the right-thing-to-do attitude. There are many people in government who also see themselves as taxpayers. There are many people who also see themselves as loyal Americans. They believe that instituting a better way to conduct government business is in the best interest of all Americans, including themselves. These are the people who will improve a process and suffer the consequences if necessary. We have observed teams who develop systems that in the long run would mean that some of them would have to find different jobs or, as a consequence of their work, their budget would decrease rather than increase. Of course, when we observed associates willing to make personal sacrifices for the betterment of their government, the top management team took the position that there will always be a place in the organization for quality people, and some of them even got promotions. Our appeals that TQM was the right thing to do for government were heard by many associates. One associate remarked, "I have worked in government for 30 years, and this is the first time (after TQM) I've felt good about what I am doing. I wish we had had TQM 30 years ago."

The frustration of doing rework, correcting mistakes day in and out, seeing money wasted, seeing people frustrated and being frustrated provides motivation for change to TQM. There are many people in government who are willing to change for the benefit of the customers government serves. Appealing to these people is an effective method for change.

Overcoming Trickle Down Fear

At the initial stage of TQM implementation, there will be associates who will openly reject TQM. Even though it's annoying to deal with the associates' outright rejection it is not as irritating as trying to persuade those who aren't as forthright. These people present a difficult obstacle. They pretend to understand TQM and that it might work in the workplace, but they do very little to help the TQM initiative.

Most of the associates who give the impression that they are accepting TQM, but in reality are rejecting it, are top managers. They are people who are in powerful positions and see TQM as a process that interferes with their need to control other people. There are many people in top management in government who have an extremely high need to control people and not necessarily processes. They focus on "getting people in line," and their approach to management is that if people will do what they are told to do, the organization will be effective.

They reject the notion that the system is the problem and not the people. In fact, leaders who have a high need to control people say that the system would be much better if they could hire more people, hire better people, and pay them more. They reject the principles of TQM, but are fearful of losing their power if they don't appear to go along with the TQM initiative. Therefore, their strategy is to derail the TQM effort by controlling the people below them. They use a method we call "trickle down fear."

The top managers who use the trickle-down-fear approach do so by instilling fear into the associates who report to them. They may openly tell their associates that TQM is a high priority in the department, but then say that meeting production goals better not go down as a result of TQM. For example, one top manager who gave the appearance that he was for TQM, told those people reporting to him that they could go ahead and meet as teams, but there "better not be any loss of production any week they have a team meeting." Also, they may inject other negative stimuli, such as, "remember the federal government requires quotas, therefore get all your reports to me on time or someone will pay." The manager may go on to say, "If you get your quotas completed, then you can spend time on TQM."

The associates who report to managers who have an excessive need to control people become extremely frustrated by TQM. They get mixed signals. They get a signal from the department that teams can form to improve their processes, but if they take the risk of forming a team they will not have the support of their managers. The trickle-down-fear approach is a very effective method of sabotaging TQM.

To overcome the sabotage, we instituted the submarine approach to change described earlier in this chapter.

One of the most effective submarine methods we used was to visit offices throughout the state. When we visited these offices, we would soon find out that top management did not truly support TQM. When top managers found out that we might be visiting some of the offices that they were responsible for, they would order the managers of those offices to make up displays to show that this office was participating in the TQM initiative. In fact, when a memorandum went out to all divisions that the Secretary and the Deputy Secretary would be visiting offices to review their progress in TQM, the top managers who were appearing to be going along with the TQM initiative, but rejecting TQM, ordered all of the offices to generate data and display data that would persuade the Secretary and the Deputy Secretary that TQM was "happening" in that office.

Many associates in these offices became angry by this phony display and the extra work required of them just to impress the Secretary and the Deputy Secretary. These associates found ways to complain so that it was easy for the Secretary and the Deputy Secretary to determine which top managers were supporting the department's TQM initiative and those who were not. Even though the Secretary and Deputy Secretary were not always able to remove leaders who did not support them, they made it very difficult for top management to continue with their behavior.

Subordinate Evaluations

One of the most effective methods of determining whether managers are supporting a TQM initiative is to have subordinates evaluate their managers. It provides a true perspective of which managers truly support the TQM initiative.

Management Expectations—Job Description

One of the most effective methods of instituting change is to describe the behaviors expected from leaders. In our efforts to initiate TQM in the Department, we waited too long to use job descriptions as an instrument of change. We were into our initiative for more than two years before we clearly defined the manager's role in TQM. Clearly outlining what is expected from them is not only an effective instrument of change but it's also good management practice.

We would advise any organization that is implementing TQM to address management performance expectations early in the initiative. When we instituted the management performance expectations, we received some resistance. It was easy to determine which of our top executive managers were on board and those who weren't. Those who initiated the management performance expectations immediately gave a clear signal that they were on board. Those who found many excuses not to implement the performance expectations were clearly resisting TQM. Some senior management made statements to the effect that they would implement the performance expectations when they "felt like it." This was a clear indication of which divisions were moving forward and those that were resisting.

Since it is very difficult to remove even top management in government who are not supporting departmental management policies, establish ways to work around them. By being persistent and maintaining what Deming refers to as "constancy of purpose" even top management resistance can be overcome.

Enlightenment

In the movie *Rising Sun*, a Japanese character says, "When Americans find something wrong, they look to blame someone. In Japan when they find something wrong, they look to improve the process." In changing an organization from traditional management practices to Total Quality Management, there is often tremendous resistance. The approach to dealing with resistance can take two extremes—enlightenment or punishment.

It is tempting to try to punish those who provide barriers to change. It is easy to say, "If I could only remove that person, we could be successful." Removing an individual, first of all, is not always an option. Second, a better option is one of enlightenment, to work with people to see whether they can change their management perspective. They should be provided with opportunities to learn more about and work within TQM on a daily basis so that they can conclude that TQM is an effective management system.

In the beginning of a TQM initiative, most people are not willing to accept TQM beliefs and principles. It takes time. The best approach to change is enlightenment. Time should be spent convincing associates that the goal is to meet or exceed customers' expectations and the best way to do that is to improve processes, collect data, and work in teams. Thomas Jefferson was correct when he said that a democracy can only survive if it is composed of people who are enlightened. Similarly, TQM will survive only if all associates are educated and understand the principles of TQM.

Jefferson felt that if leaders were faced with the choice between enlightening the ignorant or punishing the ignorant, there was only one solution and that was one of enlightenment. When Jefferson spoke of enlightenment, there were many people who believed that only the rich and the brightest knew what was best for all people and therefore only the rich and the brightest needed to be enlightened. The ones who were not enlightened were told what to do, and if they didn't do what they were told to do, they were punished. The same applies to TQM. There are still many people in organizations who believe that only those who are at the top of the organization know what's best for all people.

Eventually with the evolution of TQM in the organization, these attitudes will be dispelled, and all associates will come to the conclusion that an enlightened workforce is the most effective workforce.

Publishing a Departmental TQM Booklet

Breaking the mold in government is not an easy task. It requires persistent verbal and nonverbal communication. One of the most effective methods of change is to prepare a short booklet describing the change the organization is attempting to initiate. Soon after we began implementing TQM, the co-authors published a short booklet that described TQM beliefs, principles, and tools. Since the booklet was very brief and easy to read, many associates requested the book. We did not dispense the book to all associates, but rather distributed it at training seminars and then tracked requests made by associates.

We first began to realize that we were having a significant impact upon the culture when about two to three months after we published the booklet, there was a huge demand for the booklet in the department. We recommend to any organization that is initiating TQM that one of the first actions that organization takes is to publish a simple, readable book that clearly states the beliefs and principles of TQM.

Knowing and Understanding Key Processes

A late convert and an early critic of TQM introduced the Deputy Secretary to a large group of associates by saying, "Even though I gave resistance to TQM and the notions of the Deputy Secretary when I first came aboard, the one thing I did admire about the Deputy Secretary was that he started out by first learning our processes, rather than coming into the department with ideas on how he was going to change our department without knowing what we do. He first found out what we did and then focused on helping us to improve the way we do work."

We recommend that this is perhaps the only approach to changing an organization. It requires a lot of work to understand how work gets done in any organization. We believe the best way to understand the processes in the organization is to be able to explain them. To begin by understanding how work is done and how work flows is extremely important.

The Process of Change

Our approach to planned organizational change followed the model developed by Curt Lewin, where he suggested unfreezing the culture, changing the culture, and then refreezing the culture. We would estimate that it took approximately one year just to "unfreeze" the thinking of most of the associates in our organization. It was in the second year that we actually began to change to a TQM culture. It's difficult to project when the organization would ever reach the point where TQM was so successful that we could refreeze the environment.

Our approach to change began with a vision of what the organization should look like in the future, its future state. Then we analyzed the present state, and from there developed a plan on how we could move from the present state to the future state. To make the transition from the present state to the future state, we continually developed hypotheses and tested them along the way.

Organization Structure

The potential for using the organization structure as a potential instrument of change has significant merit in the workplace. However, we decided intentionally not to focus on structure, but rather allow structure to follow naturally. Our rationale was that government is constantly being changed by top management, and one of the simplest methods top management can use is to restructure the organization. We felt that any significant attempt at reorganization during our TQM initiative would only serve to distract focus. It would give top managers a good feeling that if we reorganized, they were still in control of people. Since we wanted to assist managers in becoming process focused rather than people controllers, we made every effort to stay away from reorganization. However, as divisions began improving their processes, they made small incremental changes in structure.

Associates: Investing in Themselves

One of our change strategies was to assist all associates in understanding the effects of change on them personally. Most people in government respond like a frog who is placed in a kettle of warm water. If you continually increase the heat to the point where the water is boiling, the frog will not jump out and will become a victim of the boiling water. On the other hand if you take a frog and throw it into boiling water, it will immediately jump out.

Government employees tend to respond the same way. When hit with immediate change, they respond quickly and intelligently. For example, when catastrophes occurred in Florida such as Hurricane Andrew or the closing of a major company, the personnel in the Department of Labor and Employment Security responded in an almost unbelievable manner. State workers are proud to work all night, proud to handle extremely difficult situations, work together magnificently, and use their brains to serve their customers. They do all of this without complaining.

On the other hand, when the same personnel approach day-to-day work in the department, they spend much of their time doing routine tasks without putting forth significant energy to improve what they are doing, to increase customer satisfaction, or making personal improvements in themselves. The daily routine is to do their work, complain, make fun of management, and frequently lament on why they are not paid more.

Like the frog that's placed in warm, soothing water only to be boiled, state workers frequently don't see how fast the world is changing and how quickly they may find out that they are without skills needed by government organizations. Many believe because of career service protection they will be able to whether the storm. Many state workers realize that technology is not a threat to their job and are willing to take the necessary steps to make technology a friend and not an enemy. On the other hand, others fear technology and believe it is the enemy, but either fail to realize or don't take the steps necessary to develop the skills that will help them cope with technology. Technology is beneficial if one has the requisite skills. Technology is an enemy to those who don't.

In our TQM initiative, we continually sent messages to all of our associates that if they were going to be prepared for work in today's environment, let alone the future, they needed to develop many new skills. We encouraged them to continue their education and develop themselves so they could assist organizations in improving quality. For state workers to be successful today, they must invest in themselves and be willing to put forth the energy required to learn.

Government workers want taxpayers to give them the recognition they deserve and pay them more. Some have an attitude that since the taxpayers don't appreciate them and the Legislature ignores their pay requests, then they will just take the easy road. We tried to point out that they may have been able to take the easy road in the past 30 years, but in the next decade if they ignored their own personal development, they would be out of luck.

We also appealed to our associates by discussing the enjoyment of learning and how learning the skills required of a TQM organization would not only be beneficial to their own career advancement, but that the concepts were exciting in themselves. We asked our associates to demand more education and training from their organization. We asked them to demand for themselves, to increase their own personal expectations about what they could personally achieve and make a commitment to improving themselves daily.

The Sterling Award

Applying for the Sterling Award was a very effective change strategy. In surveying the participants who participated in filling out the Sterling Award criteria, we found there are many positive results that come from having a team work together in evaluating their organization. Involving many people in analyzing an organization against quality criteria established by major quality award agencies is an effective method to bring about change in the organization.

Focus Groups

Focus groups consist of invited people to provide feedback about a process. For example, in our Division of Unemployment we assembled a representative group of customers to communicate with us on how well we were doing. We asked the group to evaluate our organization, and then tell us what we might do to better meet or exceed their expectations. Focus groups can be created for every process, not just customer service. The groups could be "suppliers," "suppliers and customers," or could be a group of people assembled just to focus on improving one specific part of a process. To make focus groups effective, we suggest the following: (1) invite people who are interested in improving processes; (2) establish a mission; (3) agree on fundamental values which will guide participants' behavior; (4) provide very brief reviews of recent data collected on quality indicators; (5) ask participants to review the organizations' strengths, weaknesses, and opportunities for improvements; (6) ask participants what actions are necessary to make improvements; (7) ask: "What is it that we are able to do better? and (8) ask: "What are behaviors you want to see? New skills? New processes? How will these be demonstrated?"

Benchmarking against Other Government Agencies

Benchmarking with the Sterling Award, Baldridge Award, Deming Criteria, etc., helps people measure their organization against criteria essential for a quality organization. Further, it helps develop internal benchmarks for monitoring customer satisfaction, continual improvement, the relationship with external suppliers, leadership, etc. Benchmarking is a process of measuring services, practices, and products against organizations that are recognized as the best in a specific category.

Baseline data, the information collected by an organization, is often compared to the benchmark. One of the problems that we experienced in our department was not only the lack of a benchmark, but the lack of baseline data to even establish a benchmark. Further, there was significant resistance by state workers to collect "meaningful" baseline data. Most workers felt they never had time to collect real data. Therefore, government is overloaded with mere guesses of what they really do. Furthermore, there seems to be no agreement between what the agency reports and what the computer printout shows when senior management raises questions about specific results.

Also, there are thousands of excuses as to why one office can't be compared to another office, one program with another, one agency with another, etc. Therefore, the department set out to develop baseline data that was meaningful. Then, we identified the benchmark within the state. This had an extremely positive effect. Even though there were thousands of excuses as to why offices throughout the state could not compete against the benchmark, it was very clear to all associates that we were going to recognize the office that did establish the benchmark and that we were going to be comparing each office to the benchmark.

What is difficult for a quality initiative is that government organizations are excellent at collecting lots of data, most of which is not meaningful and much of which is irrelevant to the quality initiative. For example, data may show how many jobs an agency has secured for customers. The data, however, is often difficult to break down into each office, and even after analyzing which offices got specific jobs, the offices that are shown to be doing a poor job will more than likely reject the data. They will claim that they counted the way they get jobs differently than the one that's ranked at the top. In other words, it just becomes management by excuses or what's also referred to as "management by mystery."

In a quality initiative, data is collected that's important to the customer, to processes, and to the team. When benchmarking begins, the organization members initially identify what they are trying to observe by asking the question, "What data outside the organization or outside the process is available and relevant in order to make a comparison?" The goal is to look outside the organization or process so that the effectiveness of the organization process can be measured against the best. In the Department of Labor and Employment Security, we looked at agencies within our state and to other states for comparison.

Our strategy was to form teams who would monitor data from many sources and establish what we referred to as "quality indicators." Once we identified relevant benchmarks, the team would start comparing our baseline data to the benchmark. This is not an easy task since benchmarking in government is relatively new. Even though government has significant baseline data, identifying benchmarks is relatively new.

One of the advantages of benchmarking is that it causes attention to the system that is doing an effective job. By highlighting those who do the best in state agencies, it draws attention to what can actually happen if one has an effective process. Other people in the state who do similar work may offer many excuses as to why they aren't as good as the office that establishes the benchmark. These excuses are probably acceptable to individuals, but they are not acceptable to a process improvement team. In fact, it's quite the contrary. The more often benchmarks are published, the more teams are energized to see if they can move towards establishing a new benchmark or at least compare favorably to the benchmark.

We recommend that in government benchmarking should be done initially, not against other agencies, but internally within a division. Then benchmarks should be published, discussed openly, and the teams that establish the benchmarks and those who compare favorably to the benchmarks should be recognized. In government, there are many agencies against which to compare, even if there is only one process in a department. For example, the travel process can easily be compared to the best travel process within the state. Each department should have established benchmarks for each process. It doesn't necessarily have to be a benchmark that's in another state or in another division. It's important to set a benchmark so that baseline data can be used to compare one process to another.

12 ORGANIZATION ASSESSMENT AND SUSTAINING TQM

"In God We Trust, All Others Must Use Data."

Assessing progress in implementing Total Quality Management is an ongoing activity. Daily assessments come mainly from observations from your TQM leaders who understand TQM beliefs and principles and are able to visualize a TQM organization. We believe that you should use internal observations, documented activities, internal surveys, and evaluations from external sources to evaluate progress.

Any organization that desires to implement TQM will be extremely interested in determining progress. At first only those members of the TQM planning team, which in our organization was referred to as the internal consultants, will be interested in charting initial progress. Later, as more and more associates become interested in the TQM initiative, organizational progress will become a frequent discussion at many meetings.

INTERNAL OBSERVATIONS

The following observations were tracked from the beginning of our TQM initiative:

I. Top Management

    A. Took the lead in creating a TQM environment.

    B. Encouraged change, innovation, and risk taking.

    C. Focused on continual improvement.

    D. Provided resources, time, and training to improve quality.

    E. Led by example.

F. Encouraged open communication.

G. Removed barriers for associate participation in TQM activities.

H. Established trust and encouraged cooperation.

I. Rewarded behavior that reflected TQM beliefs and principles.

J. Role modeled values.

K. Attended TQM training.

L. Recognized and reinforced associates who participated in TQM activities.

M. Communicated quality vision to associates.

N. Incorporated TQM beliefs and principles into organization goals and plans.

O. Participated on TQM teams.

P. Used TQM tools to gather data.

Q. Allowed data to drive decision-making in the organization.

II. Strategic Management

A. Short- and long-term goals established for quality improvement.

B. Managers-leaders held accountable for TQM.

C. Customer needs and expectations played an essential role in quality improvement planning process.

D. Resources allocated to support the quality initiative.

E. Core processes flow charted, and suppliers and customers identified for each process.

F. Continual improvement plans created with milestones.

G. Customers and key suppliers participated in improving organizational processes.

H. Software technology used to support continual improvement activities.

    I.   Associates, customers, and suppliers involved in the TQM planning process.

    J.   Planning performed by quality teams.

III. Measurement and Analysis

    A. Quality measures tracked and monitored.

    B. Quality measures used by associates to identify problems and to determine root causes.

    C. Quality measures used in the plan, do, check, and act cycle.

    D. Cycle-time reduction made a goal.

    E. Problems detected and documented at the earliest possible point.

    F. Data analysis performed on nonconforming areas.

    G. Supplier information recorded and tracked.

    H. Customer information and results recorded and tracked.

    I.   Key operating quality measures for processes monitored.

    J.   Internal support services, such as personnel, administrative services, monitored and tracked.

IV. Training

    A. Training designed to support the TQM vision.

    B. Requirements and goals of the corporation incorporated in all training programs.

    C. TQM training objectives assessed, documented, and periodically updated.

    D. Training budgeted.

    E. Training tracked.

    F. Training delivered just in time and evaluated for effectiveness.

    G. Training visibly supported by management.

    H. Orientation training established for new associates.

    I.   Organization created a structured curriculum for TQM training.

    J.   All associates received training.

    K. Associates believed that TQM training is important, useful, and effective.

V. Communication

    A. Associates understood and accepted vision.

    B. Leaders provided meaningful and timely feedback to their associates.

    C. Leaders wrote articles on TQM for organization newsletter.

    D. Leaders were accessible.

    E. Newsletter contained articles pertaining to TQM.

    F. Associates and teams shared continual improvement progress.

    G. Graphic displays of data and continual improvements provided.

    H. Evidence of the use of analytical techniques, such as Pareto analysis, highly visible.

    I. Organization values highly visible.

    J. Process requirements communicated to suppliers.

    K. Customer feedback encouraged and appreciated.

    L. Organization used effective and timely methods of communicating TQM quality progress.

VI. Recognition

    A. Continual improvement activities recognized and appreciated daily.

    B. Continual improvement teams formally recognized.

    C. TQM leaders recognized and rewarded as well.

    D. Team presentations before the Quality Council encouraged.

    E. Awards adequately reflected team effort.

    F. Celebration of small successes was common.

    G. Rewards and recognition were broad-based and innovative.

    H. Rewards and recognition encompassed all levels of the organization, were centered on team quality improvement.

VII. Performance Management

A. Evaluations of managers and associate performance focused on achievement of measurable quality improvements.

B. Quality criteria integrated with associate selection system.

C. Quality criteria integrated into performance appraisals.

VIII. Associate Empowerment and Teamwork

A. Culture supported associate involvement, contribution, and teamwork.

B. Teamwork provided a vehicle for cooperation and communication.

C. Associates had clear avenues for participation and involvement.

D. Hierarchies reduced in favor of cooperative teams and networks.

E. Quality improvements that require cross organization units met through cross-functional team cooperation.

F. Process improvement teams and cross-functional teams promoted optimization of the entire organization.

G. Organization members participated on quality improvement teams and contributed to the development and implementation of improvement plans.

H. Members of quality improvement teams participated in establishing performance measures, review processes, and made decisions that improved organizational processes.

I. Associates had a strong feeling of empowerment and team ownership of work processes.

J. Power, rewards, information, and knowledge moved to the lowest levels of the organization.

IX. Customer Focus

A. Met and satisfied internal and external customer expectations.

B. Customer perceptions of performance continually measured, evaluated, and documented.

C. Feedback data used to improve processes and services.

D. Measures of customer satisfaction were accurate, objective, reliable, and complete.

    E.   Trends in customer data tracked and used to make process improvements.

    F.   Associates' policies and organization procedures empowered customer contact.

X. *Quality Results*

    A.   Organizational processes benchmarked against the best.

    B.   Organization showed quantifiable improvements in processes.

    C.   Performance improved each year.

    D.   Quality indicators data showed marked improvements.

    E.   Outputs and outcomes compared favorably to other government organizations that have similar processes.

    F.   Errors and cycle time significantly reduced.

    G.   Customer expectations met or exceeded.

THE PRESIDENT'S QUALITY AWARD PROGRAM

One of the more effective assessment tools used in our TQM initiative was the President's Quality Award Program sponsored by the Federal Quality Institute. We used their award criteria in the development of our TQM initiative and to help us assess our quality progress. Their criteria embodied the core values and concepts of Total Quality Management as follows:

- Quality is defined by the customer.

- A focus on continual improvement is part of all operations and activities.

- Prevention of problems and waste is achieved through building quality into products, services, and processes.

- Success in meeting quality and performance goals depends on workforce quality and involvement.

- Senior management creates a customer orientation, clear and visible quality values, and high expectations.

- Reinforcement of values and expectations requires substantial personal commitment and involvement.

- Employees are valued and recognized for their involvement and accomplishments.

- Management decisions are made based upon reliable information, data, and analysis.

- Long-term commitments are made to customers, employees, suppliers, and the community.

- Public responsibilities are fulfilled.

- Partnerships are built with other agencies and the private sector to better accomplish overall goals.

STERLING AWARD APPLICATION

In 1995 the Division of Unemployment Compensation located in the Florida Department of Labor and Employment Security accepted the Sterling challenge. The Sterling challenge is sponsored by the State of Florida and its purpose is to recognize organizations who are successful in implementing Total Quality Management.

The Sterling challenge starts with a self-assessment document. The organization first assesses itself against the Sterling Award criteria as follows:

The Sterling Award Categories

Leadership

Senior executive's personal leadership and involvement in:

- creating and sustaining a focus on customers;

- making a visible commitment to quality;

- fostering a management system to guide the organization to excellence, and

- building quality values into the way the company operates.

Participation of union leaders in the above categories where applicable.

The organization's commitment to partnership and cooperation with employees, unions, customers, suppliers, and other organizations in the community at large.

Your organization's leadership in its public responsibilities, such as environmental protection and ethics.

Information and Analysis

The use and management of valid data and information to drive quality.

The adequacy of your data, information, and analysis system to enhance your organization's overall performance, including operational and comparative performance.

Strategic Quality Planning

Your organization's planning process.

How your organization integrates key quality and operational performance requirements into overall organization planning.

Your organization's short-term and long-term plans.

How quality and performance requirements are deployed, understood, and achieved in all work units.

Human Resource Excellence

The effectiveness of your organization's efforts to develop and realize the full potential of the workforce, including management.

Your organization's efforts to maintain a work environment conducive to full participation, empowerment, personal and organization growth, and cooperation between management and employees.

Management of Process Quality

The systematic processes used by the organization to pursue ever-higher quality and overall operational performance.

The key elements of process management, including:

- design and development of quality products, programs and services;

- management and continual improvement of process quality for all work units and suppliers;

- the organization's plans and actions to improve supplier quality; and

- regular assessment of systems, processes, products, programs and services.

Quality and Operational Results

Your organization's current quality levels and improvement trends, based on objective measures, over the past few years.

Overall operational, business process and support service performance results.

Supplier quality trends and comparisons.

Current quality and performance levels relative to those of competitors or similar providers.

Customer Focus and Satisfaction

Your organization's relationships with its customers (who may be students in the educational sector, patients in the health care sector, or constituents in the public sector).

Your organization's knowledge of and responsiveness to customer requirements.

Customer relationship management and methods to determine customer satisfaction.

Commitments made to customers to promote trust and confidence.

Current levels and recent trends in customer satisfaction.

Customer satisfaction relative to competitors or similar providers.

We accepted the Sterling challenge because we wanted to:

1. Demonstrate our commitment to Total Quality Management.

2. Focus on our customers by identifying their needs and refining our processes to exceed their expectations.

3. Empower our associates to solve problems and implement solutions.

4. Serve as a role model in improving state government.

5. Learn to initiate and accept changes in work processes, to eliminate unnecessary processes and to embrace positive adaptations.

6. Improve the quality of services provided to our customers.

7. Identify ways we could improve.

8. Assess our progress toward achieving a total quality workforce.

9. Recognize the many accomplishments of front-line associates through out the state.

10. Identify areas where additional training may be needed.

Accepting the Sterling Award challenge more than met our expectations. The self-assessment process alone provided us a method for analyzing the current status of our quality efforts against the Sterling standards. By completing the application, associates in the Division thoroughly understood their strengths and weaknesses. They realized that a lot of work remained to be done if they were going to win the Sterling Award.

More importantly, they understood from their self-assessment where there was plenty of opportunity for improvement. Their assessment gave them a clear picture of the present state of their organization and what actions were necessary to take them to their desired state.

SUSTAINING TQM INITIATIVES

Designing, developing, and implementing Total Quality Management in government is exciting, enlightening, frustrating, and rewarding. For the past four years, the authors have dedicated practically every minute of their work day towards implementing TQM in government. From the results of our work, we have concluded without any reservations that Total Quality Management is an extremely effective system for delivering quality government services.

We strongly believe that government at all levels, including the legislative and executive branches of government, should adopt the beliefs and principles of TQM as their system of management. The purpose of this book was to describe how we designed, developed, and implemented TQM in the Department of Labor and Employment Security, State of Florida. Perhaps our most difficult hurdle was to change the way government employees interpreted the direction they were to follow in doing their work.

For years most government employees thought that their job was to do what they were told to do by their superiors who were primarily driven by standards and quotas. It was indeed a difficult challenge to convince government employees that to be effective they should look not to the executive and legislative branches of government for direction, but rather to their customers. We found that government can be extremely effective if it is allowed to focus on customers, to meet or exceed their expectations.

Instituting TQM in government requires long-range planning and continuous commitment. We believe, for example, that it will take another four years to institutionalize TQM in Florida's Department of Labor and Employment Security.

Therefore, significant work and effort will be required to sustain a TQM initiative. We believe the following is necessary to sustain a TQM initiative:

1. Create Constancy of Purpose

As Deming pointed out in his first 14 points on TQM, top management must never lose sight of its purpose to improve its products and services for the benefit of its customers. We believe that top management, in order to sustain TQM, must constantly remind their associates of the cornerstones of TQM as follows:

A. Customer focus.

B. Data driven.

C. Continual process improvement.

D. Team-centered empowerment.

E. Process partnerships.

Each associate must understand that the cornerstones of TQM guide top management thinking, and they should serve to guide all associates in the performance of their work.

2. Master Plan TQM Initiative

TQM implementation is a process and requires continual improvement. Therefore, a TQM master plan team consisting of top management should be empowered to set goals and action steps for organization improvement. We found that approximately every three months, the master planning team needed to meet to renew its vision and to set forth a strategy for creating awareness and instituting actions that assisted associates in changing their orientation towards TQM. Each meeting followed the agenda described below:

A. Vision renewal.

B. Restatement of mission.

C. Restatement of values.

D. Organization analysis.

    1. Strengths.

    2. Weaknesses.

    3. Opportunities.

    4. Threats.

E. Goals, action steps, and time completion of each action step.

3. Stress Leadership Commitment to TQM

Organization leadership must continually emphasize the need for quality and that TQM is the management system the organization uses in achieving its goals. Leaders demonstrate their commitment by doing the following.

A. Communicate clearly to all of their associates orally and in writing the importance of quality.

B. Personally adhere to TQM beliefs and principles.

C. Expect all associates to perform according to TQM practices.

D. Raise quality awareness among all associates.

E. Serves as members of process improvement teams.

F. Focus on customers.

G. Use quality tools and make decisions based on relevant data.

H. Role model organization values.

4. Maintain Emphasis on Quality

One of the most difficult challenges in implementing TQM in government is to eliminate work standards that prescribe numerical quotas. For years government workers have received their direction from top management in the form of standards and quotas. It will take many years to change this orientation. Therefore, government leaders must be willing to devote many hours if they are to successfully redirect government workers. We believe at a minimum the following activities are required:

A. All associates must focus on customers.

B. All associates must focus on process improvement.

C. All associates gather and analyze data, and make decisions that benefit customers.

D. Performance standards and quotas are eliminated and replaced with performance expectations.

E. Leaders emphasize quality and demonstrate confidence and patience with teams. Leaders believe that meeting or exceeding customer expectations will also result in higher productivity over time.

F. Leaders stress outcomes and not outputs.

5. Establish Measurements for Every Process

To identify areas for improvement, it is essential that process quality indicators be identified. Further, top management maintains its control of processes by reviewing quality measurements. To establish organization-wide process indicators, we suggest the following:

A. Work flow is shown by flowcharts.

B. Specific quality indicators are identified within the work flow.

C. Quality indicators are tracked.

D. Measurement results are graphically displayed.

E. Reviews of quality indicators occur regularly.

F. Benchmark organization processes against the best.

6. Maintain Momentum by Making Annual Improvements and Outcomes the Highlight of Organization Performance

Most government organizations report with pride the outputs of their system. Generally graphs and charts show government organizations to be doing more than previous years relative to numbers. For example, Vocational Rehabilitation may report with pride that they have closed more cases than the year before. Although these reports measure the quantity of successful rehabilitations, what has been missing prior to TQM implementation was an assessment of the quality of services by VR's customers. We also need to insure that the quality of services offered by suppliers meet or exceed customers' expectations. For example, do the training schools used by VR prepare customers to meet the needs of tomorrow's employers?

To report annual improvements and outcomes, we suggest the following:

A. Identify all process improvements annually.

B. Emphasize outcomes.

C. Detail benefits to customers.

D. Provide summaries, data, and graphs that demonstrate how the Division met or exceeded customers expectations.

7. Organize Around Core Processes

As TQM becomes institutionalized, it becomes readily apparent that traditional agencies organized around Divisions, in order to be effective, need to organize around how work actually flows. Traditional models of management focused on dividing work into specific parts where each individual was given the responsibility for a specific task. When TQM is applied to an organization, the responsibility of each worker to focus on the entire process to which they are assigned, rather than a division of work, becomes the focus.

To organize around core processes, we suggest the following:

A. Establish a core process team.

B. Flowchart core processes.

C. Review core processes by analyzing how work actually flows and make suggestions on how the organization can be more effective if duplication is removed and if resources were reallocated.

D. Suggest changes in the organization that improve work flow.

E. Reorganize or even eliminate divisions within the organization.

8. Create an Organization Structure That Emphasizes Process and Teams

When people organize around processes and teams are empowered to improve processes, fewer managers are needed. The ultimate objective is not, as in traditional management, controlling people, but rather is controlling processes. Therefore, a TQM organization needs fewer managers since the aim is no longer just to control people.

To save the expense of management and, just as important, to keep management from interfering with empowered associates by trying to control them, we suggest the following:

A. Flatten the organization structure.

B. Assign managers to lead more than one process.

C. Hold managers accountable for process improvement.

D. Have managers function as team leaders and no longer be accountable for planning, organizing, directing, and controlling people.

9. Empower Quality Council

When the Quality Council is only composed of the top executive team, empowerment is not an issue. However, in a TQM organization where all levels of the organization should be represented on the Quality Council, empowerment becomes a significant issue. In the early stages of the Quality Council, the role and scope of the council is rather clear. The Quality Council establishes the TQM mission, sets forth the department values, establishes beliefs and principles, develops criteria for individual and team presentations before the council, and provides recognition for those who appear before the council.

The council primarily signals the rest of the organization that quality is a high priority with top management. As the council matures, the role and scope are less clearly defined. Top management is somewhat reluctant to empower the Quality Council because of a lack of trust and, perhaps even just as important, many top managers are unwilling to seek advice regarding all organization matters from subordinates. We believe there will be significant differences in all Quality Councils.

Enlightened leaders will perceive their associates on the Quality Council as a resource to be tapped. If the latter is the case, the Quality Council will take on a significant role in organization development and change. The ultimate goal of TQM organization is to have the Quality Council replace the traditional executive staff meeting. To empower the Quality Council, we suggest that the goals of the Quality Council be as follows:

A. To recognize teams and individuals who contribute to process improvement.

B. To review core process measurement data.

C. To develop the long-range plan for the department.

D. To identify and implement organization strategies for continual improvement.

E. To develop performance assessment criteria.

F. To develop quality policy.

G. To publish quality results.

H. To conduct organization surveys.

I. To structure the organization for team-centered empowerment.

J. To review department, division, and bureau quality performance.

K. To supervise and direct organization training.

L. To sponsor quality forums.

10. Constantly Communicate

Since all associates are valued members of the organization, show them respect by sharing information. Associates should be treated as though they are top executives. Providing them with significant information is a requirement for a TQM organization. We suggest the following actions to improve communication:

A. Publish numerous articles on TQM, preferably articles written by associates.

B. Share ideas, tools, and methods.

C. Create a common language that assists associates in understanding and communicating in a total quality organization.

D. Re-emphasize values.

E. Publicize TQM cornerstones, beliefs, and principles.

F. Constantly remind associates of the department's mission and vision.

G. Publicize quality results.

H. Sponsor TQM forums.

I. Publicize quality improvements

J. Recognize teams and individuals.

K. Publish articles on TQM written by all members of the organization, from the top executive to the front-line.

L. Publicize quality forums.

11. Vigorously Train All Associates

All associates should be exposed to the same training. A TQM organization doesn't offer courses just for management. Everyone, no matter at what level they are in the organization, has the same basic objective—to continually improve organizational processes.

Therefore, whatever course is required for front-liners is also required for senior executives. Even courses that have a management tone, such as leadership, should be available to all associates. All team members, whether or not they are designated as team leaders, must understand the role of leadership and be prepared to serve in leadership roles on their teams.

To vigorously train all associates, we suggest the following:

A. All associates are required to attend and demonstrate their knowledge in the core TQM training courses.

B. Advanced TQM courses such as Advanced TQM Tools, Advanced Decision-making, Team Dynamics, Advanced Flow Charting, Statistical Process Control, etc. are made available to all associates

C. Associates visit other TQM organizations.

D. The agency publishes materials written by associates and distributes leading TQM books to all associates.

E. Leaders develop and offer a Total Quality Management assessment center where associates can evaluate their strengths and weaknesses.

F. Training teams seminars are held where associates can learn from other teams. Associates are sponsored for seminars outside of the organization.

12. Promote and Develop Quality Process Partners

To sustain total quality initiatives, processes must extend beyond traditional organization boundaries. Government organizations must learn what business organizations learned in the 1980s, that it is difficult to build a quality product if suppliers provide products with defects. It required business organizations to take a preventive approach by assisting their suppliers in developing quality organizations so that when the products arrived, they were free of defects.

Supplier partnerships in government are just as important. Rarely does a government department or division function within a vacuum. Personnel actions, financial transactions, policy development, budget authority, etc., generally require cooperation from other organizations. Further, effective government requires customer partnerships.

To develop successful process partners, we suggest the following:

A. Identify suppliers, and if necessary require suppliers to implement Total Quality Management. Suppliers should be expected to provide error-free products and services. Rather than waiting to see if a supplier meets this goal through inspection methods, the TQM organization should assist them to prevent organization dissatisfaction with suppliers.

B. Flow chart processes to include suppliers and customers.

C. Share information with partners.

D. Share flow charts with suppliers, customers, and partners.

E. Develop customer councils, share data with them, and use their knowledge in making process improvements.

F. Recognize process partners with awards.

13. Accent Leadership and Teamwork

For TQM to work effectively, leadership and teamwork are required. Personal commitment and involvement are vital ingredients. Leaders must work effectively in teams and support team-centered empowerment. Leaders must set aside their personal agendas and create win-win situations. This is a difficult challenge for government managers who have been trained to use their power to control others. Also, it's extremely difficult for many government managers to look to the customer for direction, since they have grown used to the notion that their only job is to keep their boss happy and out of trouble. Also, it is easier to work for a superior than to take personal responsibility for process improvement. Being "just" an effective member is sometimes a difficult chore. We suggest the following actions to accent leadership and teamwork.

A. Leaders should perceive themselves as change agents.

B. Leaders are highly visible, committed, and promote quality.

C. Leaders are team members.

D. Leaders role model organization values.

E. Leaders are highly informed about processes and are knowledgeable about TQM.

F. Leaders are accessible to all associates, suppliers, customers, and partners.

G. Leaders are personally involved in education and training. They teach, model, and are continually learning.

H. Leaders spend considerable time in recognizing associates, suppliers, customers, and partners for their efforts.

I. Leaders clearly understand customer expectations and quality improvement objectives.

14. Encourage Self-Assessment

When organizations adopted management by objectives, or management by results, as their management methodology, organization assessment was relatively easy since results were the only key indicators. If management was dissatisfied with the results, then they would change people. It was a relatively simple way to manage an organization— provide managers with objectives and hold them accountable.

In a TQM organization the importance of results remains a high priority; however, results of key processes along with quality indicators form the foundation for assessment. Furthermore, process performance is the focus of management attention, not the performance of individuals. Process improvement teams are held accountable. Consequently, organizations do not have to wait for overall performance to determine whether they have a quality organization.

Organization assessment is an ongoing activity and processes can be evaluated against the intended performance levels and can be benchmarked against similar processes. To sustain TQM initiatives, we suggest that each year government organizations apply for a quality award primarily for the purpose of having organization members assess their organization relative to quality criteria by doing the following:

A. Select quality criteria. For a government organization, we suggest the Federal Quality Institute Criteria. State organizations may wish to choose criteria used by their state quality award program.

B. Empower a quality assessment team.

C. Allow teams substantial time to collect data relative to the criteria.

D. Prepare and present final report to Quality Council.

E. Use quality assessment team members as internal consultants who assist the organization to improve processes.

The challenge to change government organizations into quality organizations is a difficult one. It takes years of relentless effort. It is a very slow process that requires patience and self-confidence. Those who lead will no doubt endure criticism and be mocked, and attacked by those who are comfortable and want to be "let alone so they can just do their job."

On the other hand, those who lead TQM initiatives will experience what Maslow referred to as "self-actualization." The thrill of transforming an organization is exhilarating. To design, develop, implement, and sustain a TQM initiative is a challenge, but also personally rewarding. It's fun to come to work every day knowing that government customers are benefiting from hard work. It's also enjoyable to watch people develop, processes improve, and organization outcomes meet or exceed customers expectations.

BIBLIOGRAPHY

Aguayo, Rafael. *Dr. Deming: The American Who Taught the Japanese About Quality.* Secaucus, NJ: Carol Publishing Group, 1990.

Barker, Joel A. *Future Edge.* New York, NY: William Morrow and Company, Inc., 1992.

Barry, Thomas J. *Management Excellence Through Quality.* Milwaukee, WI: ASQC Quality Press, 1991.

Beckhard, R. and Pritchard, W. *Changing the Essence, The Art of Creating and Leading Fundamental Change in Organizations.* San Francisco, CA: Jossey-Bass Publishers, 1992.

Bennis, W. and Nanus, B. *Leaders: The Strategies for Taking Charge.* New York, NY: Harper & Row, 1985.

Block, Peter. *The Empowered Manager: Positive Political Skills at Work.* San Francisco, CA: Jossey-Bass, 1987.

Boyett, Joseph. *Workplace 2000: The Revolution Reshaping American Business.* New York, NY: Dutton, 1991.

Byham, William C. *Zapp!: The Lightning of Empowerment: How to Improve Productivity, Quality and Employee Satisfaction.* New York, NY: Harmony Books, 1990.

Caropreso, Frank, ed. *Making Total Quality Happen.* New York, NY: Conference Board, 1990.

Carr, David K. *Excellence in Government: Total Quality Management in the 1990's.* Arlington, VA: Coopers & Lybrand, 1990.

Covey, Stephen R. *Principle Centered Leadership.* New York, NY: Simon & Schuster, 1990.

————. *The Seven Habits of Highly Effective People.* New York, NY: Simon & Schuster, 1989.

Crosby, Philip B. *Completeness: Quality for the 21st Century.* New York, NY: Dutton, 1992.

————. *Quality is Free: The Art of Making Quality Certain.* New York, NY: McGraw-Hill, 1979.

————. *Quality Without Tears: The Art of Hassel-Free Management.* New York, NY: McGraw-Hill, 1984.

————. *Running Things: The Art of Making Things Happen.* New York, NY: McGraw-Hill, 1986.Crosby, Philip B. *The Eternally Successful Organization.* New York, NY: Penguin Books, 1988.

Cullen, Joe and Hollingum, Jack. *Implementing Total Quality.* Bedford, MA: IFS Publications, 1987.

Deci, E.L. and Ryan, R.M. *Intrinsic Motivation and Self-Determination in Human Behavior.* New York, NY: Plenum Press, 1985.

Deming, W. Edwards. *Out of the Crisis.* Cambridge, MA: MassachusettsInstitute for Technology, Center for Advanced Engineering Study, 1982.

————. *The New Economics.* Cambridge, MA: Massachusetts Institute for Technology, Center for Advanced Engineering Study, 1993.

Dimack, H.G. *Intervention and Collaboration, Helping Organizations to Change.* San Diego, CA: Pfeiffer and Company, 1993.

Dobyns, Lloyd. *Quality or Else: The Revolution in World Business.* New York, NY: Houghton Mifflin, 1991.

Ernst & Young Quality Improvement Consulting Group. *Total Quality: An Executive's Guide for the 1990's.* Homewood, IL: Dow Jones-Irwin, 1990.

Feigenbaum, A.V. *Total Quality Control.* New York, NY: McGraw-Hill, 1991.Fellers, Gary. *The Deming Vision: SPC/TQM for Administrators.* Milwaukee, WI: ASQC Quality Press, 1992.

Forsha, Harry I. *The Pursuit of Quality Through Personal Change.* Milwaukee, WI: ASQC Quality Press, 1992.

Francis, Dave. *Improving Work Groups: A Practical Manual for Team Building.* La Jolla, CA: University Associates, 1979.

Gabor, Andrea. *The Man Who Discovered Quality: How W. Edwards Deming Brought the Quality Revolution to America.* New York, NY: Times Books, 1991.

Gitlow, Howard S. *The Deming Guide to Quality and Competitive Position.* Englewood Cliffs, NJ: Prentice-Hall, 1987.

——. *Planning for Quality, Productivity, and Competitive Position.* Homewood, IL: Dow Jones-Irwin, 1990.

Guaspari, John. *I Know It When I See It: A Modern Fable about Quality.* New York, NY: American Management Association, 1985.

——. *It's About Time: A Fable about the Next Dimension of Quality.* New York, NY: AMACON, 1992.

Harrington, H. James. *The Improvement Process: How America's Leading Companies Improve Quality.* New York, NY: McGraw-Hill, 1987.

Harvey, Jerry B. *The Abilene Paradox and Other Meditations on Management.* Lexington, MA: Lexington Books, 1988.

Hempden-Turner, C. *Creating Corporate Culture, From Discord to Harmony.* Reading, MA: Addison-Wesley, 1990.

Hickman, Craig R. *Creating Excellence: Managing Corporate Culture, Strategy and Change in the New Age.* New York: New American Library, 1984.

——. *Mind of a Manager, Soul of a Leader.* New York, NY: Wiley, 1990.

Howard, Robert. *Brave New Workplace.* New York, NY: Penguin Books, 1986.

Hudiburg, John J. *Winning With Quality: The FPL Story.* White Plains, NY: Quality Resources, 1991.

Hunt, V. Daniel. *Quality in America: How to Implement a Competitive Quality Program.* Homewood, IL: Business One Irwin, 1992.

Hutchins, David C. *Achieve Total Quality.* Englewood Cliffs, NJ: Director Books, 1991.

Imai, Masaki. *Kaizen: The Key to Japan's Competitive Success.* New York, NY: Free Press, 1986.

Ishikawa, Kaoru. *Guide to Quality Control.* White Plains, NY: Quality Resources, 1986.

Jablonski, Joseph R. *Implementing Total Quality Management: An Overview.* San Diego, CA: Pfeiffer, 1991.

Juran, J. M. *Juran on Leadership for Quality: An Executive Handbook.* New York, NY: Free Press, 1989.

———. *Juran on Planning for Quality: An Executive Handbook.* New York, NY: Free Press, 1988.

Juran, Joseph M., and Gryna, Frank M. assoc. ed. *Juran's Quality Control Handbook, 4th Edition.* New York, NY: McGraw-Hill, 1988.

Juran Institute. *Quality Improvement Tools: Desk Guide.* Washington, DC: Department of the Treasury, Internal Revenue Service, 1992.

———. *Quality Improvement Tools: Instructor's Guide.* Washington, DC: Department of the Treasury, Internal Revenue Service, 1992.

Kanter, Rosabeth Moss. *The Change Masters: Innovation for Productivity in the American Corporation.* New York: Simon and Schuster, 1983.

Kilmann, R.H., Covin, T.J. & Associates. *Corporate Transformation: Revitalizing Organizations for a Competititve World.* San Francisco, CA: Jossey-Bass, Inc., 1988.

Kouzes, James M. *The Leadership Challenge: How to Get Extraordinary Things Done in Organizations.* San Francisco, CA: Jossey-Bass, Inc., 1987.

Lam, K.D. *Total Quality Management: A Resource Guide.* Colorado Springs, CO: Air Academy Press, 1990.

LeBoeuf, Michael. *How to Win Customers and Keep Them for Life.* New York, NY: Berkeley Books, 1989.

Lewis, Ralph G. Smith, Douglas H. *Total Quality Management in Higher Education.* Delray Beach, FL: St. Lucie Press, 1994.

Lowenthal, Jeffrey N. *Reengineering the Corporation.* Milkauwee, WI: Quality Press, 1993.

Mackay, Harvey. *Swim With the Sharks Without Being Eaten Alive: Outsell, Outmanage, Outmotivate and Outnegotiate Your Competition.* New York, NY: Morrow, 1988.

McLaughlin, Dave. *Take the High Ground: An Executive's Guide to Total Quality Management.* Tampa, FL: Manicorp Publishers, 1990.

Naisbett, John. *Megatrends 2000: Ten New Directions for the 1990's.* New York, NY: Morrow, 1990.

———. *Re-Inventing the Corporation.* New York, NY: Warner Books, 1985.

Oakland, John S. *Total Quality Management.* New York, NY: Nichols Publishing, 1989.

Osborne, David. *Re-Inventing Government: How the Entrepreneurial Spirit is Transforming the Public Sector.* Reading, MA: Addison-Weslery, 1992.

Parkinson, C. Northcote. *Parkinson's Law and Other Studies in Administration.* Boston, MA: Houghton Miffin, 1957.

Peters, Thomas J. *In Search of Excellence: Lessons from America's Best-Run Companies.* New York, NY: Warner Books, 1982.

———. *Thriving on Chaos.* New York, NY: Knopf, 1987.

Pierce, Richard J. *Leadership, Perspective, and Restructuring for Total Quality: An Essential Instrument to Improve Market Share and Productivity, by Eminent Leaders of America's Most Competitive Companies.* Milwaukee, WI: ASQC Press, 1991.

Pirsig, Robert M. *Zen and the Art of Motorcycle Maintenance.* New York, NY: Bantam Books, 1981.

Potts, Mark. *The Leading Edge: CEO's Who Turned Their Companies Around.* New York, NY: McGraw-Hill, 1987.

Rummler, G.A. and Brache, A.P. *Improving Performance: How to Manage the White Space on the Organization Chart.* San Francisco, CA: Jossey-Bass, 1990.

Ryan, Kathleen D. and Oestreich, Daniel K. *Driving Fear Out of the Workplace.* San Francisco, CA: Jossey-Bass, 1991.

Sashkin, Marshall. *Putting Total Quality Management to Work: What TQM Means, How to Use It, and How to Sustain It Over the Long Run.* San Francisco, CA: Berrett-Koehler, 1993.

Saylor, James H. *TQM Field Manual.* New York, NY: McGraw-Hill, 1991.

Scherkenbach, William W. *The Deming Route to Quality and Productivity: Road Maps and Roadblocks.* Milwaukee, WI: ASQC Quality Press, 1991.

Scholtes, Peter R. *The Team Handbook: How to USe Teams to Improve Quality.* Madison, WI: Joiner, 1988.

Schonberger, R.J. *World Class Manufacturing: The Lessons of Simplicity Applied.* New York, NY: Free Press, 1986.

Senge, Peter M. *Managing Quality: A Primer for Middle Managers.* Redaing, MA: Addison-Wesley Publishers, 1992.

Shores, A. Richard. *Survival of the Fittest: Total Quality Control and Management Evolution.* Milwaukee, WI: ASQC Quality Press, 1988.

Spendolini, Michael. *The Benchmarking Book.* New York, NY: AMACON, 1992.

Steeples, Marion Mills. *The Corporate Guide to the Malcolm Baldridge National Quality Award: Proven Strategies for Building Quality into Your Organization.* Milwaukee, WI: ASQC Quality Press, 1992.

Stratton, A. Donald. *An Approach to Quality Improvement that Works.* Milwaukee, WI: ASQC Quality Press, 1991.

Talley, Dorsey J. *Total Quality Management: Performance and Cost Measures; The Strategy for Economic Survival.* Milwaukee, WI: ASQC Quality Press, 1991.

Townsend, Patrick L. *Commit to Quality.* New York, NY: Wiley, 1990.

Townsend, Robert. *Up the Organization.* New York, NY: Knopf, 1970.

Varney, Glenn H. *Building Productive Teams: An Action Guide and Resource Book.* San Francisco, CA: Jossey-Bass, 1989.

Walton, Mary. *The Deming Management Method.* New York, NY: Perigee Books, The Putnam Publishing Group, 1986.

Wellins, Richard S. Byham, William C. and Wilson, Jeanne M. *Empowered Teams: Creating Self-Directed Work Groups that Improve Quality, Productivity and Participation.* San Francisco, CA: Jossey-Bass Publishers, 1991.

Westland, Cynthia Lane. *Quality: The Myth and the Magic.* Milwaukee, WI: ASQC Quality Press, 1990.

Wright, Russell. *A Little Bit at a Time: Secrets of Productive Quality.* Berkeley, CA: Ten Speed Press, 1990.

Zuckerman, M.R. and Hatala, L.J. *Incredibly American: Releasing the Heart of Quality.* Milwaukee, WI: ASQC Quality Press, 1992.

INDEX